Developing Annuities Markets
The Experience of Chile

Developing Annuities Markets
The Experience of Chile

Roberto Rocha
Craig Thorburn

THE WORLD BANK

1818 H Street NW
Washington DC 20433
Telephone: 202-473-1000
Internet: www.worldbank.org
E-mail: feedback@worldbank.org

1 2 3 4 5 10 09 08 07

ISBN-10: 0-8213-6666-1
ISBN-13: 978-0-8213-6666-0
eISBN: 0-8213-6667-X
DOI: 10.1596/978-0-8213-6666-0

Cover photo: Train station, Santiago, Chile by Marcelo Montecino.
Cover design: Naylor Design.

Library of Congress Cataloging-in-Publication Data

Rocha, Roberto Rezende.
Developing annuities markets : the experience of Chile / Roberto Rocha, Craig Thorburn.
p. cm. – (Directions in development. Finance)
Includes bibliographical references and index.
ISBN-13: 978-0-8213-6666-0
ISBN-10: 0-8213-6666-1
1. Annuities—Chile. I. Thorburn, Craig, 1964- II. Title.

HG8790.R63 2006
368.3'700983—dc22 2006048571

Contents

Figures

Tables

Acknowledgments

This study of the Chilean annuities market consists of seven chapters, two technical annexes, and one statistical annex. It is part of a broader project on annuities coordinated by the Operations Policy Department (OPD) of the World Bank and designed to identify best regulatory practices and institutional arrangements, capable of promoting the sound development of annuities markets in member countries.

Roberto Rocha and Craig Thorburn were the main authors of this report. During the elaboration of the report the authors benefited from the collaboration of Thomas Glaessner, Sara Zervos, Gregorio Impavido, Diego Sourrouille, and Ying Lin. Marco Morales, of Diego Portales University in Chile, co-authored Annex 2. The authors initiated this study during a first visit to Santiago de Chile in October 2003, where they held meetings with pension and insurance regulators, numerous insurance companies and pension fund administrators, and other market participants. The authors had the opportunity to visit Santiago in two subsequent missions in the context of the IMF/World Bank Financial Sector Assessment Program (FSAP). During those two occasions, the authors obtained additional information and discussed the preliminary findings of the report with market participants and regulators.

The authors would like to acknowledge the cooperation and support received from the managers and the staff of the Central Bank of Chile

(CBC) the Chilean Insurance Supervisory Agency (Superintendencia de Valores y Seguros—SVS), and the Pension Supervisory Agency (Superintendencia de Administradoras de Fondos de Pensiones—SAFP). The authors feel particularly indebted to Klaus Schmidt-Hebel and Jorge Perez (CBC); Alejandro Ferreiro, Ernesto Rios, Osvaldo Maciel, and Sebastian Gonzales (SVS); and Guillermo Larrain and Solange Berstein (SAFP).

The authors would also like to acknowledge the substantial technical and logistical assistance provided by Augusto Iglesias and Guillermo Martinez of Primamerica Consultores in Santiago de Chile, during the first visit to Chile and during the elaboration of the report. During the elaboration of the report the authors also benefited from substantive discussions and comments provided by Augusto de le Torre, Dimitri Vittas, Eduardo Walker, Estelle James, Richard Hinz, and Salvador Valdés. The remaining errors in this report are the sole responsibility of the authors.

Acronyms and Abbreviations

ADF	Augmented Dickey-Fuller test
AFPS	*Administradoras de Fondos de Pensiones*
AIC	Akaike Information Criterion
ALM	asset-liability management
AP	average premium
AP (EARLY)	average premium of early retirement annuities
AP (OLD)	average premium of old age annuities
APV	*Ahorro Previsional Voluntario* (Voluntary Pension Plans)
AR	annuity rate
ASSAL	Latin American Insurance Association
BFR	Basic Financial Reserve
BG	Breusch-Godfrey (Lagrange Multiplier statistic)
BIC	Bayesian Information Criterion
BP	Breusch-Pagan (Lagrange Multiplier test)
bps	basis points
BTR	Basic Technical Reserve
CALCE	the denomination of the risk-based capital rule for annuity providers in Chile
CBC	Central Bank of Chile
CPI	Consumer Price Index

CR	commission rate
DB	Defined Benefit
DC	Defined Contribution
DKK	Danish Krona
EU	European Union
FF	fully funded
FSAP	IMF/World Bank Financial Sector Assessment Program
GDP	gross domestic product
GLS	Generalized Least Squares
HER	Herfindahl index
HER (EARLY)	Herfindahl Index in the market for early retirement annuities
HER (OLD)	Herfindahl Index in the market for old age annuities
IAIS	International Association of Insurance Supervisors
ILONA	Irish Life of North America
IMF	International Monetary Fund
INP	*Instituto de Normalización Previsional*
IPS	Im, Pesran, and Shin
LAC	Latin America and the Caribbean
LEV	Financial leverage ratio
LICO	Life Insurance Company
LLC	Levin, Lin, and Chu
MA	Moving Average
MAIC	Modified Akaike Information Criterion
MIS	measure of duration mismatch
MPG	minimum pension guarantee
MSHARE	market share measured by the stock of technical reserves
MWR	money's worth ratio
NT	number of effective observations
OECD	Organisation for Economic Co-operation and Development
OLS	Ordinary Least Squares
OPD	Operations Policy Department (World Bank)
p.a.	per annum
PAYG	pay as you go
PRC-20	twenty-year indexed bonds issued by the Central Bank of Chile
PW	programmed or phased withdrawals

RC	*Reserva de CALCE*
RF	risk-free (rate)
RIM	Retirement Income Modeling
ROA	Return on Assets
ROE	Return on equity
ROFI	real return measured by the interest rates on corporate and mortgage bonds
RV	*Renta Vitalícia*
SAFP	*Superintendencia de Administradoras de Fondos de Pensiones*
SCOMP	*Sistema de Consultas y Ofertas de Montos de Pensión*
S.E.	Standard Error
SOA	Share of Other Assets
SOFI	Share of Fixed Income Instruments
SPV	Special Purpose Vehicle
SVS	*Superintendencia de Valores y Seguros*
tasa de venta	annuity rate reported by annuity providers to the SVS
TIAA-CREF	Teachers Insurance and Annuity Association—College Retirement Equities Fund
TR	Technical Reserve
TW	temporary withdrawal
UF	*unidades de fomento* (a unit of account indexed to prices)
U.K.	United Kingdom
U.S.	United States
VAR	value at risk

Glossary

Annuity Rate The internal rate of return on the annuity contract. The annuity rate should be computed with a mortality table that reflects accurately the mortality experience of the annuitant population. The reported annuity rate in Chile has been calculated with an outdated mortality table, the RV-85, which implies an underestimation of the true or effective annuity rate.

Asset Margin The hidden margin held by life insurance companies as a result of valuating assets at book value on their balance sheet, equivalent to the unrealized capital appreciation of the assets.

Calce Rule The generally recognized name for the rule that regulates provisioning and capital requirements with respect to annuities written by life insurance companies in Chile.

Deferred Annuity In contrast to an immediate annuity (see below), a deferred annuity commences the payment of the income stream after a period of deferment defined at the point of issue of the contract provided that the annuitant or annuitants are alive at the time that the payments are made.

Defined Contribution (DC) The type of pension system where the final benefit depends on the contributions and the net investment returns.

Gearing Ratio The same as leverage ratio. For a life insurance company, the ratio of other liabilities to capital.

Guaranteed Annuity Normally an annuity would have payments made as long as the annuitant or surviving spouse is alive. However, as an added benefit, a guaranteed annuity can have a term defined where, until the expiry of that term, the payment is made independent of survivorship. After the guaranteed term, payments would be made dependent on survivorship as usual.

Immediate Annuity An annuity where the payments commence "immediately" on the issue of the contract. In the case of a monthly annuity, the first payment would occur one month after the issue of the contract provided that the lives had met the survivorship conditions.

Joint Annuity An annuity where the payments are dependent on the survivorship of more than one life. In Chile, these take the form of "last survivor" joint life annuities where the payments are made provided that at least one of the beneficiaries is alive.

Minimum Pension Guarantee (MPG) A minimum benefit defined in UFs and accessible to all workers who have contributed for at least 20 years. The MPG is a top-up benefit, raising the levels of a PW or an annuity to a defined minimum level in the event that these benefits would, otherwise, fall below this level.

Mortality Table A table that shows the probability of death at each age. It can be built in two different versions, a period table and cohort table.

Programmed Withdrawal (PW) A periodic series of payments taken from an account balance based on a determined formula and methodology. Sometimes this is also termed as a "phased withdrawal."

Mortality Drag If an annuity is deferred, the individual misses the mortality profit, or the mortality cross-subsidy (see below). The extra return required to compensate the investor for the absence of this subsidy is called the mortality drag. The impact of the mortality drag increases with age. This means that annuities become more attractive at older ages and that the risks associated with phased withdrawals increase (in the absence of any guarantees, such as the minimum pension guarantee).

Mortality Profit Annuity providers make a "profit" from the fact that some members die sooner than expected, without receiving their residual fund value (the funds remain with the provider after death). This results in a profit that is either provided to the surviving annuitants, through higher annuities (compared with the situation where the individual generates his own annuity from his own balances), or the insurer. The mortality profit is also frequently called the mortality cross-subsidy, as it involves a transfer from those that die young to those that remain alive.

Reversion/Reversionary Annuity Where more than one life is involved in the survivorship determination, after the first death the remaining payments are described as the reversion. In the case of joint life annuities in Chile, during the survivorship of the first life, regardless of the survivorship of the second life, the annuity is paid at the full level. After the death of the first life, if the second life is still surviving, the reversion is payable at the rate, in this case, of 60% of the previous level. This is described as a 60% reversion to the surviving spouse.

Single Life Annuity An annuity where the payments depend on the survivorship of one life only.

Temporary Withdrawal (TW) That part of an income stream taken by a retiree as a drawdown from his or her AFP account. The TW is taken along with a deferred annuity, the AFP account balance being reduced initially by the premium for the deferred annuity and the balance paid through a programmatic drawdown during the period of deferment of the annuity as the TW.

Executive Summary

The Payout Challenge and the Importance of Chile's Experience

The increasing awareness of a looming pension crisis has led to a wave of pension reforms, particularly in the last decade. Pension reforms have frequently involved a combination of changes in the parameters of the public pay-as-you-go (PAYG) scheme with the introduction of mandatory and fully funded (FF) schemes operated by the private sector. The role of the private sector in the provision of retirement income has generally increased, and even countries that have restricted the core reform to changes in the PAYG scheme have also made efforts to promote voluntary and complementary private pension arrangements.

The increased involvement of the private sector in pension provision has led to a substantial volume of research on the structure, performance, and regulation of private pension funds. However, most of the analytical effort has been focused on the accumulation phase of private pension provision. There has been less effort to examine the challenges in the payout phase. This is cause for concern, because many countries that have enhanced the role of the private sector in pension provision will start facing the "payout problem" in the near future, i.e., the problem of converting the individual balances accumulated in defined contribution schemes into streams of retirement income, such as phased withdrawals (PWs) and annuities.

One of the central questions faced by policy makers in these countries is whether it is possible to develop an efficient market for retirement products from a low initial base. A more specific and critical question is whether the insurance sector can effectively deliver relatively complex products such as annuities, and honor contracts that may span a period of 40 years or longer. This is not a trivial question, given the lack of reliable mortality data in many emerging countries, their less developed institutional and regulatory frameworks, and their less developed capital markets.

Chile provides one of the most relevant experiences for countries that have reformed their pension systems and have to develop markets for PWs and annuities. This is due to its well-known pension reform of 1981, which involved a move from a public PAYG system to a FF system operated by the private sector. At the start of its pension reform in the early 1980s, Chile was a middle-income country without a pension industry, an incipient insurance sector, little regulatory and supervisory capacity, and undeveloped capital markets. By 2004, Chile had reasonably developed markets for retirement products, as shown by 200,000 PWs, 320,000 annuity policies, and 6,000 temporary withdrawals (TWs)—the combination of a withdrawal with a deferred annuity.

By the same time, there were about 17 life insurance companies providing annuities and managing assets of 20 percent of GDP, and 6 pension fund administrators (AFPs) providing PWs and individual accounts for active workers, and managing assets of more than 60 percent of GDP. Moreover, the assets of pension funds are mostly related to the accumulation phase, indicating that Chile's market for retirement products should grow further in the future.

The Demand for Retirement Products in Chile

The fact that more than 60 percent of all pensioners have selected annuities implies one of the highest rates of annuitization in the world, quite in contrast with the experience of many other countries. It is also noteworthy the strong association between annuitization and early retirement—nearly two-thirds of pensioners that retire at the normal age of 65 and 60 (for men and women, respectively) choose PWs, while 90 percent of all early retirees select annuities. Workers can retire early if they meet certain conditions—their balances must generate a pension equal to at least 70 percent of their average real wages in the past 10 years and 150 percent of the minimum pension guarantee (MPG), a basic guarantee that has been set around 25 percent of the economy-wide average wage.

Pensioners who choose PWs are exposed to longevity and market risk, but maintain full ownership of their retirement balances, which goes to the heirs as a bequest upon death. Annuitants are insured against longevity, market, and inflation risk (annuities in Chile have been fixed and indexed to consumer prices, variable annuities have been allowed only recently). Moreover, married males need to buy joint annuities, implying that their spouses are also insured against longevity risk. Furthermore, the great majority of annuitants have opted for annuities with guaranteed terms, which provide a lower initial payout but preserve these payout levels upon the death of the main beneficiary, and also allow bequests during the guaranteed period.

The high rate of annuitization and its relation to early retirement is the result of several factors, including regulations that restrict access to lump sums, the lack of a front-ended PAYG benefit, the design of the minimum pension guarantee (MPG) consisting of a low level of top-up, back-ended benefits, regulations that force low income pensioners with small balances to take PWs and the MPG, and the influence of insurance brokers.

Restrictions on lump sums are an important explanation for the observed outcomes, as they increase the demand for all retirement products, including annuities. The lack of a front-ended social security benefit means that pensioners in Chile are more exposed to longevity and market risk than pensioners in most other countries. The MPG provides insurance against longevity and market risk, but at low levels, implying that middle and higher income pensioners that choose PWs are still substantially exposed to market risk. Therefore, it is not surprising that annuities have become popular among most retirees. The availability of guaranteed annuities allowing some room for bequests has probably enhanced the attractiveness of this instrument. The PW option is primarily attractive for low income workers already close to the MPG.

Finally, the marketing of retirement products is strongly biased towards annuities and early retirement. Life insurance companies market annuities aggressively because they account for a large share of their total business. Moreover, insurance brokers have had an incentive to induce higher income workers with larger balances to retire early because they receive larger commissions. By contrast, AFPs generate most of their income from the accumulation phase and have little interest to market PWs.

The Structure and Performance of the Chilean Market for Retirement Products

Chilean annuitants have generally got a good value for their premiums, as indicated by average money's worth ratios (the ratio of the expected present value of annuity payouts to the premium) on their indexed annuities around 1.04–1.06 in recent years, which are significantly higher than the unitary value considered as an actuarially fair annuity. Money's worth ratios increase with age, and are lower for joint annuities and guaranteed annuities. These results generally reflect the exposure of the provider to mortality and reinvestment risk, the higher risks in contracts with longer duration, and the imposition of a load to cover these risks.

Average money's worth ratios in Chile have been high by international comparison. In most other countries money's worth ratios range from 0.9 to 1 for nominal annuities, and from 0.8 to 0.85 for indexed annuities, in the few developed countries that offer inflation protection, such as the United Kingdom. The higher money's worth ratios of indexed annuities in Chile are in part due to the availability of a wide supply of financial assets indexed to prices, including higher yield assets such as mortgage, corporate, and infrastructure bonds. This has allowed annuity providers to hedge inflation risk efficiently while also extracting higher real returns. Moreover, providers have been able to extract an increase in risk-adjusted returns from these instruments, as they are much less liquid than Government bonds and therefore contain a liquidity premium that investors with long horizons can extract. An econometric analysis of the annuity rate suggests that providers have partly shared the higher returns with annuitants.

The high money's worth ratios are also due to a very competitive annuities market. Quite in contrast with the pensions market, which became extremely concentrated during the 1990s, the Chilean annuities market became very competitive in the same period, due to the entry of several life insurance companies. In more recent years providers seem to have engaged in aggressive pricing strategies, as indicated not only by the high money's worth ratios but also the very thin intermediation spreads. Some life insurance companies have left the market in recent years, as a result the strong competitive pressures, the thin spreads, and the low returns on equity.

The high money's worth ratios (MWRs) of the recent years probably cannot be sustained for a longer period, as they indicate that at least some providers may have experienced losses in their annuity business in this period. The industry could absorb these losses, because of the strong capital buffer accumulated in the 1990s, and which was due to the introduction of a strict capital regulation early in that decade. However, the continuation of aggressive pricing strategies could lead to further erosion of capital and an excessive increase in gearing ratios. An adjustment in MWRs is likely, although it is also likely that these ratios will remain attractive by international comparison, especially by comparison with MWRs of indexed annuities in other countries. This is because Chilean providers will retain an advantage over providers in most other countries—their access to a wider and more diversified supply of indexed financial instruments.

The Quality of the Regulatory Framework

The regulatory framework for the annuities market is reasonable and has evolved positively over the past 20 years. Product regulation has included a number of restrictions designed to prevent an early exhaustion of real incomes at retirement, and might be considered excessively restrictive by comparison with other countries. However, these restrictions have been justified as appropriate for Chile, where the second pillar plays a fundamental role in social protection. Annuities have been fixed and indexed, and married males need to buy joint annuities. These features imply relatively lower payments in the early stages of retirement but ensure adequate payments for beneficiaries in later stages. The PW formula follows the same conservative approach, by preventing a depletion of the balance in a finite period of time and distributing payments according to life expectancy. The regulation of providers has supported a sound development of the market in the past 20 years. In particular, innovative capital rules introduced in the early 1990s, linking capital requirements to the exposure to reinvestment risk, provided an initial capital buffer that has provided stability to the industry.

A new Pension Law approved by Congress in 2004 has addressed several regulatory deficiencies that were identified during the 1990s and early 2000s. The conditions for early retirement have been tightened. The new Law has introduced new products such as variable annuities, but through combinations that always include a minimum fixed and indexed annuity, thus ensuring minimum insurance against investment and longevity risk. The pension and insurance supervisors have removed deficiencies in product and capital regulations caused by the prolonged use of an outdated mortality table by adopting an updated cohort table. Questionable selling practices have been addressed by the introduction of an innovative electronic quotation system for annuities and PWs. The new system has improved market transparency and has ensured that retiring workers have effective access to the best quotes.

At the same time, there are still some weaknesses that would need to be addressed in the future. The separation of the accumulation and retirement phases implies that neither pension funds nor annuity providers are effectively maximizing the individuals' pension wealth over the entire lifecycle. In particular, workers in the preretirement phase are subject to some risks such as annuity rate risk that have not yet been properly addressed. Management of longevity risk by annuity providers remains a challenge in Chile, as it is in other countries. In addition, although annuity providers in Chile have access to a wider range of financial instruments than providers in other emerging countries, they still face a duration mismatch problem that needs to be continuously addressed. Providers also lack access to important risk management tools such as derivatives and reinsurance.

Although product regulation is generally satisfactory, the use of a backward-looking technical rate for PWs still produces a residual bias in selection, and additional annuity designs could be considered. Marketing regulation has evolved significantly, but there are still challenges to be faced, particularly regarding the riskier products. Investment and capital regulations have not yet been revised to accommodate the introduction of new products and the changes in risk patterns. Finally, the experience in handling the first bankruptcy case has revealed some gaps in resolution rules that have not yet been fully addressed.

Recommendations for Further Improvements in Regulation

The investment regime for pension funds should be reviewed, as it has remained unnecessarily complex and probably ineffective in addressing several types of risk. A judicious relaxation of several quantitative restrictions could open more room for asset managers to operate without any meaningful increases in risk, benefiting both active workers and PW holders. Allowing a small share of equity in Fund E (the fixed income fund chosen by many retiring workers and PW holders) would probably improve its efficiency. Reducing the exposure of retiring workers to annuity rate risk would require an increase in average portfolio duration. This might be difficult to achieve through regulatory tools, but policy makers may consider allowing a special fund more tailored to the needs of these workers.

Chile has achieved considerable progress in developing its capital market, but annuity providers still lack access to sufficient tools for risk management, especially longevity and market risk. The introduction of special arrangements to share longevity risk (such as those adopted by Danish companies or the TIIA-CREF fund in the United States) does not seem feasible in the Chilean context. However, regulators should examine the recent efforts to issue longevity bonds in the United Kingdom and assess the possibility of developing this instrument in Chile.

Management of market risk could be seriously complicated by an excessive de-indexation of the stock of financial instruments resulting from aggressive new issues of peso- or U.S. dollar-denominated instruments. The critical role of indexed financial instruments for the asset-liability management of annuity providers cannot be sufficiently emphasized. Annuity providers must retain access to a substantial volume of long-term indexed instruments, and would also benefit from access to a more developed derivatives market, including interest options, swaps, and bond futures.

Policy makers may consider the introduction of additional annuity designs, such as adjustable annuities, or the staggered purchase of fixed annuities. Adjustable indexed annuities would allow retirees some room to address annuity rate risk by benefiting from future increases in interest rates in a scenario of low interest rates at retirement. It would also allow retirees to enjoy higher initial payouts, as the provider would be less exposed to reinvestment risk. The annuitant would be exposed to the risk of a further fall in future annuity rates, but several annuitants might prefer this option to a pure fixed indexed annuity, given their planned consumptions paths at retirement. If this option is allowed, however, it should probably be combined with a minimum fixed indexed annuity providing minimum protection against investment risk, in line with the combinations allowed by the new Pension Law. Staggered fixed annuities could allow retiring workers to address annuity rate risk more effectively. Real escalating annuities could prove attractive to early retirees who continue working and saving.

The updating of the parameters used in the PW formula should be completed, in order to remove the residual bias in selection. The technical rate should be forward-looking, and possibly consist of the yield of a mix of fixed income instruments in Funds D and E.

The new quotation system has improved market transparency, but some retirees may still select instruments based on a comparison of initial payouts only, without proper knowledge of the risks involved. For example, an excessive emphasis on initial payouts may lead several retirees to choose variable annuities, without proper knowledge of the risks involved in this instrument. Information on risks cannot be easily inserted in the quotation system, but participants in the new system should be required to provide brochures highlighting the basic aspects of each retirement instrument.

The investment and capital regimes for insurance companies may need to be reviewed to accommodate the introduction of new products that introduce more sharing of investment risk between the provider and the annuitant. In the longer term, a move from a rules-based approach to a risk-based approach would be of benefit.

Some improvements in resolution rules may also be needed. Intervention triggers could be improved by introducing a leverage test that uses economic values rather than book values. Intervention and administration rules should be reviewed to ensure an equal treatment of different policyholders. The merit of creating a small resolution fund would be worth investigation, whether it is pre- or post-funded.

Longevity risk remains one of the most difficult issues to be addressed by regulators and participants in annuities markets, requiring a constant effort to track mortality improvements and reflect these improvements in capital and product regulation. Finally, the Government should make an effort to build an actuarial model capable of producing more robust estimates for the expenditures with the MPG, and able to provide more accurate inputs for future policy formulation

Lessons for Other Countries

One of the most important lessons that can be extracted from the Chilean experience is the feasibility of developing a market for retirement products from a low initial base. As indicated before, when Chile implemented its pension reform, the market for retirement products did not exist. Twenty years later Chile had a well-developed and rapidly growing market for PWs and annuities, judged by the number of PW and annuity policies, the size of the PW and annuity premiums, the assets of life insurance companies, and the number of market participants.

The conservative Chilean approach to product regulation is appropriate for countries that expect the new second pillar to play a major role in retirement provision. The restrictions on lump sums that Chile implemented increase the potential demand for all retirement products, including annuities. A PW formula that is based on life expectancy prevents a very premature exhaustion of funds. The imposition of fixed annuities indexed to inflation, and joint annuities for married couples all contribute to prevent an early exhaustion of funds and poverty at old age. The introduction of riskier products such as variable annuities should require a minimum fixed annuity component providing investment and longevity insurance, as in the case of Chile.

Countries that have preserved a large first pillar and introduced only a modest second pillar can adopt a more liberal product regulation, as in these cases the exposure of retiring workers to investment and longevity risk is more limited. However, very liberal rules for lump sums can hinder significantly the development of the market for retirement products, especially annuities markets. The appropriate policies in this area will vary significantly from country to country. In some cases it may be appropriate to continue restricting lump sums, but adopt a more liberal approach to the design of retirement products. For example, the regulation of PWs may be more liberal, allowing designs that enable a faster withdrawal of funds. Likewise, variable annuities may be introduced without the obligation of a fixed annuity component.

The high money's worth ratios for indexed annuities in Chile is due in good part to the existence of a large supply of indexed financial instruments, not only public sector bonds, but also other higher yield instruments such as mortgage bonds, mortgage-backed instruments, corporate bonds, and infrastructure bonds. There is evidence that Chilean providers operating in a competitive environment have shared the higher real yield of these instruments with annuitants, in terms of higher annuity rates. In many countries annuities do not need to be indexed, while in others indexation is required but there is no effort to develop proper hedging instruments for providers. Even a temporary bout of inflation can lead to inadequate incomes at retirement. In countries where indexation is required but providers cannot properly hedge the inflation risk, the result will be lower rates of return for indexed annuities.

The computation of money's worth ratios for different classes of annuitants shows that providers in Chile price the higher risk involved in annuities with longer expected duration. This indicates the importance of developing long-term financial instruments, in order to reduce providers' exposure to reinvestment risk and enable them to offer better annuity rates to all classes of annuitants.

Product regulation can introduce unintended biases and influence the selection process. While annuity providers should be able to price their annuities freely, PW payments are typically determined by formulas with regulated parameters. These parameters must be as up-to-date and market related as possible, in order to minimize biases in selection. Chile segmented the provision of the two major classes of retirement products, with pension funds providing PWs and life insurance companies providing annuities, but this segmentation does not have any obvious justification. Therefore, regulators could allow life insurance companies to offer PWs as well, as in the case of most OECD countries.

The Chilean experience with marketing regulation also provides important lessons for other countries. Brokers and sales agents can influence significantly the selection of products and providers, and in the case of Chile this influence has produced mixed outcomes. The new electronic quotation system has been designed to improve market transparency and ensure that retirees effectively get the best quotes. It is an innovative and promising reform, whose results should be closely monitored by regulators in other countries.

Chilean regulators have addressed reinvestment and mortality risks by imposing strict capital regulations on providers. The capital rules introduced in 1990 were innovative, being based in a formula that links the level of reserves to the extension of the duration mismatch, and that also uses a low discount rate for valuing liabilities. This approach to capital regulation enabled the early buildup of a strong capital buffer that has proved very important for the sound development of the industry. In other countries, providers are probably subject to even more severe mismatches and reinvestment risk. A capital regulation that penalizes mismatches can not only strengthen the capital buffer but also promote the adoption of appropriate asset-liability management strategies in the early stages of market development.

At the same time, the Chilean experience also indicates the need to make an early effort to produce appropriate mortality tables that will be used for regulatory purposes, including the regulation of PWs and the computation of technical reserves and capital. The Chilean PW design is attractive because it incorporates life expectancy, but it was weakened by the prolonged use of an outdated mortality table. Likewise, capital regulations were innovative in many aspects but their power was eroded by the prolonged use of outdated mortality tables. These problems can be avoided through more frequent efforts to examine mortality experience and update the tables used for regulatory purposes.

Intervention and bankruptcy rules should prevent an early depletion of provider assets by life policyholders in a bankruptcy scenario, as this will reduce the residual value of assets left to honor annuity payments, and will increase the cost of any Government guarantee. Annuitants should not be less favorably treated than other policyholders, particularly in a system of mandatory savings. Countries that have introduced a mandatory second pillar may have to introduce an annuity guarantee as Chile did. The guarantee should not be total, including a reasonable amount of coinsurance by annuitants in order to minimize the possible loss of market discipline at the point of purchase. In Chile, this guarantee is backed by budgetary resources, but other countries may consider the introduction of a small fund financed by the industry.

CHAPTER 1

Introduction

Background

Demographic aging strains pension systems around the world, leading frequently to large pension expenditures and deficits. The increasing awareness of a looming pension crisis has led to a wave of pension reforms, particularly in the last decade. Pension reforms have frequently involved a combination of changes in the parameters of the public pay-as-you-go (PAYG) scheme with the introduction of mandatory and fully funded (FF) schemes operated by the private sector. Some countries have adopted a more radical approach, replacing the PAYG scheme entirely by a private, FF scheme. The role of the private sector in the provision of retirement income has generally increased, and even countries that have restricted the core reform to changes in the PAYG scheme have also made efforts to promote voluntary and complementary private pension arrangements.

The increased involvement of the private sector in pension provision has led to a substantial volume of research on the structure, performance, and regulation of private pension funds, both in developed and emerging countries. However, most of the analytical effort has been focused on the accumulation phase of private pension provision. There has been less effort to examine the issues and challenges in the payout phase. This is cause for concern, because many countries that have enhanced the role of the private sector in pension provision will start facing the "payout problem" in the near future, i.e., the problem of converting the individual balances accumulated in defined contribution (DC) schemes into streams of retirement income, such as annuities and phased withdrawals (PWs).[1] The absence of more substantive analytical work on annuities is particularly worrisome, as this is an instrument that involves more complex regulatory and supervisory issues.

The theoretical and empirical research on annuities has expanded in recent years, but has remained focused on specific issues and countries. Researchers have examined the adverse selection problem that may hinder the growth of annuities markets, have documented the thinness of voluntary annuity markets, have calculated the implicit returns to annuitants, have identified some of the major risks facing workers, retirees, and providers, and have offered some solutions designed to deal with these risks. However, there is a wide range of issues in the regulation of products and intermediaries that have not been properly examined. Moreover, the bulk of the empirical research has been restricted to a few developed countries, primarily Australia, the United Kingdom and the United States. Research on other countries has been usually limited to a general overview of the institutional and regulatory framework.[2]

Therefore, although the existing body of research has produced useful insights, it has not addressed many questions that are critical for policymakers in emerging countries. This is particularly true for countries that have undergone a pension reform entailing an important role for the private sector, and where regulatory restrictions on lump sums imply that PWs and annuities will become important vehicles of retirement income. One of the central questions faced by policy makers in these countries is whether the insurance sector can effectively deliver relatively complex products such as annuities, and honor contracts that may span a period of 40 years or longer. This is not a trivial question, given the lack of reliable mortality data in many emerging countries, their less developed institutional and regulatory frameworks, and their less developed capital markets.

Policy makers and regulators in many countries would benefit from a more in-depth analysis of the markets for retirement products across a greater number of countries, as this would enable them to identify best practices in the regulation of products and intermediaries, and institutional arrangements that may work better, particularly in less sophisticated environments. Policy makers would also benefit from the analyses of more adverse scenarios, involving failures and bankruptcies of annuity providers, as well as the identification of solutions to protect retirees and minimize disruptions to the market.

The Importance of Chile as a Case Study

Chile provides one of the most relevant experiences for countries that have reformed their pension systems and that are trying to develop markets for annuities and PWs. This is due to its pioneer and well-known pension reform of 1981, which involved a radical move from a public PAYG system to a FF system operated by the private sector. At the start of its pension reform in the early 1980s, Chile was a middle income country without a pension industry, an incipient insurance sector, little regulatory and supervisory capacity, and undeveloped capital markets.[3] Twenty years later Chile had reasonably developed markets for retirement products, as shown by 320,000 annuity policies and 200,000 PWs, and about 17 life insurance companies providing annuities and managing assets of almost 20 percent of GDP. Moreover, the large size of Chile's pension sector (assets exceeding 60 percent of GDP) indicates that Chile's market for retirement products should grow further and rapidly in the future.

The Chilean case does not enable the assessment of one of the issues that has attracted the interest of many researchers—why the voluntary demand for annuities seems so weak in many countries, and why many retiring workers favor taking a lump sum whenever this option is allowed.[4] This is because lump sums in Chile are subject to strict constraints that limit most workers' access. However, the Chilean experience allows the examination of the demand for annuities versus PWs, which provides many interesting insights and lessons. Most importantly, the Chilean experience allows the examination of all the regulatory issues faced by a country that had to develop its market for retirement products literally from scratch, and that has made considerable progress in this endeavor.

The Purpose and Structure of the Report

The purpose of the report is to examine the Chilean experience in developing the market for retirement products, including PWs and annuities, and to draw lessons for other countries that are also making efforts to develop such markets or anticipate the need to do so. The report examines the performance of the market and the evolution of the regulatory framework since the implementation of the pension reform of 1981, but with a focus on the past 10 years.

The report is structured as follows. The second chapter provides an overview of the market for retirement products in Chile. It describes briefly the main products, examines how the demand for these products has evolved over time, and then examines the structure and performance of the pension and life insurance industries, with a focus on the life insurance companies that have provided annuities. The third chapter identifies the main risks faced by workers, retirees, intermediaries, and the Government as the ultimate guarantor of the system. The overview of the market for retirement products in Chapter 2 and the analysis of risks in Chapter 3 together provide a useful starting point for the more in-depth analyses of key regulatory issues, which are presented in subsequent chapters.

The fourth chapter examines the internal risk management strategies followed by the providers of PWs and annuities, which in the Chilean case are the pension fund managers and the life insurance companies, respectively.[5] The chapter starts by examining the range of financial instruments available in Chile and then analyzes the main components of the asset-liability management strategies followed by pension fund managers and insurance companies. The analysis is focused on life insurance companies, because of the more complex technical issues involved in the management of annuities. This includes an examination of the pricing of annuities, the strategies to manage the long duration of annuity contracts, and the solutions to deal with the risk of specific asset classes. The section highlights the problems faced by risk managers in environments where there may not be sufficient assets and risk management tools available.

The fifth chapter examines in more detail the regulation of retirement products, including not only the design and regulation of PWs and annuity products, but also marketing regulations and the guarantees offered by the Government. The chapter also examines the problems in the marketing and distribution of annuities that emerged in the 1990s and the efforts to find a solution, culminating in the passage of a new Pension Law in 2004 that, among other measures, introduces an electronic quotation system and a ceiling on brokers' commissions.

The sixth chapter analyzes the regulation of intermediaries, including licensing, investment rules, and capital rules. The chapter places special emphasis on capital regulation, especially the innovative regulation put in place in the early 1990s to deal with the duration mismatch in the balance sheet of annuity providers. The chapter also examines resolution rules, and the experience gained in 2003 in handling the first bankruptcy of an annuity provider. Finally, the seventh chapter summarizes the main findings and conclusions, and presents a number of policy recommendations and lessons for other countries.

The report contains two technical annexes and one statistical annex. The technical annexes contain critical analytical work, whose results substantiate the analysis in the main report. Annex 1 provides a detailed analysis of money's worth ratios, based on an extensive panel of roughly 6,500 individual annuities. Annex 2 provides an econometric analysis of the annuity rate, based on a panel of 20 annuity providers and 40 quarters. Finally, the statistical annex provides more detailed statistical tables.

Notes

1. These are also called programmed withdrawals and drawdowns.
2. See, e.g., Blake (1999); Brown et al. (2001); Cardinale, Findlater, and Orszag (2002); Davis (2002); Fornero and Luciano (2004); Impavido, Thorburn, and Wadsworth (2003); James, Song, and Vittas (2001); Mitchell (2001); Orszag (2000); Palacios and Rofman (2001); and Valdés-Prieto (1998).
3. Chile did not have a voluntary pension system before 1981, aside from a few pension plans sponsored by international companies operating in Chile. These plans were offered to their Chilean employees but managed overseas.
4. This is labeled as the "annuity puzzle." See, e.g., Brown et al. (2001), and Mitchell (2002).
5. In many countries insurance companies provide both types of products.

CHAPTER 2

The Market for Retirement Products: An Overview*

The Evolution and Current Size of the Market for Retirement Products

Chile's market for retirement products has its origins in the well-known pension reform which was implemented in 1981, involving the gradual replacement of the public pay-as-you-go (PAYG) system by a private and fully funded (FF) system that operates on a defined contribution (DC) basis. Under the new system, workers contribute 10 percent of their wages to an individual account, up to a ceiling of 60 *unidades de fomento* (UFs), the equivalent of about three times the average wage. The UF is a unit of account indexed to prices which is widely used in the valuation of contracts and tax parameters.

Workers can choose freely among different pension funds managed by dedicated pension fund administrators (Administradoras de Fondos de Pensiones—AFPs). In addition to the 10 percent contribution, workers

*Sara Zervos provided valuable inputs to this chapter in the early stages of the analysis.

also pay about 2.2 percent of their wages to AFPs, part of which is used to pay for disability and survivorship insurance. At the time of retirement, workers use their accumulated balances to purchase an annuity from an insurance company or a phased withdrawal from a pension fund. Disabled workers are entitled to a disability pension and the dependents of deceased workers and pensioners are entitled to a survivor's pension. Both disabled and survivorship pensioners can also choose between annuities and phased withdrawals.

As participation in the pension system is mandatory, the State provides four types of guarantees. The first two apply to the accumulation phase and include a minimum relative return guarantee and a guarantee of coverage against disability and death risks. The minimum relative return guarantee involves the obligation for all AFPs to ensure a minimum return relative to the industry's average. If the AFP cannot honor this obligation, it is submitted to supervisory intervention and the Government provides the required resources to raise the return to the minimum. The second guarantee ensures that workers remain properly covered against disability and death risks, in case the insurer defaults in its obligations. (AFPs need to insure all members against these risks through a contract with a licensed life insurance company.)

The third and fourth guarantees apply to the retirement phase, and include a minimum pension guarantee (MPG) and a guarantee against the bankruptcy of annuity providers. The MPG entails an income floor for those workers who have contributed for at least 20 years and whose pensions do not reach or fall below the minimum. Changes to the MPG are discretionary, but its level has varied between 20 and 25 percent of the average covered wage, and has exceeded the poverty line by a growing margin, as shown in Figure 2.1.

The fourth is a guarantee in the case of institutional failure—if a worker's annuity provider defaults, the Government covers 100 percent of his/her annuity up to the MPG and 75 percent of the amount above this level up to a maximum of 60 UFs per month. The MPG is the most prominent guarantee and plays a major role in the Chilean pension system, not only for the minimum pension that it provides, but also for being a key parameter in the regulation of retirement conditions and retirement products.[1]

The new system was made mandatory for new entrants to the labor force and voluntary for existing workers, but most workers opted to switch to the new system, as they received recognition for their accrued rights (in the form of recognition bonds issued by the Government) and

Figure 2.1. Minimum Pension and Poverty Line in UF and Minimum Pension as % of the Average Covered Wage, 1990–2005

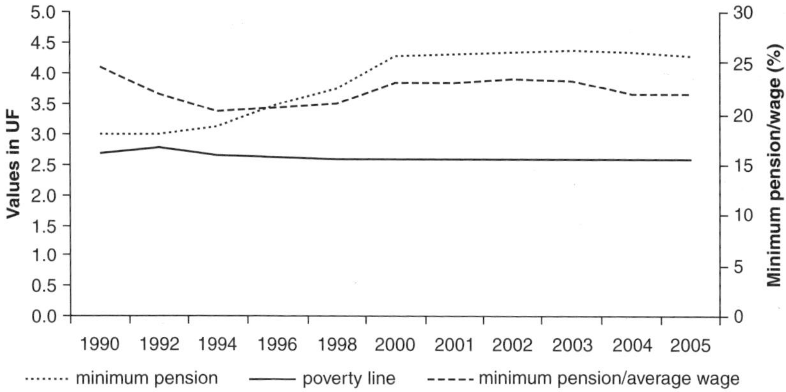

Source: SAFP.

enjoyed a reduction in contribution rates. The transition from the old to the new pension system is virtually completed—by 2004 nearly 97 percent of contributors were enrolled in the new pension system. The number of active contributors is 3.5 million workers, or the equivalent to about 55 percent of the labor force, as shown in Table 2.1. This coverage ratio is much higher than the Latin American average of 35 percent, although still low by comparison with the Organisation for Economic Co-operation and Development (OECD) average of about 90 percent. The number of pensioners under the new system has increased significantly, reaching 520,000 in 2004, the equivalent of 15 percent of the number of contributors and 38 percent of the number of total pensioners, as shown in Table 2.2.

The increase in the number of pensioners has led to a strong demand for both annuities and PWs, and a fast growth of the Chilean insurance sector in the past decade. As shown in Figure 2.2, total insurance premiums increased from 2.4 percent of GDP in 1990 to more than 4 percent of GDP in 2004, driven primarily by the life sector. The increase in life business has been driven in turn by the expansion of the annuity business. By the early 2000s total sales of immediate life annuities had reached almost 2 percent of GDP. The rapid expansion of the insurance sector is also reflected in its total assets, which grew from about 5 percent of GDP in the mid-1980s to about 20 percent of GDP in 2004. As shown in

Table 2.1. Coverage in the Chilean Pension System, 1990–2004

Year	*AFP Members*	*AFP Contributors*	*Employment*	*Labor Force*	*Members/ Labor Force*	*Contributors/ Labor Force*	*Contributors/ Employment*
1990	3,739,542	2,642,757	4,539,040	4,896,680	76.4%	54.0%	58.2%
1995	5,320,913	2,961,928	5,206,650	5,596,630	95.1%	52.9%	56.9%
2000	6,280,191	3,196,991	5,366,570	5,857,030	107.2%	54.6%	59.6%
2004	7,058,895	3,477,500	5,746,200	6,285,400	112.3%	55.4%	60.5%

Sources: SAFP, INP.

Table 2.2. Number of Pensioners in the Old and New Pension Systems, 1990–2004

Year	*Pensioners in Old Systems*	*Pensioners in New System*	*New Pensioners/ AFP Members*	*New Pensioners/ AFP Contributors*	*New Pensioners/ Total Pensioners*
1990	894,359	57,119	1.5%	2.2%	6.0%
1995	872,946	190,400	3.6%	6.4%	17.9%
2000	859,303	343,965	5.5%	10.8%	28.6%
2004	835,593	520,793	7.4%	15.0%	38.4%

Sources: SAFP, INP.

Figure 2.2. Insurance Premiums: Total, Life, Non-Life, and Annuities (in % of GDP), 1990–2003

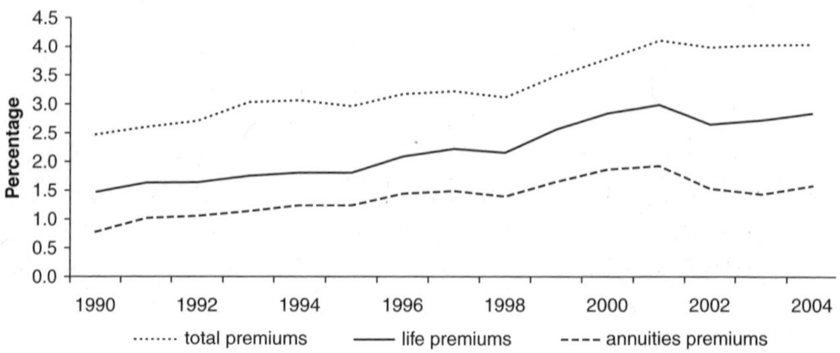

Source: SVS.

Figure 2.3, the assets of the insurance sector are still much smaller than the assets of the pension sector, but have generally grown at a faster pace—between 1990 and 2004 the ratio of insurance assets to pension assets increased from about 25 percent to 33 percent.[2]

Chile has today the highest life insurance premium relative to GDP in Latin America, and compares well with high income OECD countries. As shown in Table 2.3, life insurance premiums in 2001 were five times larger

Figure 2.3. Pension and Insurance Assets (% of GDP), 1990–2004

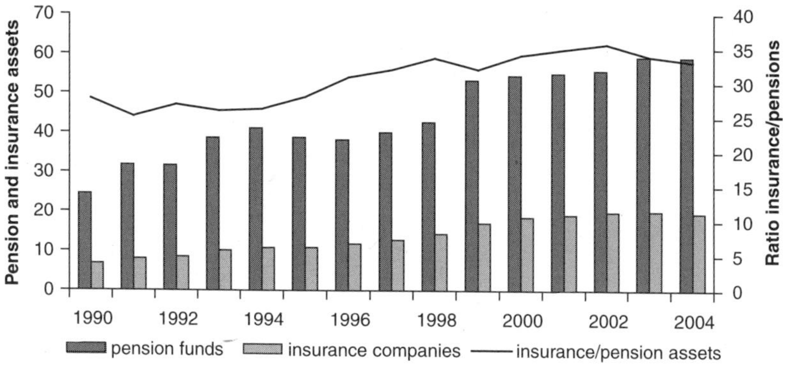

Source: SVS, SAFP.

Table 2.3. Insurance Premiums (% of GDP) in Chile, LAC, and OECD, 2001

	Chile	*Latin America*	*High Income OECD*
Insurance Premiums	4.6	2.2	7.9
Life	3.5	0.7	4.6
Annuities	1.9	-	-
PWs in AFPs[a]	0.5	-	-
Other	1.1	-	-
Non-Life	1.1	1.5	3.3

Sources: SVS, SAFP, OECD, Swiss Re, ASSAL.
a. Estimated.

than the Latin American average and not much smaller than the OECD average. This was essentially due to the large size of annuity and PW premiums, which amounted to about 2.4 percent of GDP and almost 70 percent of life premiums.[3] The lack of accurate information on annuity and PW premiums in OECD countries does not allow a straight comparison, but the size of annuities and PW markets in the OECD is known to be much smaller than Chile's. For example, in Australia (a country with a mandatory, private, and DC pension system like Chile) premiums on PWs and annuities amount to only 0.8 percent of GDP and 16 percent of life premiums. In the United States, the share of single immediate life annuities is only 7 percent of life business, excluding variable annuities in the accumulation stage.[4]

Comparing total insurance assets in Chile with the relevant benchmarks yields similar conclusions. As shown in Table 2.4, the ratio of insurance assets to GDP in Chile is about six times larger than the Latin

Table 2.4. Assets of Insurance Companies and Pension Funds (% of GDP) in Chile, LAC, and OECD

	Chile (2003)	*Latin America (2001)*	*High Income OECD (2001)*
Total Insurance Companies	20.1	3.4	48.8
Life	18.8	-	39.7
Annuities	15.0	-	-
Other	3.8	-	-
Non-Life	1.3	-	9.1
Pension Funds	59.7	11.1	33.8
Insurance + Pension Funds	79.8	14.5	82.6

Sources: SVS, SAFP, OECD, ASSAL.

American average, and the difference is primarily due to the large volume of annuity assets in Chile. The ratio of insurance assets to GDP is still smaller than the OECD average, but the share of annuity-related assets is probably larger than most OECD countries (a straight comparison of annuity assets is not possible due to the lack of information). Moreover, combining pension and insurance assets places Chile at the same level of OECD countries, and indicates that insurance assets in Chile should continue growing strongly in coming years, as these are pension accounts that will need to be converted into annuities and PWs at retirement. All in all, the numbers indicate that the Chilean market for retirement products is already large by international comparison, and should continue expanding rapidly in the coming decades.

The Conditions for Retirement

Workers can retire from the pension system at the normal retirement age of 65–60 for men and women, respectively. A worker can retire early if he or she has accumulated a sufficient balance in his or her account. This is defined as the balance needed to generate a pension equal at least to 50 percent of his or her average real wage in the past 10 years, and at least 110 percent of the MPG. The new Pension Law adopted in 2004 raised these parameters to 70 and 150 percent, respectively, and also introduced a stricter definition of the average real wage, excluding periods of no contributions.

These changes were introduced in reaction to the rapid growth of early retirees and the decline in the average age of retirement. As shown in Tables 2.5 and 2.6, by 2004 roughly 520,000 workers had retired under

Table 2.5. Breakdown of the Stock of Pensioners, by Type of Retirement, 1990–2004

		Normal Old Age		*Early Retirement*		*Disability + Survivors*	
Year	*Total*	*Number*	*% of Total*	*Number*	*% of Total*	*Number*	*% of Total*
1985	7,609	2,647	34.8%	-	0.0%	4,962	65.2%
1990	57,119	23,876	41.8%	5,790	10.1%	27,453	48.1%
1995	190,400	55,591	29.2%	69,537	36.5%	65,272	34.3%
2000	343,965	93,152	27.1%	132,221	38.4%	118,592	34.5%
2004	520,793	133,343	25.6%	220,929	42.4%	166,521	32.0%

Sources: SAFP.

Table 2.6. Average Retirement Age, by Type of Retirement, 1988–2003

	1988–1990	*1991–1995*	*1996–2000*	*2001–2003*
Old Age	65	65	65	64
Men	67	67	67	66
Women	63	62	62	62
Early Retirement	58	57	56	55
Men	58	57	56	56
Women	56	55	54	53

Source: SAFP.

the new system, the share of early retirees had increased to more than 40 percent of the total, and the average age of retirement had declined by three years among early retirees. Early retirement in Chile does not necessarily imply withdrawal from the labor force, and the average pension of early retirees is higher then the average pension of normal old-age retirees, because their incomes are higher (Table 2.7). Nonetheless, there was a concern that the retirement rules were too liberal, that many workers were induced to retire early by insurance brokers, and that there was a risk of low replacement ratios in the future, with possible fiscal consequences through access to the MPG. The stricter conditions for early retirement were part of a broader package of reforms that also included changes in marketing rules and that will be examined in more detail in the following chapters.

Disabled workers are entitled to a full or partial disability pension, depending on the severity of their case and after medical examination. All disabled pensioners need to be recertified after a period of three years. Unlike old-age and early retirement pensions, disability pensions are determined according to a defined benefit formula and amount to 70 percent of the average real wage of the member in the 10 years preceding disability. Survivor pensions are defined as 50 percent of the average wage of the member who dies before retirement, paid to the surviving spouse

Table 2.7. Average Monthly Pensions by Type (in UF), 1990–2004, Period Averages

	Old Age	*Early Retirement*	*Disability*	*Survivorship*	*Total*
1990–94	5.6	9.5	7.4	2.7	5.7
1995–99	6.1	9.8	7.7	3.2	6.8
2000–04	6.8	10.2	8.2	3.7	7.4

Source: SAFP.

and 15 percent to each surviving child under 21 years of age. In the early phase of the new pension system most pensioners were disability and survivor pensioners and there were few old-age retirees. This is expected, as most retiring workers in the early 1980s preferred to stay in the old system because of their acquired rights. The share of disability and survivor pensioners has recently stabilized around one-third of the total.[5]

The Menu of Retirement Products

Retiring workers can take a partial lump sum subject to strict conditions and can also choose among three basic retirement products: a PW, an annuity, and a temporary withdrawal (TW) combined with a deferred annuity. This section provides a brief description of these products. (A much more detailed analysis of product regulation is provided in Chapter 5.) Workers can take a partial lump sum if they meet strict conditions, namely, the remaining balance must finance a pension equal at least to 70 percent of the average real wage of the worker in the 10 years preceding retirement and 120 percent of the MPG. In 2004 the second condition was raised to 150 percent of the MPG. Relatively few workers draw partial lump sums and the amounts are generally considered to be small.

The basic condition for buying an annuity at the normal retirement age is that it must be higher than the MPG. Workers who do not meet this basic condition must buy a PW and receive the MPG from their own balance until it is exhausted, and after that point, receive the MPG from the State via the AFP. Annuities are provided by life insurance companies and are freely priced according to age, gender, and market conditions, particularly the level of interest rates. Workers can choose among all licensed companies upon retirement. Until recently, all annuities were fixed and indexed to prices (denominated in UFs). The new Pension Law introduced other options, including combinations of PWs and fixed indexed annuities, and combinations of variable and fixed indexed annuities. Married males still have to buy joint life annuities. Annuities with a guarantee period are optional, entitling the spouse to receive the same levels as the main beneficiary, if the main beneficiary's death occurs within the guarantee period.

In the PW option, the individual balance remains in the AFP and is drawn according to a formula that takes into consideration life expectancy. In the past, PW holders had no choice of the fund—their balances were invested in the same diversified portfolio of assets as active workers. Since 2002 PW holders can choose from three different funds, which are differentiated according to the share of equity that they can hold – 40, 20, and 0 percent, respectively (as described in Chapter 4, active workers have access to two additional funds that can hold more equity). At the end of each year PW payments are recalculated based on the residual balance and the drawdown formula. PW holders can decide to draw less than the formula, provided it is at least equal to the MPG, but not more. PW holders can also switch to an annuity at any time during retirement provided that the annuity exceeds the MPG. Upon death of the main beneficiary, the spouse continues receiving the PW payments, and upon his/her death, the residual balance goes to the heirs as a bequest.

TWs involve a fixed drawdown for a predefined number of years (most commonly one year) followed by a deferred annuity. The size of the two types of payouts is defined jointly at the time of retirement and the balance is split accordingly between the AFP and the selected insurance company. The TW payout cannot be lower than either the MPG or the eventual annuity and cannot be higher than twice the level of the eventual annuity. TWs differ from PWs by the fact that they involve a deferred annuity, and can be considered as an annuity for all practical purposes.

These three retirement products have different strong and weak aspects, and appeal to workers with different needs and risk profiles. Fixed and indexed annuities provide protection against investment and longevity risk, but do not allow bequests, unless they are guaranteed. The holder is subject to the risk of bankruptcy of the annuity provider, although this risk is reduced by the annuity guarantee. PWs allow the holder to share the gains in the capital market. If returns are high, PW payments may even increase in the initial years. They also allow bequests. However, PWs expose holders to investment and longevity risk. PW payments decline to very low levels over time, and eventually reach the MPG. Therefore, the PW holder still retains basic longevity insurance through the MPG, but at this stage he or she receives the minimum pension. TWs offer the possibility of larger initial payouts in the early years, combined with longevity insurance when the deferred annuity is received.

The Demand for Retirement Products

The number of retirees choosing annuities has increased considerably in the past 20 years. As shown in Table 2.8, only 3 percent of the stock of pensioners had chosen annuities in 1985, while in 2004 this percentage had increased to more than 60 percent, including the small stock of TW holders. Excluding disability and survivor pensioners, the share of annuities increases to roughly 70 percent. These numbers imply one of the highest rates of annuitization in the world. The average annuity payment is significantly higher than the average PW payment, as shown in Table 2.9, showing that the average income of the annuitant population is higher. The average TW payment is much higher, reflecting a segment of higher income annuity holders.

A dataset containing information on all the new annuities issued in March 1999, 2002, 2003, 2004, and 2005 provides more insights into the selection of retirement products. As shown in Table 2.10, most annuities are joint life, reflecting the regulation that forces married males to take this type of annuity. The share of deferred annuities in the flows of annuities increased slightly from 20 to 30 percent, but the period of deferment has remained short, roughly around one year. The short period of deferment helps explain the low share of TWs in the total stock of retirement products.

The share of guaranteed annuities is surprisingly large, and most of these annuities are guaranteed for periods of 10–15 years and even longer. The strong demand for guaranteed annuities reveals a voluntary insurance/income smoothing arrangement within the family unit, as well as a preference for bequests. The main beneficiary accepts a lower payment in exchange for the maintenance of the same payment to the surviving spouse upon his/her death during the guaranteed period (when the guarantee expires the payment is reduced to 60 percent of the main annuity). If both die, the heirs keep receiving the payments during the guaranteed period. In the case of single annuities, payments go directly to the heirs during the guaranteed period.

There is a very strong association between annuitization and early retirement in Chile. As shown in Figure 2.4a, approximately 65 percent of normal-age retirees take PWs and only 35 percent take annuities. By contrast, 90 percent of early retirees take annuities and only 10 percent take PWs. Examining the distribution from the point of view of the retirement product (Figure 2.4d), 60 percent of all annuitants are early retirees and only 15 percent are normal-age retirees (the remainder are disabled

Table 2.8. Breakdown of Stock of Pensions, by Type of Instrument, 1990–2004

		PWs		*TWs*		*Annuities*	
Year	*Total*	*Number*	*% of Total*	*Number*	*% of Total*	*Number*	*% of Total*
1985	7,609	7,373	96.8%	—	0.0%	236	3.2%
1990	57,119	36,696	64.2%	148	0.3%	20,275	35.5%
1995	190,400	98,699	51.8%	6,803	3.6%	84,898	44.6%
2000	343,965	147,532	42.9%	6,632	1.9%	189,801	55.2%
2004	520,793	196,242	37.7%	6,193	1.2%	318,358	61.1%

Sources: SAFP.

Table 2.9. Average Pensions by Instrument (in UF), 1990–2004, Period Averages

Period	*PWs*	*Annuities*	*TWs*	*Average*
1990–04	3.8	7.5	25.0	5.7
1995–09	4.8	7.5	23.4	6.6
2000–04	5.0	7.9	26.7	7.0

Source: SAFP.

Table 2.10. Types of Annuities Issued in March 1999, 2002, 2003, 2004, and 2005

	March 1999	*March 2002*	*March 2003*	*March 2004*	*March 2005*
Number of annuities issued	937	1,517	1,193	1,490	1,391
Number of joint annuities	670	1,069	823	973	763
Number of deferred annuities	199	331	307	409	419
(% of total)	(21.2%)	(21.8%)	(25.7%)	(27.5%)	(30.1%)
Number deferred for 12 months	164	275	238	322	315
Number of guaranteed annuities	708	1,191	948	1,153	1,093
(% of total)	(85.6%)	(78.5%)	(79.5%)	(77.4%)	(78.6%)
Number guaranteed for 10 and 15 years	666	1088	846	1016	912

Source: SVS.

retirees and survivors). If disability and survivors are excluded, the share of early retirees in the stock of annuities increases to 80 percent.

The high rate of annuitization in Chile, and its relation to early retirement, is the result of several factors (which are examined in more detail in Chapter 5). First, restrictions on lump sums increase the demand for all retirement products, including annuities. Second, the absence of a front-ended first pillar benefit and the low level of the back-ended MPG imply that middle and higher income retirees who take PWs are substantially exposed to investment and longevity risks. These retirees have no

Figure 2.4. Shares of PWs and Annuities in the Stock of Normal Old-Age Pensions (in %), 1990–2004

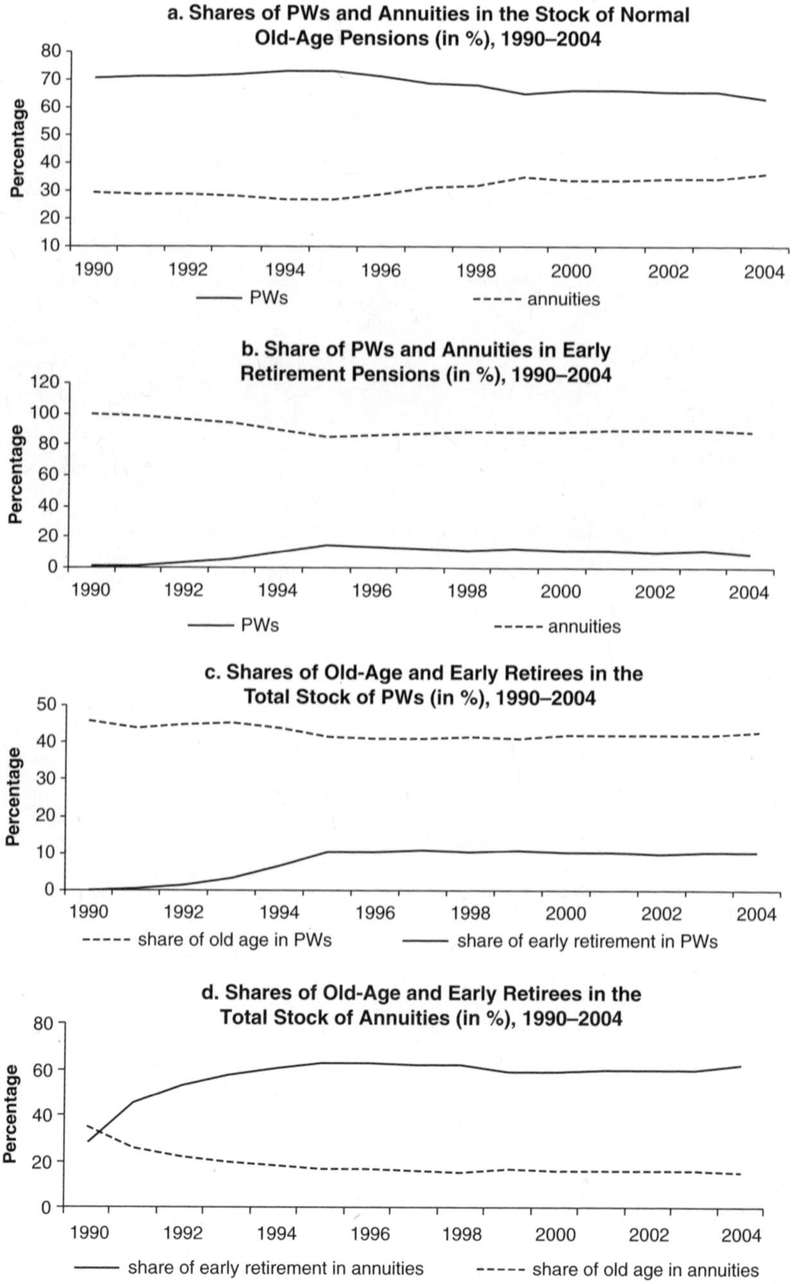

Source: SAFP.

other stable source of retirement income and can experience a large erosion of the real value of their pensions if they take a PW. Therefore, they may find attractive the protection provided by annuities. Moreover, these retirees tend to be early retirees precisely because only higher income retirees can meet the conditions for early retirement.

Third, low income workers who retire close to the MPG find PWs more attractive, because they can enjoy any high returns in the early phase while not being exposed to downside risk – if returns prove weak they will receive the MPG anyway. Moreover, PW holders tend to be lower income workers retiring at the normal age, precisely because they cannot meet the conditions for early retirement. The PW population also includes low income workers who are forced to take PWs because of their very small balances.

Finally, the marketing of retirement products is one-sided. AFPs focus on the accumulation phase of the pension business and do not market PWs actively. By contrast, life insurance companies depend on the annuity business and have marketed their products aggressively. Insurance brokers obtain their income from commissions on annuity premiums, and market primarily to higher income workers, frequently inducing these workers to retire early and annuitize. Brokers do not receive any commission from a client or provider in the case of the client taking a PW.[6]

The Structure of the Market for Retirement Products

The structure of the pension and life insurance sectors evolved very differently in the past 20 years. As shown in Figure 2.5, the pension sector became very concentrated during the 1990s, with the number of AFPs declining from 20 to 8 in the decade, and to only 6 more recently. This reduction in the number of participants was reflected in a sharp increase in concentration ratios. As shown in Figure 2.6, the three largest AFPs increased their combined market share significantly and now account for more than 70 percent of total assets. The increase in the Herfindahl index was even more pronounced.

By contrast, the fast increase in the number of annuity contracts in the 1990s attracted new entrants to the life insurance market, increasing the total number of life insurance companies to 34 by the late 1990s, 23 of which were providing annuities. At that time foreign participation was substantial, accounting for two-thirds of total capital. The annuities market was very concentrated in its early stages—by the end of the 1980s the share of the three largest firms in the annuity business amounted to 87 percent.

Figure 2.5. Number of Life Insurance Companies, Annuity Providers, and AFPs, 1988–2005

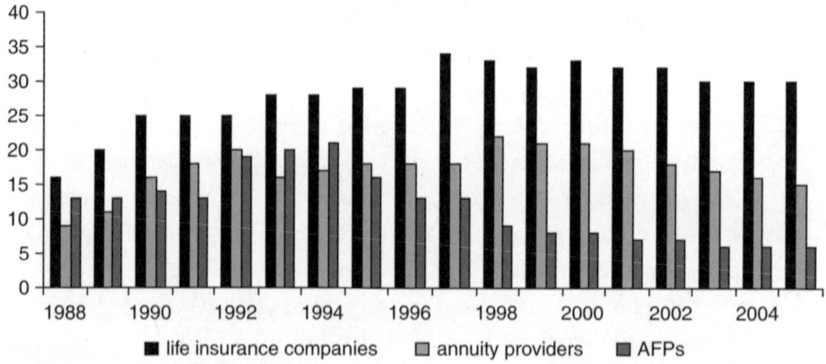

Source: SVS, SAFP.

Figure 2.6. Market Concentration Ratios in Herfindahl Pensions and Annuities, and Share of the Three Largest Firms, 1988–2005

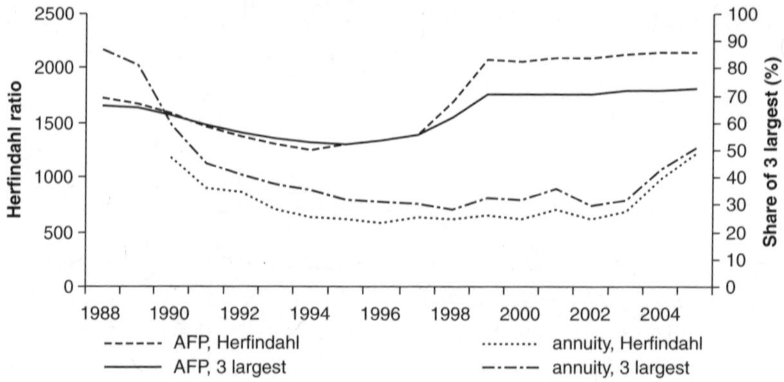

Source: SVS, SAFP.

The increase in the number of participants in the 1990s led to a continuous decrease in concentration ratios, and one decade later the share of the three largest firms had declined to less than 30 percent (about 10 percent each).

In recent years some life insurance companies have decided to exit the annuities segment of the life insurance market, discouraged by the very intensive degree of competition, the thin intermediation spreads and the relatively low returns on equity (see the next section). The new electronic quotation system introduced in 2004 (Chapter 5) has contributed to more transparency and price competition, opening room for some firms to gain market shares and inducing others to leave the market. These factors have resulted in an increase in concentration ratios, whether measured by the three-firm concentration ratio or the Herfindahl index. However, the annuities sector in Chile today still remains more competitive than the AFP sector, whether measured by the number of participants or concentration ratios. It is also important to note that life insurance companies that decide to exit the annuities market can enter the market again if the conditions prove attractive, that is, the annuities market not only remains less concentrated than the AFP market, but also looks more contestable.

The Performance of the PW Market

This section examines briefly the performance of AFPs in providing PWs. The pension market has been extensively examined in the literature, with most researchers concluding that AFPs have generated high real returns on managed funds, but still charge high fees on contributors. Gross and net real returns have averaged 10 and 7 percent p.a. since the creation of the system in 1981, well above the average growth of real wages of 2 percent p.a. in the same period. At the same time, the wedge of 3 percent reflects the high fees that have been charged. This wedge reflects the high costs and very high profit margins during this period—in the past 10 years AFPs have always earned real returns on equity (ROE) above 20 percent, and in some years the average ROE reached 50 percent.

AFP costs and fees have declined significantly in the past 20 years, but still remain high. In 2003 total fees amounted to 1.0–1.1 percent of assets, including the large fees of about 100 basis points paid to foreign asset managers, which are not visible because they are netted from the returns. By comparison, the average costs of U.S. occupational pension funds of similar size are about 0.5 percent of assets. The average fees of U.S. mutual funds of similar size are about 1 percent of assets, but these include equity funds with high turnover. Bond funds and equity funds with low turnover have much lower fees.[7] These figures indicate that there is still scope for reducing costs, profit margins and fees.

The AFP market has generally performed better for PW holders than active contributors, because they earn the same rates of return as active workers in the three portfolios where they can invest, but are charged much lower fees. Since the multiportfolio regime was created in 2002, active workers and PW holders can choose among five and three different portfolios, respectively. PW holders are not allowed to invest in the two riskiest funds but still have access to a reasonable range of portfolios, and can expect to earn real rates of return of 4 to 7 percent p.a. depending on their tolerance to risk (Chapter 4). At the same time, PW holders are charged much lower fees for the management of their accounts. As discussed in more detail in Chapter 5, AFPs do not maintain a sales force for the distribution of PWs, and charge a fee of only 1 percent on PW benefits paid, an amount that is designed to cover just marginal administration costs. AFPs have been able to generate high returns on equity, but these returns derive from the accumulation phase, not the payout phase.

The Performance of the Annuities Market: The Consumer's Side

Assessing market performance in the annuities market involves the use of more elaborate indicators, given the different nature of annuity contracts and their very long duration. One indicator that is commonly used is the money's worth ratio (MWR), defined as the ratio of the expected present value of benefit payments to the annuity premium. This indicator measures how much the annuitant gets back for the premium paid. A ratio equal to one is usually interpreted as an actuarially fair annuity. Table 2.11 provides information on MWRs for all annuities issued in March 1999, 2002, 2003, 2004, and 2005. A detailed analysis of MWRs is provided in Annex 1.

Table 2.11. Average MWRs for Annuities Issued in March 1999, 2002, 2003, 2004, and 2005

	March 1999	*March 2002*	*March 2003*	*March 2004*	*March 2005*
All cases	0.978	1.080	1.036	1.064	1.062
maximum	1.148	1.222	1.181	1.276	1.223
minimum	0.755	0.872	0.872	0.876	0.706
Male, Age 55	0.981	1.081	1.056	1.036	1.042
Male, Age 65	0.996	1.098	1.066	1.042	1.067
Female, Age 55	0.994	1.105	1.056	1.060	1.064
Female, Age 60	1.021	1.120	1.066	1.074	1.083
Joint Life (Male 65, Female 60)	0.998	1.089	1.058	1.062	1.069
Premium up to UF1,000	0.980	1.078	1.045	1.068	1.067
Premium above UF3,000	0.997	1.099	1.047	1.075	1.071
Non-guaranteed	0.990	1.092	1.045	1.071	1.073
Guaranteed	0.974	1.076	1.033	1.062	1.059
Without deferment	0.979	1.079	1.035	1.063	1.061
With deferment	0.974	1.080	1.036	1.067	1.064

Source: Annex 1.

As shown in Table 2.11, the average MWR was slightly lower than 1 in 1999 and has been above 1 since then, indicating that Chilean annuitants have generally got a good value for their premiums. However, the spread between the maximum and minimum ratios has been wide, amounting to 40 percent in some years, and suggesting that some annuitants may have not obtained as good a deal. Average money's worth ratios are lower for younger retirees, consistent with the greater investment and longevity risks involved in annuities with longer durations. MWRs are lower for joint annuities by comparison with single annuities consistent with their longer duration as well.

MWRs are higher for larger premiums, indicating that insurance companies are willing to pay higher annuity rates for larger balances, just like banks pay higher interest rates for large deposits, because unit costs are lower and profit margins are higher in these cases. Single female annuities are higher than MWRs of single male annuities, despite their longer expected duration. This result may be partly due to the higher average premium in the case of single females. MWRs of guaranteed annuities are lower than those of non-guaranteed, because long guaranteed periods change the time path of payments and increase duration. Finally, the MWRs of deferred annuities are higher than those of non-deferred, but the difference is marginal.

The availability of a large dataset on individual annuities in Chile allows the formal testing of these relationships.[8] As shown in Table 2.12, MWRs are positively and significantly related to age and the size of the premium, and negatively and significantly related to the length of the guaranteed period. The sign of the deferred coefficient is also positive and

Table 2.12. Money's Worth Ratios as a Function of Selected Variables
(Pooled data; Least squares with robust standard errors)

Variable	*Coefficient*	*t-statistic*	*p-values*	*Other statistics*
Constant	62.39	86.31	0.000	Dep. Variable: MWR*100
Age	0.41	45.700	0.000	No. Observations = 6,526
Log (premium)	1.62	22.07	0.000	
Guarantee	−0.13	−16.04	0.000	$R^2 = 0.639$
Deferment	0.02	2.24	0.025	Adj. $R^2 = 0.638$
Male	1.35	8.98	0.000	Prob. > F = 0.000
Female	4.02	40.59	0.000	Mean Dep. Variable: 104.9
2002	10.66	76.10	0.000	S.D. Dep. Variable: 5.60
2003	5.70	38.72	0.000	
2004	8.25	58.67	0.000	
2005	6.51	44.72	0.000	

Source: Annex 1.

significant, but this was the only variable that became non-significant when the MWR equation was estimated for each year separately. In any case, the result should be qualified by the short length of deferment. Finally, the MWRs of single male and female annuities are significantly higher than those of joint life annuities, as indicated by the statistics of the respective dummy variables.

Overall, the major conclusions to be drawn from this analysis are that, in Chile, there is evidence that annuities with longer expected durations get lower MWRs than annuities with shorter expected durations, and that larger premiums get better value on average than smaller ones. This is consistent with the view that insurers are concerned with the higher reinvestment and longevity risks presented by long durations and, in the case of size, the effect of fixed expense loadings is more significant in the Chilean market than attempts to differentiate mortality between annuitants of different income levels.

At the same time, the regression results also show that nearly 40 percent of the variations in individual MWRs are not explained by these individual characteristics. The wide spread between the highest and the lowest annuity is intriguing, and is especially wide for lower premiums, as shown in Annex 1, indicating that market search may be inefficient among lower income retirees. Further examination of the dataset reveals that annuitants with the same characteristics such as age, premium, and gender frequently receive materially different annuities.

Comparing average MWRs in Chile with those estimated for other countries suggests that Chilean annuitants have generally got a better deal than annuitants in other countries, especially considering that Chilean annuities are indexed. As shown in Tables 2.11 and 2.13, average MWRs in Chile are higher than the average nominal MWRs estimated for other countries, which range from 0.9 to 1. The differences are striking in the case of indexed annuities – buyers of indexed annuities in the United Kingdom get a much lower annuity value of 86 percent of the premium, and pay a charge of about 5 percent of the premium to obtain inflation protection. The cost of inflation protection in the United States is even higher, amounting to more than 20 percent of the premium. This result is at least in part explained by the larger supply of indexed instruments in the Chilean case, including not only indexed Government bonds, but also other higher yield fixed interest instruments that allow providers to hedge inflation risk while obtaining more attractive returns.[9]

While the differences between MWRs of indexed annuities in Chile and other countries can be reasonably explained, other differences cannot

Table 2.13. Average Money's Worth Ratios in Selected Countries

	Australia (James)	*Canada (James)*	*Switzerl. (James)*	*UK[1] (James)*	*UK (Cannon)*	*UK (James)*	*US[2] (Brown)*
Nominal Annuities							
Male, Age 55	—	—	—	—	—	—	0.934
Male, Age 65	1.013	0.981	1.046	—	0.977	0.908	0927
Female, Age 55	—	—	—	—	—	0.928	0.927
Female, Age 65	1.002	0.976	1.037	—	0.979	0.907	0.927
Joint	0.988	0.980	0.985	0.981	0.987	—	0.929
Indexed Annuities							
Male, Age 55	—	—	—	—	—	0.867	
Male, Age 65	—	—	—	—	0.887	0.854	0.822
Female, Age 55	—	—	—	—	—	0.876	—
Female, Age 65	—	—	—	—	0.877	0.857	0.782
Joint	—	—	—	—	0.880	—	—

Note and sources: Annex 1.

be easily interpreted. For example, the relationship between MWRs and age is negative in the U.K. and U.S. cases, quite the inverse of the Chilean case. As mentioned before, the positive relationship in the Chilean case can be explained by the higher reinvestment and mortality risks associated with annuities with longer expected durations. The same factor also explains the lower MWRs of joint annuities in Chile, and it is noteworthy that joint annuities have similar or lower MWRs than single annuities in other countries as well. Therefore, the inverse relationship between MWRs and age in the U.K. and U.S. cases probably reflects factors specific to those countries.[10]

Market performance can also be measured by the relationship between the annuity rate (defined as the internal rate of return on the annuity) and the risk free rate. As shown in Figure 2.7, the average annuity rate measured by the recently built RV-04 mortality table tracked the interest rate on 20-year Central Bank bonds reasonably well during the 1990s, with the difference between the two rates averaging 0.7 percent p.a. in this period.[11] It would be tempting to conclude that retired workers could have obtained a better deal by investing directly in risk-free bonds, but this conclusion would need to be modified considering the costs and the risks to retirees, especially the exposure to longevity risk.

In 2001 the difference between the two rates inverted, and the annuity rate has exceeded the risk-free rate since then. This negative difference between the risk-free rate and the annuity rate is unusual. For example,

Figure 2.7. Average Annuity Rate and the Risk-Free Rate (% p.a.), 1993–2005

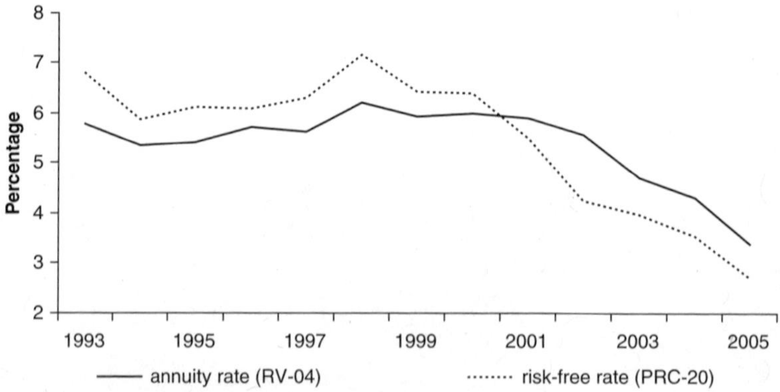

Source: SVS, Central Bank.

Brown et al. (2001) calculate the internal rates of return on U.S. annuities and obtain rates ranging from 5.9 to 6.5 percent p.a., lower than the yields of 10 and 30-year Treasury bonds—which were 7.1 and 7.3 percent p.a. in the same period. James, Song, and Vittas (2001) perform the same exercise for several countries and obtain similar results.

The average MWRs estimated for March 1999, 2002, 2003, 2004, and 2005 are consistent with the movements in the two rates. The MWR is slightly lower than 1 in 1999, consistent with a slightly higher risk-free rate, and higher than 1 in the following years, consistent with a higher annuity rate. The highest MWRs were obtained for 2002, the period when the annuity rate exceeded the risk-free rate by the widest margin. The MWRs for 2004 and 2005 are similar, consistent with a stable relationship between the two rates. We have not estimated MWRs for previous years, but the relationship between the two rates suggests that MWRs were lower in the 1990s and increased significantly after 2000. All in all, these results suggest that today annuitants in Chile are getting a better value for their premiums, and are also getting a better deal, on average, than annuitants in other countries.

The Performance of the Annuities Market: The Provider's Side

The question that arises in Chile is whether the high MWRs can be sustained. Annuity providers could in principle pay high annuity rates and still achieve positive spreads by investing in higher yield paper, and Table 2.14

Table 2.14. Portfolio of Life Insurance Companies (in % of Total), 1991–2005[a]

	1991	*1995*	*2000*	*2003*	*2005*
Government Sector	38.3	40.3	28.7	17.6	16.5
Financial Sector	23.0	28.4	45.1	37.6	34.6
Mortgage Bonds	13.9	18.6	24.2	18.8	12.8
Mortgage-Backed Securities	3.0	6.0	10.1	10.1	9.1
Company Sector	29.0	22.1	15.3	33.4	38.5
Shares	8.9	10.2	3.4	2.9	3.9
Bonds	20.1	10.7	10.7	29.3	33.5
Real Estate	7.8	7.7	7.4	7.3	7.5
Other Assets	2.0	1.5	3.6	4.1	6.8
Total	**100.0**	**100.0**	**100.0**	**100.0**	**100.0**

Source: SVS.

[a] December values in 1991–2003 and June values in 2005.

indicates that the industry has shifted towards higher yield mortgage-backed securities and corporate bonds since 1995. The move towards corporate bonds since 2000 is particularly noteworthy, with the share of this instrument increasing from 10 to almost 35 percent of the portfolio. These instruments are also indexed and pay a higher yield than Government and Central Bank bonds, allowing providers to match their liabilities while extracting a higher return.

Annuity providers may have been able to extract a higher return adjusted for credit risk, as these instruments are much less liquid than Government or Central Banks and probably pay a liquidity premium. Providers may be able to extract this premium due to their much longer investment horizon. Moreover, providers have only held bonds issued by banks and corporations with very good credit standings—usually rated AA and higher, and sometimes with specific credit enhancement features, thus maintaining credit risk at relatively low levels.

This pursuit for higher yields has been observed in other countries as well. For example, the TIAA-CREF pension fund, which is the largest annuity provider in the United States, only holds privately issued, fixed income instruments offering higher yields in order to match its fixed annuities, including a large share of less liquid instruments bought through private placements (Annex 2). The Chilean situation is different not because of the shift towards fixed income instruments issued by the private sector, but because these instruments are also indexed, allowing providers to match their indexed liabilities while extracting higher yields (Chapter 4 reviews asset and liability management strategies in greater detail).

This portfolio strategy has apparently succeeded in preserving positive financial spreads. As shown in Figure 2.8, the marginal return on the fixed income portfolio, measured by the corporate bond rate, has exceeded the annuity rate every year, with the difference amounting to about 100 basis points after 2001. However, this spread was still thin considering the need to cover all costs and risks and still generate a positive return on equity.

Providers' costs include the commissions paid to annuity brokers and all operating costs. As shown in Figure 2.9, commissions averaged 3 percent of the premium in the early 1990s, increased continuously to almost 6 percent at the end of the decade, and then decreased sharply to levels around 2 percent. The increase in the 1990s reflected the practice of

Figure 2.8. Annuity Rate, Adjusted Annuity Rate, Central Bank Bonds and Corporate Bonds (% p.a.), 1993–2005

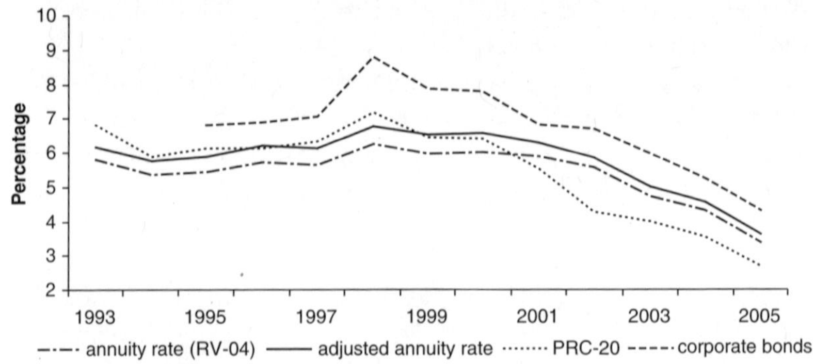

Source: Central Bank of Chile, SVS, SAFP.

Figure 2.9. Commission Rates (% of the Premium) 1990–2005

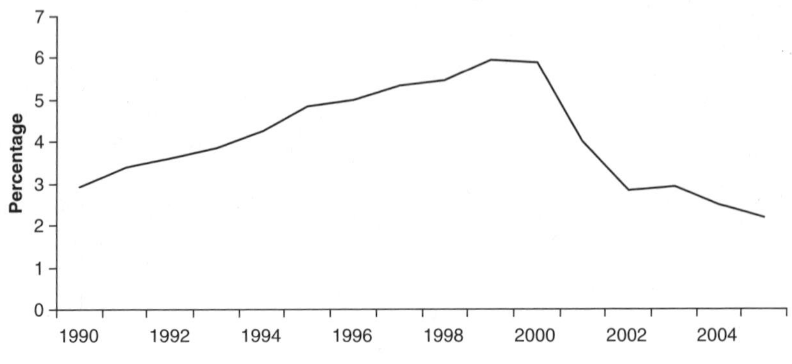

Source: Central Bank of Chile, SVS, SAFP.

charging higher commissions and providing an informal (and illegal) cash rebate to the retiree. This cash rebate amounted de facto to a partial lump sum and proved a popular marketing device, but it was also inconsistent with the intention of the law and prompted a reaction from policy makers, who at the end of 2000 submitted a draft new Pension Law to Congress, that, among other things, capped broker's commissions and proposed a new electronic quotation system. Although the new Pension Law was only passed in 2004, the threat of the Law and political pressures induced a change in behavior, as indicated by the sharp decline in commissions (Chapter 5 examines product and marketing regulation in more detail).[12]

The commission cost has added about 30 basis points to the annuity rate, as shown by the adjusted annuity rate line in Figure 2.8, reducing the intermediation spread commensurately.[13] In addition, providers also need to cover their operating costs, which in 2003 amounted to more than 1.5 percent of assets, implying a negative spread overall. As shown in Figure 2.10, life insurance companies have reduced their operating costs and may continue reducing them further, but even if cost ratios decline to 0.6 percent, which is lowest cost ratio among OECD countries (see Annex 3), prospective profit margins would appear to remain unattractive.

The analysis of money's worth ratios and intermediation spreads suggests that at least some providers may have experienced some losses from the annuities issued in the past four years. These losses did not result in financial problems for the companies because of the strong capital and

Figure 2.10. Administrative Costs of Annuity Providers, as % of Total Assets, 1989–2003

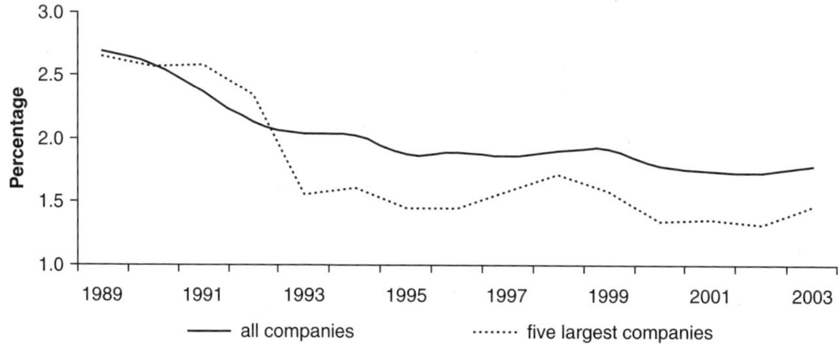

Source: Central Bank of Chile, SVS, SAFP.

reserve buffer accumulated from previous years, and which was due to strict capital regulations implemented in the early 1990s (Chapter 6 examines the regulation of providers in more detail). However, the analysis also suggests that the high MWRs of the past four years probably cannot be sustained, as they would imply further erosion of capital, at least for some companies.

The question arises as to why profit-maximizing companies have issued annuities with such thin financial margins. It is unlikely that insurance companies have incorrectly priced their annuities due to outdated mortality tables, because most companies seem to have sufficient technical capacity, including well-trained actuaries. It is more likely that companies have priced their annuities counting on a future increase in interest rates from the low recent levels. The intermediation spreads shown in Figure 2.8 do not capture the spread earned over the entire life of the annuity contract because assets have a shorter duration than liabilities. If interest rates increase (above the levels implicit in the current yield curve) margins earned on currently issued contracts would increase as well.

There is also the possibility that some companies are deliberately adopting aggressive pricing strategies in order to drive competitors out of the market and gain market share. All the industry participants acknowledge that intermediation margins have been thin and returns on equity low, and that is probably the reason why some life insurance companies have decided to exit the annuities market in recent years. The industry has become more concentrated as noted above, and the possibility that the annuities market will undergo a process of consolidation similar to that observed in the pension sector in the 1990s cannot be entirely discarded.

The availability of quarterly data on all annuity providers over the 1993–2003 period allows the examination of some of these issues in greater detail. Table 2.15 presents the results of a regression of the average annuity rate of early retirement annuities (the bulk of the annuities market) against a number of variables that include the risk-free rate (RF); the share of higher yield fixed income instruments in the fixed income portfolio of providers (SOFI); the share of riskier assets such as equity and foreign assets in the portfolio (SOA); the leverage ratio (LEV) as an indication of the available capital and level of risk to the annuitant; the market share measured by the stock of reserves (MSHARE); the average premium (AP[EARLY]); the broker's commission rate (CR); and the Herfindahl concentration index (HER[EARLY]). The annuity rate equation and the econometric results are discussed in greater detail in Annex 2.

Table 2.15. Main Determinants of the Average Annuity Rate

Fixed effects estimation, with robust standard errors; Total panel observations: 693; R2 = 0.7995; Adj. R2 = 0.7890; F-Statistic = 76.2162 ; p-value(F-Statistic) = 0.0000

Variable	*Coefficient*	*Std. Error*	*t-Statistic*	*p-value*
C	3.0760	0.2187	14.0668	0.0000***
RF	0.3639	0.0209	17.4077	0.0000***
SOFI	0.0029	0.0009	3.1772	0.0016***
SOA	0.0086	0.0038	2.2509	0.0247**
LEV	0.0110	0.0039	2.7967	0.0053***
MSHARE	−3.4900	0.5727	−6.0937	0.0000***
AP(EARLY)	0.0002	$2.57 \times e^{-5}$	6.8931	0.0000***
CR	−0.0441	0.0180	−2.4431	0.0148**
HER(EARLY)	−5.1390	0.7219	−7.1191	0.0000***
TREND	−0.0005	0.0020	−0.2244	0.8225
D	−1.2547	0.2437	−5.1479	0.0000***
RF × D	0.4118	0.0457	9.0149	0.0000***
AP(EARLY) × D	−0.0001	$3.95 \times e^{-5}$	−3.0191	0.0026***
CR × D	−0.0808	0.0351	−2.3035	0.0215**

Source: Annex 2.

*** = significant at the 1% level, ** = significant at the 5% level.

As shown in Table 2.15, the coefficients have the expected sign (or signs that cannot be determined a priori but that can be reasonably explained) and are significant. The annuity rate responds positively to the risk free rate, although the elasticity is lower than 1 for the sample period as whole. The positive and significant coefficient for SOFI suggests that the portfolio shift from Government and Central Bank bonds towards higher yield mortgage and corporate bonds led to higher annuity rates overall, and also that companies with a higher share of these assets pay higher rates. It is possible that companies operating in a very competitive environment have shared part of the liquidity premium paid by these assets with annuitants. It is also possible that annuitants may demand a risk premium from companies with riskier fixed income portfolios.

The coefficient for SOA is also positive, possibly capturing the decline in the share of equity in the mid-1990s (Table 2.14) and its impact on the annuity rate. The decline in the share of equity resulted mostly from the sales of utility shares bought during the privatizations of large state companies the late and early 1990s. These shares were sold to foreign strategic investors in the mid-1990s at very attractive prices, which reflected exceptional capital gains in the early 1990s and possibly a control premium. The perspectives of much lower returns on this asset class after the sale may have led providers to revise downward the annuity rate.

The sign of the LEV coefficient indicates that more leveraged companies pay higher annuity rates. This result is consistent with the existence of a risk premium in the annuity rates of more leveraged companies, and has been obtained despite the fact that leverage ratios should be ideally measured at economic values, not book values. As discussed in Chapter 6, it is possible that leverage ratios measured at economic and book values have not differed too much, after all the proper adjustments are considered. The existence of an annuity guarantee would tend to weaken the impact of bankruptcy risk on the annuity rate, but the fact that the guarantee is partial may explain the result.

The MSHARE coefficient could be either positive or negative. Larger companies would tend to have lower operating costs due to economies of scale and would be able to pay higher annuity rates. On the other hand, larger companies tend to have more established reputations and brand names, and also more extensive distribution networks that could allow them to sell the same amount of annuities for a lower rate. The negative coefficient suggests that the reputation/distribution network effect is more important. This result could also capture the attempts of smaller companies to price more aggressively in order to gain market share. The AP(EARLY) coefficient is positive, indicating that companies pay higher annuity rates for larger premiums, a result that was also obtained in the estimation of MWRs shown in Table 2.12.[14]

The coefficient of the commission rate (CR) is negative and significant, showing that broker activity can substitute for the annuity rate as a marketing device. This substitutability is even stronger when the commission rate is increased to provide resources for an informal cash rebate, as observed in the 1990s. The coefficient of the Herfindahl concentration index is negative and significant, indicating that the increasing degree of competition in the 1990s did translate into higher rates of return for all annuitants. Finally, the level and multiplicative dummies indicate that there was a structural break in the 2000s, and that the elasticity of the annuity rate vis-à-vis the risk-free rate increased in recent years.[15]

The econometric results are consistent with the previous analysis, indicating overall the existence of a very competitive market for annuities in the Chilean case. The differences between the degrees of competitiveness of the pension fund and insurance sectors are also reflected in the returns on equity (ROE) of AFPs and life insurance companies. As shown in Figure 2.11, while AFPs have generated ROEs above 20 percent and in some years above 50 percent, the life insurance companies have earned much lower rates of return on equity, despite bearing much higher levels of risk.

Figure 2.11. Returns on Equity (ROE) of AFPs and Life Insurance Companies (%), 1992–2004

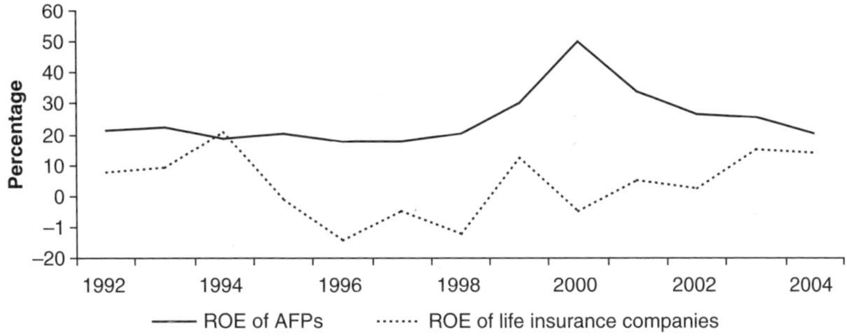

Source: Central Bank of Chile, SVS, SAFP.

The ROEs of the two sectors are not directly comparable year by year, because the returns of pension funds and the ROEs of AFPs reflect a mark-to-market valuation, whereas the portfolios of insurance companies are valued by a combination of book and market values, largely book values. Moreover, the accounting ROEs of annuity providers are affected by a strict capital rule that imposes large provisions when the company sells an annuity and that leads to accounting losses at the point of sale. However, the two indicators are more comparable over longer periods of time, and the numbers indicate clearly a more competitive annuities industry.

In sum, annuitants in Chile seem to have obtained a better deal for their premiums than annuitants in most other countries, especially considering that all annuities in Chile are indexed. This difference is in part due to the existence of a wide range of indexed financial instruments in Chile. The good deal obtained by annuitants in Chile is also explained by the existence of a very competitive life insurance sector, much more competitive than the pension sector. Money's worth ratios are probably too high, reflecting the adoption of aggressive pricing strategies in recent years. It is likely that money's worth ratios will decline to levels closer to one and that intermediation spreads will widen, to allow for the coverage of costs, risks, and the generation of positive profit margins. However, if the annuities market remains competitive, annuitants in Chile may still get a good deal for their premiums, relative to annuitants in most other countries, given the wider range of indexed financial instruments in the Chilean case. If this outcome materializes, the performance of the annuities sector would still be judged satisfactory for both consumers and providers.

Notes

1. More detailed background information on the Chilean pension reform is provided in Acuña and Iglesias (2001) and Yazigi et al. (2002).
2. The true ratio is higher than 33 percent, because insurance assets are measured by a combination of market and book values, while pension fund assets are measured at market values.
3. In Chile, PWs are provided by pension funds, and the PW premiums (the initial balance) are not reported. The PW premium was estimated and included in Table 2.3 to allow for international comparisons. The PW premium was estimated assuming a ratio of the average payout to the average premium similar to that observed for annuities.
4. Premiums on variable annuities are large, but these products are mostly in the accumulation stage and may not be converted into actual life annuities at retirement. See, e.g., Brown et al. (2001).
5. Although disability and survivor pensions play a critical role in any pension system, they involve specific issues that require a separate examination and which are beyond the scope of this report. The focus of this report is on old age and early retirement.
6. James, Martinez, and Iglesias (2006) provide an insightful analysis of the demand for PWs and annuities in Chile.
7. Collins (2003) and the Investment Company Institute (2004) provide a detailed analysis of costs and fees of pension and mutual funds in the U.S.
8. Other researchers have computed MWRs for other countries based on a smaller number of annuity quotes rather than actual annuities issued.
9. As discussed in Chapter 4 and Annex 2, Chilean providers probably succeed in extracting an increase in returns adjusted for risk due, inter alia, to the existence of a liquidity premium in higher yield bonds.
10. Brown et al. (2001) report the negative relationship between MWR and age for the United Kingdom and the United States but do not provide a clear explanation for this outcome.
11. Until 2005 insurance companies had to report their average annuity rates using an outdated mortality table, the RV-85. During 2005 annuity rates were calculated and reported with both the RV-85 and the recently built RV-04. Past annuity rates were recalculated with the RV-04 on the basis of the relationship between the two rates in 2005. This resulted in an average increase of 60 basis points in the annuity rate. Annex 1 provides a more detailed analysis of mortality tables, MWRs, and annuity rates.
12. Walker (2005) examines the relationship between the annuity rate and the risk-free rate and concludes that the threat of the new Pension Law did produce a change in behavior.

13. The commission rate is transformed into an interest rate (i.e., capitalized) by calculating the difference between the internal rates of return of an annuity with the gross and the net premiums.
14. The premium is the only variable that is present in both datasets.
15. The hypothesis that the long-run elasticity has become equal to 1 could not be rejected, a result which is consistent with Walker's (2005). Note that the results shown in Table 2.15 were obtained from a panel of 17 companies and 38 quarters, while Walker investigated the monthly relationship of the annuity and the risk free rates.

CHAPTER 3

Major Risks in the Market for Retirement Products

Introduction

This chapter identifies and examines the major potential risks faced by the four players in the market for retirement products, namely, workers, pensioners, providers, and the Government. The material in this chapter provides the elements for assessing the effectiveness of the internal risk management strategies followed by the providers (Chapter 4), the quality of product regulation (Chapter 5), and the quality of the regulation of intermediaries (Chapter 6). It is also an essential input for assessing whether the risk sharing arrangements in Chile are reasonable overall, or whether major regulatory and institutional reforms are called for (Chapter 7).

The chapter is structured as follows. The next section examines the risks borne by workers, including younger workers and older workers approaching retirement. The third section examines the risks borne by pensioners, which comprise PW and annuity holders. The fourth section examines the risks borne by the providers of PWs and annuities, which in the case of Chile are the pension fund managers and the life insurance companies. The fifth section analyzes the risks borne by the Government, as the ultimate guarantor of the system. Finally, the sixth section summarizes the main points and paves the way for the following chapters.

Major Risks Faced by Workers

The risks faced by workers in the accumulation phase are summarized in the first column of Table 3.1. During the whole contribution phase workers in a defined contribution environment face the risk of sharp drops in asset prices and a resulting decline in the value of their retirement savings. Recognition of this risk has led to an intense debate on the optimal portfolio composition for workers in the accumulation phase, particularly the optimal share of equity. One of the major issues under debate is whether equity risk declines with the lengthening of the time horizon, due to mean reversion in equity returns, which would justify significant shares of equity during the accumulation period.[1]

The evidence on mean reversion is not conclusive, providing insufficient guidance to the optimal share of equity in the accumulation phase. However, there are other arguments that justify sizable equity investments during the accumulation phase, at least for younger workers. One well-known argument takes into consideration the value of human capital during the life cycle and concludes that the portfolio of young workers should contain larger shares of equity because they can offset equity losses by working harder later in their lives. Older workers do not have this option and should hold much smaller volumes of equity (the value of human capital decreases over time and approaches zero at the time of retirement).[2] Although the optimal share of equity remains difficult to determine, policy makers and market participants seem to have reached a consensus that the optimal portfolio composition probably involves larger shares of equity for young workers and lower shares for older workers, a strategy that has been labeled as the "lifestyle" or "lifecycle strategy."[3]

Workers who follow the lifestyle strategy would be subject to only modest equity losses in the period preceding retirement, as they would be holding primarily a portfolio of fixed income assets. However, they would still be exposed to other risks. One of the most important risks in the pre-retirement phase is the risk of falling annuity rates, or the risk of having to buy an annuity at a time of low interest rates and suffer from low payouts during the whole retirement period. To immunize the

Table 3.1. Major Risks in the Market for Retirement Products

Workers	*Pensioners*	*Providers*	*Government*
Accumulation phase: Market risk, especially the risk associated with volatile equity prices. Preretirement phase: Market risk as above, but aggravated by the existence of a large accumulated balance near retirement. Annuity rate risk, or the risk of a drop in the annuity rate leading to low annuities.	Retirees that withdraw the whole balance as a lump sum (if this option is allowed): Longevity risk; Market risk; PW pensioners: Longevity risk; Market risk; Inflation risk; Liquidity risk; Fixed annuity pensioners: Risk of early death; Inflation risk (if annuities are not indexed to domestic prices); Liquidity risk; Bankruptcy risk; Variable annuity pensioners: Risk of early death; Market risk; Inflation risk; Liquidity risk; Bankruptcy risk; TW pensioners: Market risk in TW phase; Inflation risk (if TWs and annuities are not indexed); Liquidity risk; Bankruptcy risk;	PW providers (AFPs) are not exposed to major risks, as these risks are largely shifted to PW holders (except for operational risk and liquidity risk). Annuity providers (life insurance companies) are exposed to five major classes of risk: (i) Underwriting risks, or risk of mis-pricing due to: Longevity risk; Wrong assumptions about interest rates and operating costs. (ii) Market risks: Interest rate risk; Equity risk; Property risk; Currency risk. (iii) Specific asset class risks: Credit risk; Prepayment risk; Settlement risk; Concentration risk. (iv) Operational risks (v) Liquidity risks	Risk of large numbers of small pensions, large fiscal expenditures with the MPG. Risk of bankruptcies and large fiscal expenditures with the annuity guarantee.

worker's pension from a fall in interest rates at the time of retirement, the fixed income portfolio would need to have an average duration equal to the duration of the annuity, which could be 11–14 years, depending on the age of retirement and life expectancy. A long duration would generate a capital gain on the accumulated balance at the point of retirement that would offset the drop in the annuity rate, producing the same final payout.[4]

Other solutions to deal with the annuity rate risk that have been examined in the literature include deferring the annuity by postponing retirement, deferring the annuity by purchasing a phased withdrawal, introducing adjustable annuities (i.e., adjusting the annuity rates periodically in line with changes in interest rates), introducing variable annuities, allowing protected annuity funds where a fraction of the funds would be invested in call options or bond futures (generating a capital gain that offsets the fall in annuity rates), or allowing phased purchases of fixed annuities (thus diversifying the annuity rate risk over a defined period).[5]

Major Risks Faced by Pensioners

Pensioners envisaging their choices of retirement products and providers will consider their main objectives and risks. The most important objectives are typically an adequate pension at retirement and a bequest to the heirs. The most important risks are summarized in the second column of Table 3.1, and include longevity risk, the risk of early death, market (or investment) risk, inflation risk, liquidity risk, and bankruptcy risk associated with the product provider.

Longevity risk for pensioners is traditionally defined as the risk that the retiree will outlive his/her assets, and is possibly one of the major risks perceived by most retirees. Retirees that withdraw all their balances as a lump sum (in the countries where this is permitted) are particularly exposed to this risk. PWs generally provide poor protection against longevity risk, especially when they allow retirees to consume their balances in a relatively short period of time. Annuities are the only retirement products that provide effective protection against this risk. Joint annuities provide protection against longevity risk for both the main beneficiary and his/her spouse.

The traditional definition of longevity risk fails to account for situations where the retiree has a short life expectancy due to poor health conditions. Pensioners in these conditions may be more concerned with the risk of an early death and their ability to leave a bequest to their heirs, rather than the risk of outliving their assets. Even pensioners in good health conditions cannot rule out the possibility of an early death and its consequences. Lump sums allow retirees to cope effectively with the risk of an early death. PWs also allow pensioners to cope with this risk, as the balance remains the propriety of the account holder and is bequeathed to the heirs upon his/her death. Annuities by contrast, do not allow pensioners to cope with this risk, as the funds generally remain in the pool after death.[6]

Market risk (or investment risk) for pensioners is defined as the risk that the pension will fluctuate in value due to fluctuations in asset prices. The risk that is relevant for pensioners is clearly the risk of a severe decline in the value of the benefit due to a sharp decline in asset prices. Retirees that withdraw their balances as lump sums (and then invest them in conventional savings instruments) are very exposed to this risk. PWs generally do not usually provide protection against this risk either (unless they contain a minimum guaranteed return). Usually, only fixed annuities provide effective and comprehensive protection against market risk. Variable or adjustable annuities provide protection against longevity risk but not market risk.

Inflation risk for pensioners is defined as the risk that the pension benefit will lose purchasing power over time. It is not the same as market risk, because asset returns backing PWs may be stable but negative in real terms or because payouts may not be fixed in real terms. Only annuities that are fixed and indexed to domestic inflation provide effective protection against this risk. All the other retirement instruments expose pensioners to inflation risk, including PWs, variable or adjustable annuities, and annuities fixed in other currencies.

Liquidity risk for pensioners is defined as the risk that the pensioner will not be able to build a reserve to face emergency expenses, such as large medical expenses caused by illness or accidents, and not covered by health insurance.[7] Lump sums are the only "retirement product" that enables retirees to potentially address this risk. All the other retirement products tend to impose liquidity restrictions, although to different degrees. PWs provide some limited liquidity and control over retirement wealth, relative to annuities. This is because PWs may allow faster disbursements of the balance, enabling the retiree to access some reserves for emergencies. By contrast, annuities do not provide any liquidity or control to their holders.

Bankruptcy risk for pensioners is the risk that benefits will not be fully paid due to the failure of the provider to meet their contractual obligations. The risk of bankruptcy of the provider for PW holders is low, when PWs are provided by pension funds operating in a defined contribution (DC) environment, as in the case of Chile. The risk of bankruptcy of the provider for annuitants is more severe, especially in the case of fixed annuities, as these fixed obligations are backed by the reserves and capital of the provider. If the benefits are covered by a Government guarantee, the risk will be determined by the coverage of the guarantee.

It is clearly difficult to address all these different risks effectively. One particular retirement product may provide effective protection against some of these risks but not all of them. The second column in Table 3.1 summarizes the major risks that are borne by pensioners that choose lump sums, PWs, annuities, and TWs. If pensioners had full access to lump sums they would be able to cope with some risks such as the risk of early death and liquidity risks, but would be severely exposed to longevity and market risks.

PW pensioners would also be able to cope with the risk of early death, but would be subject to longevity risk (as traditionally defined), as well as market and liquidity risks. The degree of exposure to these risks can be partially addressed by the specific design of the PW instrument. For example, PWs that allow pensioners to deplete their balances in a relatively short period of time (e.g., 5 or 10 years) expose them to more longevity risk than PWs that entail a more gradual drawdown and a slower decline of the individual balance. Likewise, market risk can be reduced by investing in a conservative portfolio. However, none of these risks can be effectively addressed by a PW instrument.

Pensioners holding fixed indexed annuities are protected against longevity, market and inflation risks, but exposed to liquidity and bankruptcy risks. In addition, they cannot leave a bequest in the event of an early death. Protection against early death can only be partly achieved by a guaranteed annuity—an annuity where the provider guarantees payments for a predefined period, regardless of the death of the main beneficiary. The price of the guarantee takes the form of lower payments relative to non-guaranteed annuities.

Fixed nominal (peso) annuities are not allowed in Chile, but annuities fixed in U.S. dollars have been recently allowed, as noted in Chapter 5. Pensioners who opt for these annuities are protected against longevity risk but exposed to market and inflation risks, through exposure to currency fluctuations. They are also exposed to liquidity and bankruptcy risks.

Variable annuities protect their holders against longevity risk and allow them to benefit from higher returns and capital gains, but at the cost of exposing them to market risk. Variable annuities may provide some hedging against inflation, but this hedge is never perfect. Therefore, holders of variable annuities are more exposed to an erosion of purchasing power than holders of fixed indexed annuities. Both holders of fixed and variable annuities are exposed to the risk of bankruptcy of the annuity provider, a risk that is not trivial considering the long duration of annuity contracts. The bankruptcy risk can be addressed by a Government guarantee, but this type of guarantee raises the question of financing and the regulations required to minimize the potential moral hazard generated by the guarantee.[8]

Major Risks Faced by Providers

A Taxonomy of Risks for Providers of Retirement Products

There have been several efforts to identify and classify the risks borne by insurance companies and other providers of financial services. This report follows the taxonomy that has been proposed by the International Actuarial Association (2004) and also utilized by the International Association of Insurance Supervisors (IAIS 2006), as it seems particularly suitable to providers of retirement products, and is at a level of detail sufficient for consideration here. Under this taxonomy, risks faced by providers are classified into five major groups, namely, (i) underwriting risks, which includes longevity risk; (ii) market risks; (iii) credit risks and other risks related to specific asset classes; (iv) operational risks; and (v) liquidity risks. As described below, AFPs do not face substantial risks as providers of PWs, but life insurance companies providing annuities face complex risks.

Risks Faced by AFPs

AFPs in Chile do not face longevity, market, or credit risks as providers of PWs, as these risks are transferred to their holders. AFPs still face operational and liquidity risks, but these two risks are less material by comparison with the first three types of risks. The only substantive risk faced by AFPs is the risk of performing substantially below the market. Chilean regulations include a relative return guarantee that obliges AFPs to maintain minimum reserves and transfer them to the individual accounts if the rate of return that they would otherwise provide falls below the minimum. However, the risk of underperforming and having to draw from their own capital and reserves only becomes significant if the AFP adopts a portfolio strategy which is very different from the industry's average.

Risks Faced by Annuity Providers

Underwriting Risks Underwriting risk entails the risk of incorrectly pricing annuity contracts due to unrealistically optimistic assumptions about future mortality rates, investment returns, and operating costs. In the case of annuities, one of the major sources of underwriting risk is longevity risk, or the risk that the annuitant will live much longer than anticipated when the contract is underwritten. This could arise due to a variety of factors, including insufficient or poor mortality data, difficulties in assessing future improvements in mortality (due, for example, to unanticipated medical advances and lifestyle improvements), or failure to differentiate annuitants according to the level of risk. Annuity contracts could also be incorrectly priced due to unrealistic assumptions about future reinvestment rates or about the company's capacity to manage its operating costs (e.g., overanticipating the effect of improvements through technological advances or gains in market share and increased economies of scale).

Market Risks Market risks for providers arise from the volatility of asset prices, its effect on the value of the provider's assets relative to its liabilities, and on the associated cash flows. Failure to design and implement efficient asset-liability management (ALM) strategies will expose the provider to significant market risks and ultimately to the risk of insolvency. Indeed, the failure to implement efficient ALM strategies is defined in some risk classification systems as a risk in its own right.[9]

The specific risks within this category include interest rate risk, inflation risk, equity market risk, property market risk, and currency risk. Interest rate risk is one of the most important risks faced by annuity providers, as they tend to invest heavily in fixed interest assets, and results from fluctuations both in the general level and in the term structure of interest rates. The exposure to this risk is greater the larger the mismatch between the duration of assets and liabilities. If the duration of assets is substantially shorter than the duration of liabilities (a common situation faced by insurance companies and DB pension funds in many countries) the relevant risk becomes reinvestment risk, or the risk that the returns on the funds to be reinvested will fall below anticipated levels.[10]

Inflation risk for the provider arises when they issue annuities indexed to prices and do not hold sufficient indexed financial instruments or the index does not track well the index of the liabilities.[11] Equity risk arises from the exposure of fluctuations in equity prices, and is greater the larger the mismatch between the size of the equity portfolio and the size of annuity contracts linked to equity prices (e.g., variable annuities).

Likewise, currency risk arises when the provider issues annuities denominated in one currency but holds assets denominated in another currency.

Credit Risks and Other Risks Related to Specific Asset Classes It is useful to separate risks that arise from deficient ALM strategies, from risks that are specific to some asset classes. The first risk category involves the failure to construct an asset portfolio consistent with the structure of liabilities, so as to protect or immunize the institution against price fluctuations. The second class of risks is specific to some asset classes, and may arise even when the provider adopts matching strategies.

One of the most important risks in this category is credit risk, or the risk of changes in the credit quality of issuers of instruments held by the annuity provider. The most obvious example of credit risk is default risk, or the risk that the issuer will not pay its obligations to investors. However, even before default the annuity provider may be subject to a downgrading of credit ratings and a capital loss on its portfolio. This type of risk is most visible in the case of instruments such as corporate bonds, but is also present in other types of financial instruments, reinsurance arrangements, and derivative agreements such as swaps. Annuity providers may also face credit risk in their arrangements with annuity brokers (e.g., payment of the broker's commission before the actual payment of the premium by the annuitant).

A second important type of risk in this risk category is prepayment risk, or the risk that issuers of instruments will opt to pay their obligations before the contracted maturity, exposing the annuity provider to a more substantial reinvestment risk when not anticipated. This risk is particularly important in the case of mortgage bonds or mortgage-backed securities, where the underlying mortgages have refinancing options, or in the case of callable corporate bonds. Note that this type of risk could also be classified under the market risk category, as it is related to movements in interest rates.

Other types of risks within this category include settlement risk (arising from lags between the value and settlement dates of securities transactions), documentation and custody risk (arising from failures in the legal documentation or custody of instruments in the portfolio), and concentration risk (arising from excessive concentration of investments in an individual entity, a sector or a geographical area).

Operational Risks Operational risks are defined as the risks of losses resulting from inadequate or failed internal controls and procedures or through fraud or administrative failure. Life insurance companies and

AFPs are subject to these risks like any other financial institution, but annuity providers may be more vulnerable to some specific types of operational risk, given the long duration of the contracts that they underwrite. For example, the failure to maintain proper internal controls may lead to improper portfolio decisions, or transactions involving conflicts of interest, and result ultimately in low returns or losses, as well as fines or other impositions by the supervisor. Providers may also suffer from larger costs than necessary due to their failure to adopt updated technology. The dematerialization of annuity payments and the lack of proper controls may result in cases of identity theft and consequent losses for the company as well.

Liquidity Risks Liquidity risks for providers are defined as the risks of losses resulting from insufficient liquid assets to meet the cash flow requirements associated with the policies underwritten. Life insurance companies specialized in annuities are generally less exposed to liquidity risks than non-life companies and life companies specializing in non-annuity lines of business. This is because the pool of annuity contracts involves cash outflows that are more easily predictable, relative to other insurance products. For example, annuity providers are not exposed to a sudden large number of claims due to a catastrophe. They are not exposed to an early and voluntary termination of insurance policies either, because, unlike most life policies, annuities are irreversible contracts.[12] Of course, they still must forecast accurately future cash outlays and build an asset portfolio capable of generating the necessarily liquidity, which may not be a trivial exercise in a small and illiquid capital market. However, this task is simpler than the one faced by companies that deal with more uncertain cash outflows.

Major Risks Faced by the Government

The Government of Chile faces two major types of risks, both related to its role of final guarantor of the pension system. The first is the risk of large expenditures associated with the MPG. Low returns in the accumulation phase and relatively short periods of contribution (due to unemployment, withdrawals from the labor force, or early retirement) may result in larger numbers of people with small balances at retirement and eligible to receive the MPG. A large number of retirees choosing PWs over annuities may lead to the same outcome, as this instrument involves decreasing payouts and a greater likelihood that the holder will eventually be eligible for the MPG.

The second major risk is the risk of large expenditures associated with the failure of providers to honor their obligations. The Government provides guarantees both to AFP members (active workers and PW holders) and to annuitants. In Chile, the first type of guarantee is triggered only if the AFP does not meet the minimum relative return guarantee. This guarantee has not been called and has a low risk of being called in the future, as examined in Chapter 4. In Chile, the second type of guarantee is more important and has a higher probability of being called, because it applies to a more complex product and to an intermediary that assumes greater risks. In fact, the resolution of the first bankruptcy case in 2003 is likely to require some fiscal expenditures.

The risk to the Government associated with the annuity guarantee can be increased by excessive aggressive pricing by the industry, which in turn can be triggered by moral hazard and insufficient market discipline caused by the guarantee itself. If reserve and capital regulations are not well designed, this can result in bankruptcies and insufficient assets to honor the annuity contracts. The risk associated with the annuity guarantee is also affected by the quality of exit and resolution rules—the Government's contingent liabilities increase if bankrupt providers are able to continue operating and underwriting additional contracts.

Addressing the Risks in the Market for Retirement Products

The potential risks in the market for retirement products should be addressed by providers, consumers, and regulators. Providers can address several of the risks identified above through the adoption of effective risk management strategies. It is expected that profit-maximizing providers operating in a competitive environment and under a reasonable regulatory framework will adopt such risk management strategies, which are capable of benefiting both shareholders and consumers. However, this positive outcome may only materialize fully if providers also have access to a sufficient range of financial instruments and risk management tools.

Consumers may also address several of the risks identified above if they have access to a reasonable range of retirement products. Different retirees will have different needs and preferences, and therefore may assign different weights to the risks identified above. A reasonable range of retirement products that also includes combinations of different products allows consumers to address more effectively the risks relevant to their own situation. Moreover, the market also needs to be transparent, providing sufficient information on the range of available products and their characteristics.

Regulators play a key role in the sound development of the market for retirement products, including capital market, insurance, and pension fund regulators. Capital market regulators must maintain a close dialogue with providers and other market participants, and promote the development of financial instruments capable of meeting the needs of both issuers and institutional investors. The existence of institutional investors with a long time horizon provides a potential demand for different financial instruments, but their actual development requires a proactive attitude from the side of capital market regulators and policy makers.

Regulators must also ensure that different retirees have access to a reasonable range of retirement products, capable of meeting most of their individual needs, while also meeting the social protection objectives of the pension system and preventing an excessive demand on Government guarantees. The achievement of these different objectives may involve tradeoffs that need to be carefully assessed.

Finally, regulators must also ensure a sound regulatory framework for providers, especially in the areas of licensing, investments, and capital. Licensing criteria should prevent entry by applicants without sufficient capital, experience, and skills. Investment and capital regulations should encourage effective risk management strategies, impose capital requirements that are robust and aligned with provider risks, and minimize market disruptions and welfare losses caused by any failed institution. The next three chapters examine whether the risks identified above have been effectively addressed by participants and regulators in the specific case of Chile.

Notes

1. See, e.g., Bodie (1995); Bodie, Kane, and Marcus (2005); Campbell and Viceira (2002); Jorion (2003); Siegel (1994); Siegel and Thaler (1997).
2. Bodie, Merton, and Samuelson (1992); Campbell and Viceira (2002); and Samuelson (1994).
3. However, Shiller (2005) presents a skeptical view of the lifecycle strategy.
4. Booth and Yakoubov (1998).
5. See, e.g., Blake (1999); Blake and Hudson (2000); Alier and Vittas (2001); and Rocha, Hinz, and Gutierrez (2001).

6. It is possible to design annuities with a residual bequest value but this type of annuity is not common.
7. It is also assumed that the pensioner will not be able to borrow to meet these expenses.
8. A Government guarantee on annuity benefits protects annuitants against bankruptcy risk, and should not be confused with a guaranteed annuity, which exists in many countries and entails a particular design of the annuity contract, where the provider commits to pay the same benefit, regardless of the death of the main holder. After the death of the main beneficiary, payments during the guaranteed period go to the heirs.
9. International Actuarial Association (2004).
10. "Interest rate risk" is defined differently in different risk classification systems. Some systems define interest rate risk in general terms, as the risk of a loss stemming from interest fluctuations, regardless of the duration of assets vis-à-vis liabilities. Other systems define interest risk as the risk of a loss caused by interest rate movements when the duration of assets is longer than the duration of liabilities, and define reinvestment risk as the risk of a loss caused by interest rate movements when the duration of assets is shorter than the duration of liabilities.
11. In this type of situation, providers are exposed to basis risk. For example, price indices used on the asset and liability sides could be different.
12. It is possible to design special variable annuities that are not irreversible contracts (Edwards and Diaz 2006), but these annuities are not common.

CHAPTER 4

Internal Risk Management by Providers*

Introduction

This chapter examines the risk management strategies followed by the providers of phased withdrawals (PWs) and annuities, the AFPs and the life insurance companies, respectively. This chapter precedes the regulatory chapters because efficient risk management by intermediaries is the first line of defense against risk and one of the most important elements of a stable market. At the same time, the analysis is performed with the recognition that risk management does not operate in a vacuum—the strategies and techniques that are employed by providers depend not only on their internal capacity and skills, but also on the availability of financial instruments and on the constraints and incentives produced by the regulatory environment.

The interactions between internal risk management and the regulatory framework need to be particularly recognized in countries like Chile, where participation in the private pension system is mandatory.

*Thomas Glaessner and Sara Zervos contributed to this chapter.

The concern of Chilean policy makers with the safety of retirement assets has led to a more complex regulatory framework than that found in other jurisdictions, including a restrictive product regulation, several guarantees, and specific regulations on portfolio composition, asset valuation, and capital. As shown below, these regulations affect the parameters within which Chilean intermediaries operate and their risk management strategies.

This chapter is structured as follows. The next section reviews briefly the range of financial instruments available for investment and risk management by AFPs and life insurance companies. The third section examines the portfolio strategies followed by AFPs, which are the sole providers of PWs in Chile. The fourth section is the core of the chapter, and examines the more complex asset-liability management (ALM) problem faced by life insurance companies providing annuities. This section analyzes the most important elements of the ALM of annuity providers, designed to address the most important risks examined in Chapter 3, and identifies remaining deficiencies and challenges in risk management. The last section summarizes the main findings and proposes some recommendations.

The Availability of Financial Instruments in Chile

Life insurance companies and pension funds have access to a large and diversified supply of financial instruments to build their portfolios. As shown in Table 4.1, the outstanding stocks of fixed income instruments added up to 80 percent of GDP, in 2003, including public sector bonds (issued primarily by the Central Bank of Chile), mortgage bonds, endorsable mortgages,[1] corporate bonds, and certificates of deposit. More recently, there have also been substantial issues of commercial paper and infrastructure bonds. In addition, institutional investors have had access to a reasonable stock of equities, as indicated by a market capitalization of 85 percent of GDP.

As shown in Table 4.2, most fixed income instruments issued in Chile are indexed to consumer prices (denominated in UFs), whether they are issued by the public or the private sector. This is an important and to some extent unique feature of the Chilean capital market. Another distinctive characteristic of the Chilean capital market is the long maturities of fixed income instruments. Public sector and mortgage bonds have maturities of up to 20 years, and there have been corporate and

Table 4.1. Financial Assets (% of GDP) and Participation by AFPs and Life Insurance Companies,[a] 1995–2003

Year	Public Sector Bonds (% of GDP)	Share of AFPs+ LICOs (%)	Mortgage and Bank Bonds (% of GDP)	Share of AFPs+ LICOs (%)	Corporate Bonds[b] (% of GDP)	Share of AFPs+ LICOs (%)	Endorsable Mortgages (% of GDP)	Share of AFPs+ LICOs[c] (%)	Bank Time Deposits/ CDs (% of GDP)	Share of AFPs+ LICOs (%)	Stock Market Capitalization (% of GDP)	Share of AFPs+ LICOs (%)
1995	27.3	64.0	10.3	79.3	3.4	85.0	0.6	100.0	23.2	9.1	101.3	11.7
1996	28.7	65.3	12.1	82.9	3.1	84.9	0.8	100.0	26.7	6.9	89.6	11.8
1997	30.3	61.9	13.4	79.5	2.4	84.9	1.0	100.0	29.8	14.5	91.0	10.8
1998	27.6	72.5	13.5	82.2	2.9	82.3	1.2	100.0	33.2	17.2	67.2	9.6
1999	29.1	70.1	14.3	94.4	3.7	80.1	1.5	100.0	36.6	22.4	97.3	6.9
2000	27.5	76.4	14.1	98.7	5.1	74.9	1.7	100.0	35.7	27.4	85.4	7.6
2001	28.1	71.5	14.6	93.8	9.3	76.1	1.8	100.0	34.7	27.9	85.7	7.3
2002	26.8	63.2	12.9	97.0	11.4	74.2	2.0	100.0	34.3	35.1	72.8	8.2
2003	20.5	71.0	12.5	84.4	13.4	71.4	1.7	100.0	30.6	29.7	84.0	10.9

Sources: Central Bank of Chile, SAFP, SVS.

a. The share of financial assets held by LICOs is probably underestimated, as these instruments are valued by a combination of market and book values on their balance sheets.

b. Includes infrastructure bonds.

c. Assumes that LICOs hold all the outstanding stock..

Table 4.2. Characteristics of Major Financial Instruments

Instrument	*Issuer*	*Denomination*	*Maturities*	*Other Characteristics*
Public Sector Bonds	Central Bank	Mostly UFs, Some Peso and US$ issues	UF: 5–20 years Pesos: 2–5 years US$: 2–10 years	Amortizing and bullet bonds, coupon and zero bonds
	Treasury	US$, UFs	4–10 years (US$) 10, 20 years (UFs)	Bullet, coupon bonds Bullet, coupon bonds
Mortgage Bonds	Banks	UFs	10–20 years	Amortizing bonds. Bank assumes original credit risk
Mortgage-Backed Securities	SPV	UFs	10–20 years	Amortizing instruments. Holder assumes credit risk
Corporate Bonds	Top Companies	UFs	10–30 years	Amortizing and bullet bonds
Bank Bonds	Banks	UFs	2–5 years	Mostly bullet bonds
Infrastructure Bonds	Utility Companies	UFs	Up to 30 years	Mostly bullet bonds
Bank CDs	Banks	UFs	1 year	Discount instruments
Derivatives	Banks	NA	Not liquid beyond 4–5 years	Non-deliverable forward contracts and some swaps (forex and peso/UF)

Source: Authors.

infrastructure bonds issued with maturities of up to 30 years. Very few emerging countries have succeeded in developing privately issued instruments with such long maturities.[2]

The development of Chile's capital market has been, to a good extent, fostered by the 1981 pension reform and the investment requirements of pension funds and insurance companies. In particular, the existence of a reasonably large supply of fixed income instruments indexed to inflation and with long maturities is partly due to the pressures of annuity providers, as these institutions need to manage liabilities with long durations indexed to inflation. However, other factors may also have contributed to these outcomes. The pervasive presence of indexed instruments is due not only to the needs of institutional investors, but is also a more general consequence of many past decades of high inflation, while the variety of private financial instruments was only made possible by a long period of fiscal discipline that opened room for the private sector to grow.

The challenge faced by policy makers and regulators is to ensure that capital markets continue developing in a sound direction, and that institutional investors retain access to the instruments and tools that they need. The decline in inflation to very low levels has already increased the demand for nominal instruments and the share of indexed instruments can be expected to decline in the future. The Central Bank has already started issuing nominal debt so as to create a yield curve in Chilean pesos to be used as a benchmark for private issues.[3] Although this can be considered a natural and positive development, a drastic decline in the supply of indexed instruments could create complications for institutional investors, especially annuity providers, which will continue issuing annuities indexed to inflation by law and will need to retain access to assets with matching characteristics.[4]

Another area that requires attention from regulators is the area of derivatives. There has not been any significant progress in the development of derivate instruments in Chile. The market of currency forwards is relatively well developed (albeit short term for annuity providers), but there has been much less progress in developing instruments such as currency and interest rate swaps, options, and futures. The lack of development of these instruments seems to have been motivated by prudential concerns, but these are instruments that enhance risk management capacity, when properly used. In fact, their absence has created difficulties for the implementation of efficient asset-liability management strategies, as noted below.

Risk Management by AFPs

As mentioned in Chapter 2, retiring workers have the option of choosing among three basic retirement products, namely PWs, annuities, and TWs followed by a deferred annuity. Workers who choose to take PW and TWs typically remain in the same AFP, although the law does not restrict them from changing to another AFP. Until 2000 both PW and TW holders and active workers had no choice of portfolio—their balances were invested in the same diversified portfolio managed by their AFP. In 2000 each AFP was allowed to offer two funds, namely, a balanced fund and a fixed income fund. In 2002 a regime of multiple funds was introduced, with each AFP being forced to offer five funds. The funds are basically differentiated by the maximum and minimum proportions of variable income instruments that they can hold, which is 80 and 40 percent for Fund A, and which decline progressively for the other funds, reaching 0 percent in the case of Fund E.

The regulatory framework for the multiple funds promotes the concept of a lifestyle investment strategy, whereby workers hold significant amounts of equity when they are young, and declining amounts as they get older. As shown in Table 4.3, active workers who are 55 years old and younger (50 years of age for women) can choose freely among the five funds. However, older active workers cannot invest their balances in Fund A, and PW and TW holders cannot invest their balances in Funds A and B. Workers who did not exercise a choice when the multiple portfolios were introduced were allocated to Funds B, C, or D, according to their age. Judging by the average age, wage, and balance of fund members, most retiring workers and PW holders seem to have their balances in Fund D, but there are also several of these workers in Funds C and E (Table 4.4).

In a defined contribution system, investment risk is borne by the individual account holder. Current and prospective PW and TW holders not

Table 4.3. Range of Fund Choices by Age[a]

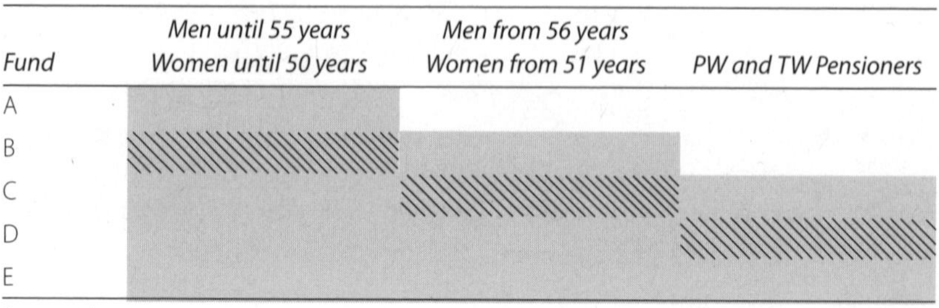

Source: Authors.
a. Shaded cells indicate eligible funds, and graded cells indicate default fund for each age group.

Table 4.4. Average Age, Wage, Balance, and Size of Different Funds, Dec. 2005

	Fund A	*Fund B*	*Fund C*	*Fund D*	*Fund E*
Average Age (years)	32	30	43	57	47
Average Wage (1,000 Pesos)	501	309	341	353	397
Average Balance (1,000 Pesos)	8,112	2,459	5,572	6,224	12,280
Number of Members (1,000)	596	3,300	3,250	741	66
Number of Active Contributors (1,000)	387	1,404	1,296	191	45

Source: SAFP.

only assume the same investment risk as any active worker investing in the same fund, but also assume longevity risk. Moreover, the investment regime in Chile sets the basic strategic asset allocation for each type of fund, involving declining shares of variable income assets for Funds A through E. Therefore, while AFPs still have room to select asset classes and individual securities, their risk management problem is simpler than that faced by insurance companies, which have to assume much greater risks associated with their long-term liabilities fixed in UFs. The only material risk that AFPs face is the risk of not meeting the minimum relative return guarantee and having to use their reserves to close the difference.

The actual portfolio allocation of the different funds clearly follows a lifestyle strategy, as shown in Table 4.5. Fund D, which is the fund chosen by many retiring workers and PW holders, contains 20 percent variable income and 80 percent fixed income instruments. Moreover, members of different AFPs selecting Fund D tend to get similar returns, due to the similarity of portfolios across AFPs. As shown in Figure 4.1, the average accumulated returns of the five funds managed by each of the AFPs are generally clustered around the same values, reflecting their similar portfolios. This convergence of returns reflects the herding behavior of pension funds that has been extensively documented,[5] and which is partly due to the incentives generated by the regulated minimum relative return guarantee.

Table 4.5. Portfolio Composition of Pension Funds, by Type of Fund (%), Dec. 2004

	A	*B*	*C*	*D*	*E*	*Total*
Claims on the Public Sector	**6.1**	**12.4**	**18.7**	**29.9**	**46.0**	**18.7**
Claims on the Financial Sector	**14.5**	**26.4**	**31.1**	**37.1**	**32.3**	**29.5**
O/w: Mortgage Bonds	1.8	4.7	7.3	9.2	14.2	6.8
Time Deposits	8.7	18.1	20.2	25.7	15.8	19.4
Claims on the Corporate Sector	**23.7**	**26.2**	**25.7**	**19.5**	**13.6**	**24.4**
O/w: Shares	19.8	18.8	14.4	9.5	0.0	14.7
Bonds	1.9	4.4	8.0	7.8	13.3	6.8
Claims on the Foreign Sector	**55.5**	**34.8**	**24.3**	**13.2**	**7.7**	**27.2**
O/w: Mutual Funds and Shares	54.6	33.9	21.1	9.2	0.0	24.4
Debt Instruments	0.9	0.9	3.2	4.0	7.7	2.4
Other Assets	**0.2**	**0.1**	**0.1**	**0.3**	**0.3**	**0.1**
Total Assets	100.0	100.0	100.0	100.0	100.0	100.0
Total Assets (US$ million)	5,455	12,646	32,205	8,698	1,802	60,806
Memo Item: Variable Income	77.7	56.9	39.7	21.0	0.0	42.8

Source: SAFP.

Figure 4.1. Real Return and Risk of Each AFP and Type of Fund, Sept. 2002–Feb. 2004

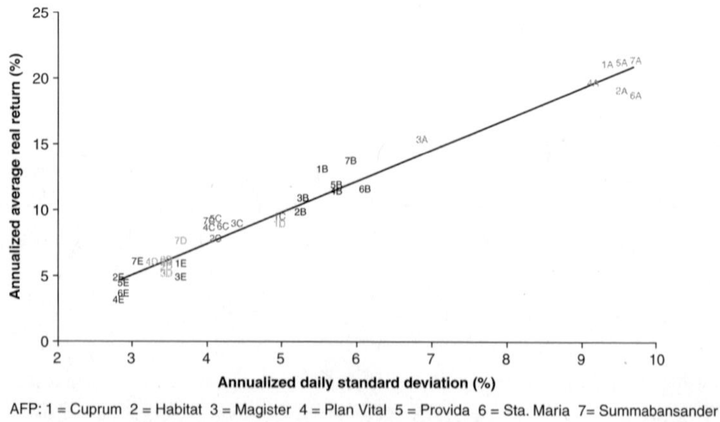

Source: AFP Habitat.

The introduction of the multiple fund regime and the lifestyle strategy have been positive developments and seem to have produced reasonable results overall. The age distribution across the five funds looks reasonable. The pattern of risk and return in the first 18 months of implementation is generally in line with expectations. Retiring workers and PW holders cannot hold higher risk portfolios but still have access to a reasonable range of choices, capable of accommodating most risk preferences. Moreover, many of them have their balances in Fund D, which provides a reasonable portfolio for members at that stage of the life cycle. The herding effect does not seem to be cause for concern—herding may be extreme in Chile, but intensive herding has been documented in other countries as well, and there is no evidence that it has produced negative effects on pension fund members or the financial sector.[6]

At the same time, there seems to exist space for further improvements in the regulatory framework. Firstly, the investment regime for AFPs in Chile remains overly complex, including numerous quantitative limits on instruments, classes of instruments, and issuers. There is scope to relax the investment regime, allowing asset managers more room to operate and possibly generate better returns without a meaningful increase in risk. The discussion of this issue is out of the scope of this report, but has been examined in detail elsewhere.[7]

Secondly, some retiring workers and PW holders select Fund E based on the perception that this is the safest fund, or the fund with the minimum variance, because it is not exposed to equity risk. However, Fund E

Table 4.6. Value at Risk of Pension Fund Portfolios, August 2003–April 2004[a]

Fund	*Aug. 03*	*Oct. 03*	*Dec. 03*	*Feb. 04*	*Apr. 04*
A	3.90%	4.03%	4.84%	4.42%	4.68%
B	2.15%	2.28%	2.91%	2.49%	2.91%
C	1.50%	1.35%	2.08%	1.93%	2.35%
D	1.02%	1.14%	1.35%	1.47%	1.13%
E	1.25%	1.07%	1.32%	1.36%	1.24%

Source: AFP Cuprum.
a. Calculated with 95% significance level and one-month horizon.

may be inefficient—there may be portfolios capable of producing higher returns with the same levels of risk. As illustrated in Table 4.6, computation of the Value at Risk (VAR) for different funds indicates that Fund D has similar levels of risk as Fund E, while also being able to generate higher returns (Figure 4.1).[8] Other simulations done by the AFPs suggest that the minimum variance portfolio would involve adding a moderate amount of equity to Fund E.

In principle, members should be able to build the minimum variance portfolio by splitting their balances between Funds D and E (members can distribute their balances in up to two different funds), but few workers do this in practice. Therefore, there seem to be two alternatives to ensure that risk-averse workers and PW holders have effective access to the minimum variance portfolio. The first alternative is to make more efforts in financial education and disclosure, showing that the minimum variance portfolio probably involves a combination of two different funds. The second is to allow Fund E to have a moderate share of equity, possibly around 10 percent of the portfolio.

Thirdly, workers are exposed to interest rate risk in the period preceding retirement, particularly to a drop in interest rates resulting in low life annuities. Workers can to some extent deal with this risk by purchasing a PW and possibly benefit from a recovery in interest rates before locking their annuity rates. The annuity rate risk could also be partly addressed by expanding the range of retirement products, such as allowing a combination of PWs and annuities, allowing the introduction of adjustable annuities, or the introduction of the phased purchase of fixed annuities. The first option has just been introduced by the new Pension Law, but the two latter options are not yet being envisaged in Chile (Chapter 5 provides a more detailed discussion of product regulation).

The annuity risk could also be addressed more effectively by AFP asset managers through portfolio strategies more tailored to the needs of retiring workers. More specifically, it would be theoretically possible to immunize the value of an indexed annuity close to retirement by holding a portfolio of indexed bonds with the same duration. This would ensure that the retiring worker would enjoy a capital gain on his/her balance, large enough to offset the fall in the annuity rate. It is not possible to address this risk completely, because this would entail highly customized portfolios, adapted to specific retirement ages, and because asset availability would present a practical challenge.[9] However, an increase in the duration of portfolios C, D, and E, from the currently low levels of 2.5–3.5 years to levels closer to the duration of annuities (10 years and higher, as shown below) would reduce exposure to annuity rate risk. Alternatively, the regulators could consider introducing a new portfolio, more geared to the needs of retiring workers, particularly those who are intending to purchase an annuity.[10]

Risk Management by Life Insurance Companies

The Overall Asset-Liability Management (ALM) Problem

Unlike defined contribution pension plans, the ALM problem facing annuity providers is far more complex. This greater complexity is due to the fact that the annuity provider assumes the risks embedded in the annuity contract, and such risks need to be assessed over a long time horizon—the provider has the legal obligation to honor a contract that can span for a period of 40 years or longer. In this case, the first major task faced by annuity providers is to measure accurately their liabilities and price them correctly. The second major task is to build an asset portfolio that matches the liabilities to the extent possible or practical and reduces exposure to fluctuations in asset values. The third major task is to assess and monitor risks specific to different asset classes, such as the risk of default. The fourth major task is to ensure operational efficiency in all aspects of the annuity business, in order to avoid unnecessary losses. Finally, the fifth major task is to generate sufficient liquidity to meet cash outflows as they come due.

Insurance companies have developed a large variety of ALM strategies in order to cope with all the five major classes of risks outlined above, namely, underwriting, market, credit, operational, and liquidity risks (Chapter 3). Particular efforts have been devoted to address the first two classes of risk, due to their analytical complexity.[11] However, the long time horizon makes standard ALM techniques, including more complex dynamic portfolio optimization and immunization techniques, difficult to implement and manage in a practical manner. Moreover, risk managers in emerging countries do not always have access to all the assets and tools required to implement these strategies. For example, assets that fully match the structure of liabilities and the related cash flows may not be available in the market, and the risk manager may not have access to other risk management tools, such as derivatives, longevity bonds, and reinsurance, that would to reduce exposure to residual risks.[12]

This section examines how annuity providers in Chile have built their ALM strategies and managed the five major classes of risk described above. Chile provides a relevant example of a high-middle-income country that has developed a critical mass of sophisticated annuity providers and that has made great strides in developing instruments and tools for risk management. At the same time, it is also a case where risk managers are still struggling with incomplete markets and the lack of sufficient tools for risk management. It also illustrates how some regulations introduced with the objective of reducing risks for members may have contributed to the growth of other risks. The policy issues that arise in this type of situation provide useful lessons for policy makers in Chile and other countries as well.

Coping with Underwriting Risk

As mentioned in Chapter 3, underwriting risk is the risk that the annuity provider may be exposed to financial losses as a result of inadequately pricing the annuity contracts it offers (or underwrites). Pricing of such long-term liabilities depends in turn on a variety of complex assumptions about the longevity of annuitants, future returns on assets, and future operating costs. Longevity risk is one of the most important risks that an annuity provider takes when it issues an annuity. In order to determine an appropriate annuity price, the company must project the annuitant's expected future survivorship, by taking into account various personal characteristics, as well as the overall health improvement that is expected to take place due to advances in medical technology and community health standards.

Estimating future improvements in longevity has proved one of the most challenging tasks faced by annuity providers and defined-benefit pension funds worldwide, due to the sharp advances in medical technology and the stricter health standards that have been introduced. The difficulty associated with this task has led providers in some countries (e.g., Denmark, the TIAA-CREF fund in the United States) to rely on risk-sharing arrangements, where unanticipated improvements in longevity trigger adjustments in benefits.[13] It has also stimulated financial innovation, such as the recent efforts to introduce longevity bonds in the United Kingdom.[14] In the absence of these risk-sharing or hedging devices, it becomes even more critical for the provider to estimate future longevity developments, as any errors need to be absorbed by its own capital.

In Chile, insurance companies are not allowed to ask personal questions (such as the personal health history, or whether he/she smokes), but are allowed to price annuities freely and differentiate risks by observable characteristics such as age, sex, wages, and the final balance (wages and financial wealth tend to be well correlated with educational levels, which in turn tends to be highly correlated with life expectancy). As examined in Chapters 5 and 6, the law only regulates the use of a mortality table to establish technical provisions and for reporting purposes. For pricing purposes, Chilean companies use their own, sex-specific, proprietary mortality tables or make adjustments to other more generally applicable tables to reflect their own expectations. Most companies indicate that these mortality tables incorporate mortality improvement assumptions, although some also indicated that this was a more recent enhancement. Overall, it is difficult to assess the extent to which all companies follow best practices and how they deal with data limitations, particularly in the tail end of the age distribution.

The choice of mortality table has a very strong impact on annuity pricing and the valuation of providers' liabilities. By way of illustration, Table 4.7 shows the effect of two different mortality tables: the RV-85 and the more recent and updated RV-04 assuming further mortality improvements. The table shows the present value of a unit annual annuity payable monthly to a single male with different age and mortality assumptions, or conversely, the monetary liability an insurance company faces when writing an annuity contract. A discount rate of 3 percent is assumed for this illustrative calculation, as this is the base rate for the reserve rule (Chapter 6). Across all ages, the increase in the annuity value (the provider's liability) would be at the order of 13 percent of the stock of liabilities, showing that faulty pricing of annuities due to the use of improper mortality tables could erode significantly the capital of the provider.

Also within the realm of underwriting risk lies the issue of future interest rate and cost assumptions. In establishing the annuity price, companies must make assumptions about the future rates of return on assets (adjusted for all the risks, including prepayment, reinvestment, and credit risks) and their operating costs, including any allowance that they will be able to reduce

Table 4.7. Impact of Different Mortality Tables on Annuity Values and LICO Liabilities

Age of Annuitant/ Mortality Table	*RV-85 without improvement*	*RV-04 with improvement*	*Percent increase in Liability*
50	17.813	20.019	12.4
55	15.943	18.050	13.2
60	13.983	15.856	13.4
65	11.974	13.548	13.2
70	9.996	11.254	12.9
75	8.023	9.049	12.8

Source: Staff calculations.

costs through greater efficiency and larger scale of business. Overly optimistic assumptions about future interest rates and about the scope for cost reductions could also lead to faulty pricing and financial losses.

There is evidence that Chilean companies take into consideration individual risk characteristics when pricing their annuities. For example, money's worth ratios (MWRs) are positively correlated with age, as shown previously in Chapter 2 and in much more detail in Annex 1. This correlation reflects the greater risks associated with annuities of early retirees, which have longer durations and expose the provider to greater mortality uncertainty and reinvestment risks.

Whereas there is evidence that companies price their annuities according to the risk characteristics of the annuitant, there is also evidence of aggressive pricing in recent years. As shown in Chapter 2 and Annex 1, average MWRs in Chile are generally higher than the average ratios in other countries, using comparable discount rates and mortality tables. The thin financial spreads shown in Chapter 2 are consistent with these results and also indicate aggressive pricing.

The high MWRs and the thin financial spreads suggest that some companies maybe be making optimistic assumptions about future reinvestment rates and operating costs. It is also possible that some companies are making a deliberate strategic decision to price their annuities aggressively in order to gain market share. The robust capital buffer accumulated in previous years has created room for more aggressive pricing in recent years, but these prices may not be sustainable for a prolonged period.

Coping with Market Risk

Market risk is another complex risk faced by life insurance companies and one of the most difficult risks to manage. Market risk is broadly defined as the risk of financial losses due to movements in inflation and asset prices, including interest rates, exchange rates, and equity prices. The degree of exposure to this risk depends primarily on the structure of the asset portfolio vis-á-vis the structure of the liabilities. In Chile, annuities account for a large share of the business of life insurance companies—they account for nearly 70 percent of life premiums and 80 percent of assets and liabilities. This implies a very particular liability structure in the Chilean case. All annuities have been fixed in UFs, which implies that they are indexed to inflation. Most annuities are immediate, and more than 80 percent of all annuities are guaranteed for five years or longer. (Variable annuities and annuities denominated in other currencies would imply a very different liability structure but were only introduced in 2004).

Most importantly, the prevalence of annuities in the operations of life insurance companies implies a very long duration of liabilities. As shown in Table 4.8, the expected duration of annuities ranges from 6.3 years for a single male aged 75 to 14.2 for a joint and deferred annuity, with most companies reporting average durations of 11–12 years on their active annuity portfolio. These are long durations for a company to manage, especially considering that they are computed in UFs.[15]

Therefore, most life insurance companies face liabilities with long durations and fixed in UFs. Life insurance companies have addressed the risks implied by this liability structure by holding primarily long-term fixed income assets denominated in UFs as well. As shown in Table 4.9, fixed income assets have accounted for about 85 percent of the portfolio of life insurance companies, and the bulk of these assets is denominated

Table 4.8. Expected Duration of Different Annuities by Age

	Age of Primary Beneficiary		
Type of Annuity	*55*	*65*	*75*
Single Male			
Without guarantee	10.9	8.6	6.3
Guaranteed for 15 years	10.8	8.7	7.1
Without guarantee, and deferred for 2 years	12.3	10.1	7.8
Single Female			
Without guarantee	12.5	10.2	7.7
Guaranteed for 15 years	12.4	10.2	7.9
Without guarantee, and deferred for 2 years	13.9	11.6	9.1
Joint (male, spouse 3 years younger, 60% reversion)			
Without guarantee	12.5	10.4	8.0
Guaranteed for 15 years	12.5	10.3	8.1
Without guarantee, and deferred for 2 years	14.2	11.8	9.4

Source: SVS, Staff calculations.

Table 4.9. Portfolio of Life Insurance Companies (in % of Total), 1991–2004

	1991	*1995*	*2000*	*2001*	*2002*	*2003*	*2004*
Government Sector	**38.3**	**40.3**	**28.7**	**21.9**	**18.9**	**17.6**	**17.1**
Financial Sector	**23.0**	**28.4**	**45.1**	**42.2**	**41.3**	**37.6**	**32.9**
Mortgage Bonds	13.9	18.6	24.2	22.0	20.6	18.8	14.7
Mortgage-Backed Securities	3.0	6.0	10.1	9.9	10.6	10.1	9.2
Time Deposits	4.0	1.9	1.6	1.6	1.9	1.2	1.8
Bonds of Financial Institutions	2.1	1.9	9.2	8.6	8.3	7.5	7.2
Company Sector	**29.0**	**22.1**	**15.3**	**24.5**	**28.0**	**33.4**	**37.8**
Shares	8.9	10.2	3.4	3.1	2.7	2.9	3.4
Bonds	20.1	10.7	10.7	20.3	24.4	29.3	33.3
Investment Fund Shares	0.0	1.1	1.1	1.0	1.0	1.1	1.1
Real Estate	**7.8**	**7.7**	**7.4**	**7.3**	**7.3**	**7.3**	**7.4**
Foreign Sector	**0.0**	**0.1**	**2.0**	**2.4**	**2.3**	**1.9**	**2.6**
Others	**2.0**	**1.4**	**1.6**	**1.7**	**2.2**	**2.2**	**2.2**
Total	**100.0**	**100.0**	**100.0**	**100.0**	**100.0**	**100.0**	**100.0**
Fixed Income/Total Assets	81.3	79.4	84.4	84.4	84.6	84.5	83.3
Total Assets (US$ million)	2339.1	6661.4	11934.1	12095.6	12392.8	14215.6	18874.3
Assets/GDP	6.1%	9.2%	15.9%	17.7%	18.4%	19.7%	19.0%

Source: SVS.

in UFs. Real estate assets account for nearly half of the variable income portfolio, while equity and foreign assets account for the remainder. These assets primarily back other life policies and voluntary pension products in the accumulation phase.

The portfolio composition of life insurance companies in Chile is unique in many aspects. As shown in Table 4.10, Chilean life insurance companies hold a much larger share of fixed income assets and a much smaller share of equity and foreign assets than their counterparts in OECD countries. This is explained not only by the much larger share of annuities in the life business in Chile, but also by the fact that these annuities are immediate (as opposed to deferred) and fixed (as opposed to variable). The life insurance sector of most OECD countries not only has a much smaller share of annuities overall, but also a larger share of variable annuities within the overall stock of annuities, including variables annuities in the accumulation phase. Fixed income assets are not a match for these types of liabilities.

The portfolios of Chilean life insurance companies are also unique by consisting primarily of instruments indexed to consumer prices. The existence of a wide range of indexed financial instruments, including higher yield instruments such as mortgage and corporate bonds gives Chilean companies an enormous advantage, allowing them to offer annuities

Table 4.10. Portfolio Composition of Life Insurance Companies (% of Total Portfolio), Chile (2003) and OECD Countries (2001)

	Cash + Deposits	*Bills + Bonds*	*Loans*	*Shares*	*Non-Financial*	*Other*	*Unspecific For. Assets*	*Total*	*Foreign Assets*
Chile	**1.2**	**83.4**	**-**	**2.9**	**7.3**	**3.3**	**1.9**	**100.0**	**1.9**
Australia	5.7	26.1	3.8	55.6	5.3	3.6	-	100.0	17.3
Belgium	3.1	49.8	8.8	33.1	2.4	2.8	-	100.0	50.1
Canada	0.9	44.1	17.0	20.7	5.4	9.8	2.2	100.0	n.a.
Denmark	1.1	59.7	0.8	33.4	0.1	4.8	-	100.0	n.a.
Netherlands	4.8	31.1	29.0	29.5	-	5.6	-	100.0	28.8
Spain	12.6	43.9	3.9	29.8	3.7	6.0	-	100.0	15.5
Switzerland	5.2	38.1	19.2	28.2	9.4	-	-	100.0	n.a.
U.K.	6.8	15.0	1.1	59.8	5.8	11.5	-	100.0	15.9
U.S.	6.9	53.6	10.8	27.9	-	0.9	-	100.0	6.0

Sources: SVS, OECD.

indexed to inflation without exposing themselves to inflation risk. The lack of sufficient indexed instruments in other countries frequently forces companies to resort to imperfect inflation hedges, such as equity and real estate, and charge heavy loads to cover the large residual risk (reflected in low money's worth ratios for indexed annuities), or even abstain from offering indexed annuities altogether.[16]

While Chilean companies have the advantage of having access to a wide range of indexed instruments, they also face some important limitations typically associated with a small and not fully developed capital market. Despite the increasing number of issues of fixed income instruments with long maturities, Chilean insurance companies still do not have access to a sufficient quantity of instruments with long maturities to match the duration of their liabilities and immunize their portfolios against interest rate risk. Most insurance companies report an average duration of the asset portfolio of 8 years, substantially shorter than the average duration of liabilities, which is 11–12 years, depending on the clientele. This implies a significant duration mismatch of 3–4 years and material exposure to reinvestment risk. Life insurance companies have been struggling to reduce such duration mismatch, not only to reduce their exposure to reinvestment risk, but also to reduce the effect of the penalty in the reserve regulations (the Calce Rule), which impose larger technical reserves the greater the duration mismatch (Chapter 6).[17]

The efforts of insurance companies to reduce duration mismatch have included a number of measures, none of which seems entirely successful. They invest in real estate and equity to match the tail end of their projected annuity payments but, as in other countries, these instruments do not provide a very good match. They have participated actively in recent issues of infrastructure bonds with longer maturities, and have also pressed corporations to structure their new bond issues more in conformity with their needs. It is possible that the average duration of the asset portfolio has increased as a result, but there is no data to enable a firm conclusion. Some companies have been attempting to increase duration to some extent by borrowing short-term and making long-term investments, which is a rather artificial strategy to increase duration.

Some companies have sought to manage the duration mismatch through the use of reinsurance, addressing the liability side rather than the asset side of the challenge. In some developed countries, companies lay off the tail end of the mismatch through a reinsurance policy with a large international company. However, regulatory restrictions still hinder the access to reinsurance in Chile. A company offering reinsurance in Chile must keep all the assets in the country, and as such, most international firms do not offer this service. Locally, this type of reinsurance is quite expensive in terms of capital and price, so that it essentially does not exist at this time to any material extent.

Chilean companies have not had access to the range of derivatives that are available to their counterparts in the OECD.[18] For example, 20-year interest rate swaps, and various interest rate option products (e.g., spread options), can help companies manage risk at longer durations. Given the earlier stage of capital market development in Chile, these types of long-dated interest rate derivatives are not available for either Chilean peso or UF contracts. The fact that Chilean law does not permit banks to write options has also hindered market development. In addition, even a conservative use of derivative operations (e.g., the writing of covered call options on stocks already held in portfolio) are not open to insurance companies as a means of earning greater returns on their existing asset portfolio.

Finally, the difficulties faced by asset managers in coping with market risk have also been due to the restrictive choice of retirement products, which has included only PWs and fixed annuities. The lack of other retirement instruments, such as adjustable annuities and variable annuities, has been a disadvantage, not only from the point of view of consumers but also from the point of the provider. Besides providing greater choice to annuitants, these products would also simplify the ALM problem, by shifting some of the risk to the annuitants who are able and willing to bear the risk. Admittedly, these products would only be appropriate to higher-income and more-sophisticated consumers, which probably account for a relatively small share of the universe of annuitants. However, the gains from issuing these products could be significant, even if they represented only a moderate fraction of the total stock of annuities.

In sum, Chilean companies have adopted appropriate strategies to cope with market risk, but still face some constraints and limitations to manage this risk completely. The matching of fixed and UF-denominated liabilities with a portfolio of fixed and UF-denominated assets is a positive aspect of risk management, and capital regulations have contributed to this outcome (Chapter 6). However, companies still face a problem of duration mismatch and the associated reinvestment risk, due to the lack of sufficient instruments with long durations, and the lack of other instruments and tools that would help them address this problem more effectively. The residual mismatch may not seem excessive but is not trivial either, and has been essentially addressed through pricing and capital regulations that impose additional reserves in line with the magnitude of the mismatch.[19]

Coping with Credit and Prepayment Risk

As shown in the preceding section, life insurance companies have held a very high share of fixed income instruments with long maturities and denominated in UFs in their portfolios, to minimize exposure to real interest rate and inflation risk. In the last 10 years, however, there was a marked reshuffling within the fixed income portfolio, away from Government bonds and towards mortgage-related securities and corporate bonds (including bonds issued by financial institutions). These two asset classes account today for 25 and 40 percent of the asset portfolio, respectively, with corporate bonds growing dramatically in recent years. As also discussed in the previous section, the strategy of building an asset portfolio of fixed income and indexed securities is appropriate, but the question arises as to how Chilean companies are coping with the specific risks in these two asset classes, namely, credit and prepayment risk.

Credit Risk. Credit risk involves primarily the risk of default by the issuers of securities. Even before actual default, investors run the risk of a decline in credit status and a loss in the value of their investments. Mortgage bonds carry a low credit risk because the issuers tend to be banks with good credit standings. Moreover, the bonds are backed by good collateral. Mortgage-backed securities carry more credit risk, as the risk of default on the underlying housing loans is borne directly by the final investor, and they are also less liquid than mortgage bonds due to the lower level of standardization. Due to their higher credit risk and lower liquidity, they provide a premium of 50–100 bps over mortgage bonds. However, the credit risk of these instruments is mitigated by the presence of good collateral, which explains why they still pay a smaller risk premium than well-rated corporate bonds.[20]

Among the main fixed income instruments held by insurance companies, corporate bonds have on average the highest credit risk. Investment regulations reduce the maximum exposure to credit risk by limiting holdings of bonds (or other securities) rated below investment grade to 5 percent of the portfolio, and capital regulations also reduce exposure to credit risk by penalizing securities with low ratings (Chapter 6). In practice, asset managers have behaved very conservatively, concentrating their holdings in corporate bonds rated AA and above. The conservative strategy seems to be partly due to reserve regulations and partly to the fear of having to sell a downgraded instrument in an illiquid market. The lack of instruments to hedge credit risk, such as credit derivatives, has also constrained asset managers.[21]

Insurance companies have to address other sources of credit risk, such as settlement and custodian risks. However, these risks are not excessive (95 percent of all securities are already under custody), and are being reduced further through ongoing improvements in custody clearing and settlement infrastructure, including the implementation of a modern payments system including real-time gross settlement.

Prepayment risk. Prepayment risk involves the risk of earlier than anticipated payment of interest and principal and the subsequent reinvestment of funds at lower interest rates. Prepayment risk primarily affects mortgage-related instruments (corporate bonds with call options are also subject to prepayment risk, but these are not prevalent in Chile), and has become a great concern due to the recent decline in interest rates where the incentive to prepay and refinance on the part of the borrower is increased markedly. In fact, most asset managers in Chile today consider prepayment risk a more important risk than credit risk. In highly developed financial systems asset managers have access to some tools to mitigate this risk, such as interest options, bond futures, swaptions, and callable debt. However, these instruments are not developed in Chile yet. The concern with prepayment risk may have contributed to the rebalancing of fixed income portfolios in recent years, away from mortgage-related securities and towards corporate bonds.

Coping with Liquidity Risk

As mentioned in Chapter 3, liquidity risk is not considered to be an important risk for annuity providers, because cash outflows associated with annuity payments can be reasonably well predicted and the annuitant is not provided with the option to commute the contract and change providers. Chilean annuity providers are not an exception to this general rule. They can afford to hold relatively less-liquid assets and still implement reasonable cash flow or duration matching strategies. Their cash surplus and their investments in more liquid instruments, such as benchmark Government debt instruments and bank certificates of deposits, offer a more than sufficient cushion to meet liquidity needs associated with their expected payouts.

Insurance companies have some concerns about the low liquidity of equity and private fixed income markets in Chile, but these concerns are primarily associated with the difficulties that lack of liquidity may cause to the implementation of ALM strategies. For example, the lack of liquidity in these markets can have an impact on portfolio valuation and the measurement of portfolio risks. Moreover, ALM strategies that call for rebalancing of the asset portfolio become more difficult to implement. The lack of liquidity in money market instruments also makes the use of derivatives to increase or reduce convexity and increase or reduce exposure to interest rates more difficult to implement. Finally, in illiquid markets it is difficult to restructure the portfolio in the event of a shock or period of financial distress in local markets. However, none of these risks is considered to be so serious as to justify larger holdings of cash or more-liquid securities with lower yields (e.g., Government bonds and bank certificates of deposits).

Coping with Operational Risks

Operational risks for life insurance companies can be broadly defined to include business continuity risks, cyber risks associated with denial of service or identity theft, and deficient internal controls that result in losses and fraud. It is difficult to make an evaluation of the performance of companies in dealing with this risk, as this would require a detailed examination of their internal controls and practices. However, the increasing use of electronic delivery of services and the dematerialization and on-line processing of annuities policies including the authentication of annuitants indicates that companies will be subject to increasing cyber risks if experience in more advanced countries (e.g., the United States and Australia) is any guide.

Summary of Findings and Recommendations

Major Findings and Conclusions

Chile has developed a relatively wide range of fixed income securities, mostly indexed to inflation, and the existence of these instruments has significantly facilitated risk management by insurance companies. There has been a symbiotic relationship between the development of the local fixed income markets and the growth in the assets and liabilities of pension funds and insurance companies. This has been especially the case in such areas as corporate and mortgage debt, where increasingly the insurance sector is driving the process of how Chilean companies come to market and structure their longer duration issues. However, there has been less progress in developing other important tools for risk management, such as derivatives, reinsurance arrangements, and other special instruments such as longevity bonds.

The introduction of multiple portfolios and a lifestyle investment regime for pension funds was a positive development and seems to have produced reasonable results. Near-retirement workers and PW holders are forbidden from holding the riskiest portfolios (especially the latter), but still have access to a reasonable range of choices. However, several members have selected to place their funds entirely in Fund E on the perception that this is the safest fund, whereas statistical simulations indicate that this fund may be inefficient. Individuals may build a more efficient portfolio by splitting their balances in Funds D and E, but there is no evidence that they follow this strategy. The short duration of fixed income assets in Funds C, D, and E is another issue that needs to be addressed, as it implies excessive exposure of retiring workers to annuity rate risk.

Most life insurance companies seem to be managing their more complex risks reasonably well, but there are some areas of concern. Their performance in coping with underwriting risk in the past three years seems mixed. The structure of annuity prices looks reasonable and consistent with efficient risk differentiation, i.e., annuities seem to be priced according to specific characteristics of the annuitants such as age and sex. However, annuity pricing has become aggressive overall, as indicated by the thin financial spreads and the high money's worth ratios. It is possible that companies are counting on future interest rate increases or on their capacity to reduce administrative costs. Some companies may be pricing their annuities aggressively as a strategy to gain market share. The strong capital buffer accumulated in past years has allowed them room to price their annuities aggressively for some time, but a prolonged period of high prices could lead to an excessive erosion of capital and high leverage ratios.

The strategies followed by life insurance companies to address market risk have been reasonable, but they still face constraints to manage this risk effectively. Their portfolio of UF-denominated fixed income assets provides a good match for their liabilities fixed in UFs, but they still face a duration mismatch of about four years, and a resulting exposure to reinvestment risk. Asset managers have explored different alternatives to reduce the mismatch, but none of these alternatives has proved entirely satisfactory. The problem lies in good part in the lack of sufficient volumes of instruments with very long duration, and also in the lack of other tools for risk management such as derivatives and reinsurance. The duration mismatch has been essentially addressed by pricing and reserve rules that penalize these gaps and impose higher levels of reserves on companies with larger duration gaps.

Companies have reshuffled their fixed income portfolios in the past 10 years, moving away from government bonds and towards mortgage and corporate bonds. This portfolio shift was motivated by the need to generate higher yields and to remain competitive in the annuities market. However, the shift into these higher yield securities implies a greater exposure to prepayment and credit risk. Prepayment risk affects primarily mortgage-related securities and has apparently become a more material risk than credit risk in recent years, due to the decline in interest rates. Companies do not have good instruments to deal with this risk, again because of the lack of development of derivatives, callable debt, and other hedging instruments more specific to the mortgage market. This helps explain the recent move from mortgage bonds to corporate bonds. Exposure to credit risk has been contained by investing primarily in highly rated instruments. Therefore, companies seem to be dealing well with these risks, considering their constraints and limitations.

Life insurance companies seem to be dealing effectively with liquidity risk, which is a particularly limited risk with respect to annuities. Finally, it is more difficult to make an assessment about their strategies to cope with operational risks, but the move to greater use of open architecture platforms to offer annuity products and the well-known problems present in the area of electronic safety including such risks as cyber-related identity theft, denial of service attacks, and other forms of cyber-related operational risk may need to be better addressed in the future.[22]

Major Recommendations

There is scope for a selective relaxation of pension fund portfolios that would open more room for asset managers to operate and possibly generate higher returns without a meaningful increase in risk. The possible inefficiency of Fund E could be addressed by allowing AFP asset managers to hold up to 10 percent of the value of the fund in equities. Reducing the exposure of retiring workers to annuity rate risk is not a trivial task as it may require, among other measures, highly customized portfolios. However, regulators may consider introducing another portfolio with longer duration more tailored to the needs of these preretirees.

The aggressive pricing strategies practiced in recent years may be simply a temporary phenomenon and the industry can suffer some erosion of capital, as it has accumulated enough of a capital buffer from previous years. However, a more prolonged period of aggressive pricing could be cause for concern. If this scenario materializes the authorities would need to consider strengthening capital rules further and possibly review some aspects of the annuity guarantee (Chapter 6 provides a more detailed discussion of capital regulations and the guarantee).

Even without aggressive pricing, managing longevity risk will remain a challenge in Chile, as it is in other countries. The introduction of direct risk-sharing arrangements, whereby annuitants would receive a higher initial pension but would be exposed to future adjustments in their payments in light with actual mortality experience, does not seem feasible under the current institutional setting. However, longevity risk could be better addressed through hedging instruments such as longevity bonds. Chilean regulators should examine the ongoing efforts to issue longevity bonds in the United Kingdom and the possibilities for introducing this type of instrument in Chile.

The difficulties that life insurance companies face in managing other risks, particularly market risks, are to some extent related to the lack of sufficient tools for risk management. Solving this problem will require relaxing regulatory limitations on the use of derivatives and making greater efforts to develop those markets. Regulatory restrictions on reinsurance should also be relaxed. The SVS is drafting new regulations that would improve access to reinsurance.

The Central Bank and the Government have been recently making an effort to diversify the range of financial instruments, by issuing nominal peso bonds and U.S. dollar-denominated bonds. A reasonable amount of these instruments is likely to contribute to the achievement of more complete capital markets and generate efficiency gains. However, a sharper move out of indexation may generate serious problems for annuity providers and have adverse consequences for the welfare of a large share of the Chilean population. The existence of a wide range of instruments indexed to consumer prices has contributed significantly to the positive outcomes observed in the annuities market. In order to be able to offer annuities with attractive conditions, providers will need to retain access to these instruments.

The recent introduction of a greater variety of products such as variable annuities and hybrid products is a welcome development from the point of view of asset-liability management, as it implies less exposure to risk and a less-complex ALM problem. As discussed in Chapter 5, the introduction of these products can also be a welcome development from the point of view of consumer welfare, depending on how they are marketed. This is because these products transfer part of the risk to the holder and may not be appropriate for many consumers. Moreover, these products need to be designed in greater detail, and some important areas of the regulatory framework such as investment and capital regulations need to be reviewed to accommodate the introduction of these new products (Chapter 6).

The apparent flaws in addressing some of the major risks may also be due to uneven quality of risk management capacity and skills across annuity providers. The regulatory framework has remained heavily compliance-based, with limited incentives for the development and assessment of risk management capacity inside institutions. A move to risk-based supervision is therefore warranted, and the SVS has already initiated a move to this approach to supervision. This change in the supervisory approach would not only introduce minimum standards and practices in risk management across all institutions, but also enable more-intensive supervision of riskier institutions.

Notes

1. Endorsable mortgages are mortgage-backed securities where the originator transfers risks and legal title to the final institutional investor.
2. Developed countries also struggle with these issues and have increased their efforts to issue longer duration instruments, both nominal and indexed. See G-10 (2005) and Wolswijk and de Haan (2005).
3. Interestingly, this is now creating a market in peso/UF swaps in the case of different entities (corporations or funds) that want to transform the extent to which their assets or liabilities are in pesos or UF.

4. Walker (2002) argues that indexation played a critical role in the development of Chile's capital market, while also concluding that the introduction of peso- and dollar-denominated instruments would contribute to the achievement of more complete markets. While this is true, an excessive move out of indexation would create problems for annuity providers, which play a key role in Chile's social protection system.
5. Yermo (2000); Rocha (2005).
6. Blake et al. (2001) and Myners (2001) show that herding has also been intensive in the United Kingdom, even without formal minimum relative return guarantee rules. Herding may have more adverse effects in a defined-benefit environment, as it implies deviations from optimal asset-liability management.
7. For example, see Rocha (2005).
8. Note that the results in Figure 4.1 and Table 4.6 are not strictly comparable. Figure 4.1 was constructed with 18 months of daily data on the returns of the five funds (since their introduction in September 2002), while the VARs reflect three years of daily data on the returns of individual instruments and asset classes.
9. These practical challenges can be seen in the similar difficulty that annuity issuers have to find assets of the duration required. There is no reason to believe that the AFPs would find it any more straightforward.
10. Booth and Yakoubov (1998) conduct numerous simulations for the United Kingdom, and conclude that the portfolio that addresses optimally annuity rate risk consists primarily of fixed income instruments with long duration, but also has some equity, because the yields of equity are highly correlated with the yields of the main matching asset (i.e., the long-term indexed bond). That is, equity could contribute to immunization and provide higher returns if the interest rates do not move in the period close to retirement. Walker (2003a) examines the risk-return properties of different portfolios in Chile and concludes that the minimum variance portfolio would be dominated by fixed income instruments with long duration but would also contain some amount of domestic equity.
11. The Society of Actuaries (2003) provides an extensive guide on all aspects of ALM. More concise reviews are provided by the Swiss Reinsurance Company (2000) and Van der Meer and Smink (1993). The IAIS (2005) proposes supervisory principles for sound ALM.
12. Risk managers in developed countries also struggle with these issues, although probably to a lesser extent. See Smink and Van der Meer (1997) for a review of ALM practices in the insurance industry and Fabbozzi et al. (2005) for a review of ALM practices among defined-benefit pension funds.
13. Andersen (2006).
14. These bonds are described in some detail in the website of BNP-Paribas.
15. The numbers in Table 4.8 refer to modified duration, which is McCaulay duration divided by $(1 + i)$, where i is the long-run interest rate (the yield to

maturity of 20-year Central Bank bonds was used). The duration of annuities is always defined in expected terms, as future payments are multiplied by the probabilities of survival.

16. A progressive change is underway to issue more nominal instruments, but annuity providers will not be material investors in such instruments.
17. Moreover, duration matching fully immunizes a portfolio against interest rate risk only when there are parallel changes in the yield curve. Immunization against changes in the slope of the yield curve also requires a particular portfolio of fixed income assets. See, e.g., Fabozzi (2000).
18. Many pension funds offering DB plans that are subject to mark to market accounting have used interest rate swaps in immunization schemes.
19. The econometric results reported in Annex 1 suggest that companies "price the mismatch" by introducing a discount in annuities with longer duration.
20. Walker (2005) provides a detailed analysis of mortgage bonds and mortgage-backed securities in Chile.
21. These instruments are used in international markets to reduce credit exposure to specific corporate issuers. Some of the very long bonds issued in Chile have included some form of credit enhancement specific to the instrument.
22. For a more detailed discussion of the issues involved see *Electronic Safety and Soundness: Securing Finance in a New Age*, World Bank (2003).

CHAPTER 5

The Regulation of Retirement Products

Background

The regulation of retirement products plays a major role in a pension system based on private individual accounts, such as the Chilean system. The regulatory framework must allow a reasonable menu of retirement products, capable of meeting the needs of workers with different risk profiles and preferences. At the same time, product regulation must also be consistent with the social objectives of the pension system, which may imply some restrictions on eligibility and on the menu of products. Whatever menu emerges as a result of these objectives, the regulatory framework must ensure in any case a maximum level of disclosure and transparency, so as to enable retiring workers to make well-informed decisions.

Analyzing the regulation of retirement products involves examining its four basic elements or components: (i) retirement rules, or the conditions for gaining access to retirement products; (ii) the menu of retirement products; (iii) the specific design features and regulations of individual retirement products; and (iv) the rules for marketing and selling retirement products.

Until recently, Chile had relatively liberal rules for early retirement and a relatively restricted menu of retirement products. Marketing regulation included a number of rules designed to ensure transparency, but these rules still opened room for companies and brokers to influence workers' choices. During the 1990s and early 2000s it became progressively apparent that these rules had allowed a number of problematic outcomes, such as a declining age of retirement, decreasing replacement ratios, dispersed benefits, and a number of questionable marketing practices, such as large broker commissions frequently combined with cash rebates, counter to the intent of the law.

In response to these problems, the Government submitted a new Pension Law to Congress at the end of 2000. The new Law introduced several substantive changes, including tighter conditions for early retirement, an expanded menu of retirement products, ceilings on brokers' commissions, and an innovative electronic quotation system for annuities, designed to increase significantly market transparency and change the way the industry operates. The new Pension Law was approved by Congress in February 2004, after an intensive and long debate, and became effective in August 2004.

Although the full impact of these changes may only be assessed in future years, the analysis of the Chilean experience with the regulation of retirement products can still provide very interesting insights and lessons for other countries. This is because the Chilean experience with product regulation reveals an evolution of policy making in response to real problems that emerged during the maturation of the pension system, and that may also emerge in other countries that are trying to develop their annuities markets.

This chapter is structured as follows. The next section reviews briefly retirement rules in Chile. The third section examines the menu of retirement products and the main features of each of these products. The fourth section examines in more detail the time path of PWs and annuities, which is crucial to gain a better understanding of these products. The fifth section examines marketing (or distribution) regulation. Finally, the sixth section summarizes the main findings and provides some policy recommendations.

Retirement Rules

Members qualify to take a pension benefit through normal age retirement, early retirement, or disability. In the event of the death of the member, benefits are also provided to surviving dependents. Retirement rules are summarized in Table 5.1, which also shows the changes introduced by the new Pension Law.

As shown in Table 5.1, normal age retirement is available on reaching age 65 for males and 60 for females. Members can retire earlier if they meet the qualification conditions. Until recently, early retirement required an accumulated pension balance sufficiently large to provide for a pension equal to at least 50 percent of the average real wage of the worker and 120 percent of the minimum pension guarantee (MPG). The average real wage was defined as the sum of all wages expressed in UFs in the past 10 years, and divided by 120. In other words, the qualification for early retirement has been focused on the adequacy of the individual replacement rate and the risk of accessing the MPG. Importantly, there is no occupational link in the qualification for early retirement, so it is not necessary to stop working. Equally, it is not compulsory to retire on reaching the normal retirement age; a member may continue working and contributing beyond the normal retirement age should their circumstances and wishes make this possible.

The new Pension Law made several parametric changes to early retirement rules. These changes have been motivated by concerns about a declining average age of retirement, a relatively low density of contributions during the accumulation phase,[1] and a perception by the authorities that the replacement ratio generated by the regime was decreasing and could become inadequate (see Chapter 2). Under the

Table 5.1. Summary of Retirement Rules

	Old Age	*Early Retirement*	*Disability*	*Survivorship*
Old Law	Men: 65 years Women: 60 years	Pension ≥ 50% of average real wage and 110% of MPG Average real wage = Sum of covered wages in last 10 years/120	Total or partial disability after medical examination. Subject to final examination after 3 years	Death of main beneficiary
New Law	Same	Pension ≥ 70% of average real wage and 150% of MPG Average real wage = Sum of covered wages in last 10 years/120 – (X – 16) X = No. of months without contributions	Same	Same

Source: Staff analysis.

new Law, the accumulated pension balance must provide for a pension equal to at least 70 percent of the average real wage in the past 10 years and 150 percent of the MPG. In addition, the new definition of the average real wage ignores months where no contribution was made, increasing the computed average and increasing further the required pension balance.

These changes will be introduced over a period of six years and will not affect male and female workers above 55 and 50 years of age, respectively. Over the long run, however, these changes will increase the average retirement age, and increase accumulated balances and replacement rates. Also, the contingent fiscal liability associated with the MPG will tend to decline. During a transition period, the number of early retirements is expected to reduce, before resuming the increasing path inherent in a maturing system. As a result, the market size for new retirement income products will also decline for a period, reflecting reduced numbers of potential customers.[2]

Eligibility for disability and death benefits has not been changed by the new Law, and these pensions will remain determined on a defined benefit basis. In the case of disability, the balance is supplemented by the proceeds of an insurance policy held by the AFP, so as to fund an annuity equal to 70 percent of the average real wage. A similar defined benefit pension also applies for death benefits paid to the surviving spouse (at 50 percent of the average real wage) and any minor dependents (at 15 percent of the average real wage for the period that they remain dependent). The defined benefit formula uses the same definition of average real wage as the early retirement test. As a result, the recent changes have increased the benefit level. Once the capital amount is made available for the benefit, the member or their surviving beneficiaries can select the benefit options in the same way as is the case for retirement.

The Menu of Retirement Products and Individual Product Design

The Menu of Retirement Products

The menu of retirement products in Chile has comprised lump sums, PWs, annuities, and TWs. However, each of these products has been subject to several restrictions to access and other specific design regulations. The new Pension Law has widened the menu of retirement products. Table 5.2 provides a summary description of the regulation of these products, and the following sections provide a more detailed discussion of their characteristics.

Table 5.2. Summary of Characteristics of Retirement Products

	Lump sums	*PWs*	*Annuities*	*TWs*
Basic description	Excess over amounts required to provide defined pension level is available for lump sum withdrawal.	Regular income stream withdrawn from own balance, in accordance with regulated formula and annually revised parameters. Payments determined in UF	Guaranteed lifetime income stream denominated in UF and providing benefits to dependents where they exist. Mandatory joint annuity for married males. Guaranteed payments for a period (in the event of death) can be added. Deferment periods available (in relation to TW cases).	Temporary withdrawals provided in combination with a deferred annuity. Balance is immediately split to finance TW and deferred annuity. TW has to be between 100% and 200% of annuity payment. No maximum period of deferral.
Access under old Law	Balance retained in the system should provide an income of at least 70% of average real wage, and 120% of MPG.	Any retiree meeting retirement conditions for normal or early retirement (Table 5.1). Mandatory for workers at normal retirement age with balances not capable of generating pension higher than MPG	Any retiree meeting minimum conditions for normal or early retirement (Table 5.1). Also, annuity must be higher than the MPG.	Any retiree meeting minimum conditions for normal or early retirement (Table 5.1). Also, deferred annuity must be higher than the MPG.
Access under new Law	Balance retained in the system must provide an income of at least 70% of average real wage, and 150% of MPG. Stricter definition of the average real wage.	Any retiree meeting new conditions for normal or early retirement (Table 5.1). Remains mandatory for workers at normal retirement age with small balances.	Any retiree meeting new conditions for normal or early retirement (Table 5.1). Balance must generate an annuity higher than the MPG.	Any retiree meeting new conditions for normal or early retirement (Table 5.1). Deferred annuity must be higher than the MPG.

(Continued)

Table 5.2. Summary of Characteristics of Retirement Products *(Continued)*

	Lump sums	*PWs*	*Annuities*	*TWs*
Provider	AFP	AFP	Life insurance company	AFP for TWs; Life insurance company for deferred annuity
Mortality table	Not applicable	Regulated: RV-85 before Feb. 2005 RV-04 after Feb. 2005	Unregulated for annuity pricing. Regulated for reserve computation and reporting to supervisors: RV-85 before Mar. 2005 and RV-04 after Mar. 2005	During TW period, not applicable. For deferred annuity component, same as for immediate annuities.
Technical interest rate	Not applicable	Regulated by formula: Rate = 0.2 X + 0.8 Y; X = average real AFP return in past 10 years Y = average annuity rate in previous year	Unregulated for annuity pricing. Regulated for computation of technical reserves under the CALCE rule (Chapter 6).	As for PWs during temporary period. Deferred annuity component as per immediate annuities.
New designs introduced by the new Law	Not applicable	Mortality table updated. Combination of PW and annuity.	(i) Combination of PW and annuity, provided that annuity component is fixed and at least equal to MPG. (ii) Combination of fixed and variable annuity, provided that fixed component is at least equal to MPG	Unchanged

Source: Staff analysis.

Lump Sums

Theoretically, the first option for a retiree would be to consider a lump sum. In Chile, this option is limited to excess funds after the provision of a minimum retirement income through a PW or an annuity. As shown in Table 5.2, the remaining balance (after deduction of the lump sum) should generate a pension equal to at least 70 percent of the average real wage in the past 10 years or 120 percent of the MPG. The first restriction was the one binding most retirees. The new Pension Law strengthened the restriction further, requiring a minimum of 150 percent of the MPG, and also strengthening the definition of the average real wage—by reducing the effect of noncontributory periods the computed average will increase.

The restricted access to lump sums in Chile reflects the central role of the second pillar (fully funded and privately managed) in the country's pension system. The Chilean pension system does not include a front-ended first pillar benefit, whether earnings-related or flat, and whether financed by contributions or general taxes. It includes the MPG, but this is a back-ended top-up benefit that was never intended to be paid to a large share of the population.[3] Therefore, the restrictions on lump sums are understandable, reflecting the social protection objectives of the pension system.

Programmed Withdrawals

In effect, the first practical option that is available to a retiring member is a PW. The main difference between this instrument and an annuity lies in the fact that PW payments are generated by the individual's PW balance throughout his/her life, and not by a common pool of funds. This implies that PW payments decline over time, as the balance is depleted. Some countries adopt liberal rules for PWs, allowing the balance to be totally exhausted in a fixed period, such as 10 years, or a slightly longer period determined by average life expectancy at retirement (around 15–20 years in many countries). The design of the PW in Chile does not allow a total and early exhaustion of the balance, reflecting the concern of policy makers with excessively accelerated PW payments leading to excessive demands on the MPG. The Chilean PW formula seeks to avoid a premature exhaustion of funds by distributing PW payments through a conversion factor that takes into account expected longevity.[4]

More specifically, retiring members who select a PW maintain their account balances in the AFP system (usually their AFP before retirement). Throughout the life of the PW, payments are determined by four elements. The first two are regulated parameters that are part of the PW conversion factor—the technical interest rate and the regulated mortality table. The conversion factor distributes the remaining PW balance over the expected remaining life of the PW holder. The other two elements are variables that affect the residual PW balance—the actual rate of return on the balance and the actual mortality experience of the member compared to the averages in the regulated mortality table.

The technical interest rate is defined as the weighted average of the average return earned by AFPs over the preceding 10 years and the average annuity rate reported by life insurance companies in the year preceding the purchase—the *tasa de venta* (Chapter 6). The weights of these two elements are 20 and 80 percent, respectively. The formula for the technical interest rate is too backward looking, especially due to its first component. Moreover, due to the declining trend of AFP returns and the general level of interest rates, the technical interest rate has been higher than both the annuity rate and the return on Funds D and E, which are selected by many PW holders. As a result, the technical rate has generally resulted in larger initial PW payments than would be justified by reasonable expectations of future market conditions.

Until 2005 the mortality table applied to the formula was the RV-85 table, which was also the table required of insurance companies to establish their annuity reserves. The table differentiates between males and females, and has separate assumptions for disability and survivorship cases. The new Pension Law empowered the SVS and the SAFP to change this table, and in February 2005 the new RV-04 table was applied to PWs issued after that date, reducing initial PW payments.[5] However, the adoption of the RV-04 to the existing pool of PW recipients has not been decided yet, because the full adoption of the new table would imply a reduction in payments for existing retirees, and could even lead some payments to fall below the MPG.

The actual (and expected) rate of return on PW balances is the most visible of the four factors, and possibly the one that most influences the choice between PWs and annuities. It is also one of the main determinants of the PW balance, and its volatility causes a commensurate volatility in PW payments (reflecting the investment risk borne by the PW holder). The actual mortality experience also affects the path of PW payments, and if PW holders live longer than predicted by the regulated table, this will imply excessive payments in the early years and what may be considered to be a premature reduction of the balance.

Each year, the recalculation of the PW payment is performed based on the residual balance and the updated conversion factor for the retiree. While the mortality table and the technical rate will be relatively stable, beneficiaries will experience variation arising from unexpectedly good or poor investment performance on their balances, as noted above. As such, following a year of particularly strong investment performance, it is possible for the PW payment to increase, while a year of weak performance can result in a sharp reduction in payments.

The PW formula sets the maximum payment that can be extracted from the account, but the PW holder can choose to receive the minimum payment, which is the MPG. The option of choosing the minimum payment and preserving a large balance may be attractive to higher income members who do not need the income and want to leave a large bequest. Where the result of the calculation is lower than the MPG, then the MPG acts as a minimum. In such cases, payments at the MPG level are made from the member's account until it is exhausted, then continue at the MPG level with the AFP provider reclaiming the funds from the Government to meet the obligations to the members who have exhausted their balance. Members on normal retirement who have an accumulated balance that is insufficient to provide the MPG are forced to take a PW.

As shown in Table 5.3, in December 2004, 63 percent of all PW holders received payments at the MPG level. Approximately 10 percent of all PW holders had already exhausted their balances and received the MPG from the Government, but 53 percent still had positive balances in their accounts. The bulk of PW holders receiving payments at the MPG level are old age retirees. This large group includes members who had to take a PW from retirement due to small balances, and members with small but sufficient balances who opted for a PW but experienced a decline in payments to the MPG level. Approximately 35 percent of PW holders were receiving PW payments according the formula, and only 1.5 percent had reduced voluntarily payments to preserve their balances. It is also clear from Table 5.3 that most PW holders with larger balances and higher payments are also early retirees.

PW holders can switch into an annuity at any time, provided that the residual PW balance provides for an annuity higher than the MPG. It is possible that some of the PW holders receiving payments according to the formula or below the formula will switch into annuities in the future. Within this group, early retirees tend to have larger balances and high PW payments and still have many years to exercise this option.

Table 5.3. Number and Average Amount of Phased Withdrawals, According to Relation to PW Formula and the MPG, Dec. 2004

	Raised to the MPG PW Balance > 0			*Raised to the MPG PW Balance = 0*			*According to PW Formula*			*PW Reduced Voluntarily*			*Total PWs*		
	Number of PWs	% of Total	Average UF Value	Number of PWs	% of Total	Average UF Value	Number of PWs	% of Total	Average UF Value	Number of PWs	% of Total	Average UF Value	Number of PWs	% of Total	Average UF Val-ue
Old Age	51,532	61.0%	4.9	10,990	13.0%	4.9	21,802	25.8%	6.7	204	0.2%	19.0	84,528	100%	5.1
Early Retirement	3,397	16.9%	4.9	1	0.0%	4.9	15,367	76.5%	12.6	1,337	6.7%	16.3	20,102	100%	12.9
Total	54,929	52.5%	4.9	10,991	10.5%	4.9	37,169	35.5%	-	1,541	1.5%	-	104,630	100%	-

Source: SAFP.

Note: MPG = 4.9 UFs.

Annuities

The only condition to buy an annuity at the normal retirement age is that it must be higher than the MPG. Members who quality for early retirement automatically qualify for an annuity, because early retirement rules are stricter. Normal age retirees who do not have an accumulated balance sufficient to provide for an annuity higher than the MPG have to take a PW. Those who qualify for an annuity can select a life insurance company. Consistent with prudent practice, annuities cannot be commuted after they are issued—once the decision is made, the beneficiaries are locked into a single provider.

The form of the annuity is prescribed, and until recently the range of choices was restricted. First, annuities were only denominated in UFs, i.e., indexed to consumer prices. Second, annuities were only issued at fixed real interest rates. Third, they had to be joint life annuities for married beneficiaries, providing for a monthly income to the member and including a 60 percent reversion to the spouse in the event of death. It also provided smaller survivorship benefits to children in the event that they were still young. Fourth, a fixed UF15 funeral benefit was also included.

As an option, the member could select a guaranteed term added to the standard annuity. For example, a member could purchase an annuity where the payment was not contingent on survivorship for a period before becoming contingent on survivorship after the end of the guarantee period. The guarantee reduced the initial payment level but the risk of loss due to the early death of the main beneficiary (or all beneficiaries) was also reduced. The guaranteed option has proved very popular in Chile, with nearly 80 percent of the annuities issued containing a guarantee. Moreover, such guarantees are issued for long periods, as shown in Table 5.4 (Annex 1 provides a more detailed analysis).

This restricted design reflected the central role of the second pillar in Chile and the social protection objectives of the pension system. The indexation of annuities was designed to protect pensioners against inflation risk, in a country that had struggled with high inflation for decades. The issue of fixed annuities protected pensioners against investment risk. The obligation of married couples to buy joint life annuities was designed to protect spouses against longevity risk and prevent their poverty at old age, or an excessive recourse to the MPG. The guarantee option provided extra protection for spouses by ensuring an income higher than the 60 percent mandated by the law (in the event of death of the beneficiary), and it is interesting to observe how many retirees have exercised this option.

Table 5.4. Annuities Issued in March of 1999, 2002, 2003, 2004, and 2005

	1999	*2002*	*2003*	*2004*	*2005*
All Cases					
Number	937	1,517	1,193	1,490	1,391
Average Age of Males	57.8	57.0	57.8	57.7	59.5
Average Age of Females	55.8	54.8	55.5	56.0	58.5
Average Purchase Price (UF)	1,971.7	1,859.6	2,116.9	2,098.8	2,454.9
Number of cases with deferment	199 (21.2%)	331 (21.8%)	307 (25.7%)	409 (27.5%)	419 (30.1%)
Of which:					
- 12 months	164	275	238	322	315
- 24 months	32	54	60	75	91
- 36 months	2	2	8	10	9
- 48 months	1	0	1	2	3
Number of cases with a guaranteed term	708 (75.6%)	1,191 (78.5%)	948 (79.5%)	1,153 (77.4%)	1,093 (78.6%)
Of which:					
- 5 years	11	19	17	18	23
- 10 years	422	701	511	636	559
- 15 years	244	387	335	380	353
- 20 years	18	64	63	93	124
- other	13	20	22	26	34

Source: SVS and staff analysis.

The new Pension Law has widened the range of retirement products while maintaining their desirable social protection features. One of the new products consists of the combination of a PW and an annuity. To access this new product, the annuity component needs to be fixed in UFs and higher than the MPG. This new product allows the retiree to capture the higher returns in the capital market while also maintaining a stable source of retirement income, as the annuity component provides insurance against longevity, investment, and inflation risks. The PW balance can be invested in Funds C, D, or E, as under the old Law. If the annuity component is sufficiently large (higher than 70 percent of the average real wage and 150 percent of the MPG), the retiree will be allowed to invest in Funds A and B as well.

A second new product consists of the combination of a fixed and a variable annuity. Again, to access this new product the annuity component must be fixed in UFs and higher than the MPG. The variable component can be denominated in pesos, UFs, or another currency (it is initially expected that some annuities may be issued in U.S. dollars), and be invested in variable income assets. While the first product will involve splitting the balance between an AFP and an insurance company, the second product will be provided entirely by the insurance company. Retirees who initially select only a PW can subsequently shift to a fixed annuity or to one of these two new hybrid products, provided that they meet the conditions.

Annuities are freely priced by insurance companies, which adopt tables for pricing that reflect their own views as to mortality by sex and type of annuity. As shown in detail in Annex 1, annuity prices (captured by the money's worth ratios) reflect in general the risk characteristics of the annuitant, such as age, gender, and the presence of a guarantee. The companies need to report the annuity rate on each annuity based on regulated mortality tables (the *tasa de venta*). Once issued, provisions are established also using regulated mortality tables and a regulated discount rate.

If an annuity falls below the MPG (because the MPG has increased in real terms) then the annuitant is paid the full MPG and the difference is recovered by the insurance company from the Government. Further, in the event of the failure of the insurance company, the annuitant receives the MPG plus 75 percent of the difference between the MPG and their annuity payment if higher, subject to a maximum on the total "insured" annuity income level of 45 UF per month[6]. As such, annuitants within the insurance company are provided with an additional form of default insurance guarantee.

Temporary Withdrawals

Retiring members can also select a combined product consisting of a temporary withdrawal (TW) and a deferred annuity. The TW payment is regulated—it cannot be lower than the MPG and cannot be higher than twice the deferred annuity. However, there are no regulatory limits on the period of deferment. Under this option, the accumulated balance is split immediately, with one fraction staying in the AFP to provide for the TW and another fraction being transferred to the selected insurance company to provide for the annuity. A TW differs from a PW because it already includes an annuity, and should be considered as an annuity for all practical purposes. The advantage of the TW over the annuity is that it allows access to larger payments in the early stages of retirement.

One would expect this product to be popular among retirees, given the restrictions on lump sums. However, TWs have accounted for only 30 percent of new annuities, although their share has increased in recent years, as shown in Table 5.4. Curiously, the period of deferment has been short, with roughly 80 percent of TW holders deferring for only 12 months, and the period of deferment has not increased over time. As discussed below, it is possible that both the relatively low share of TWs and the short period of deferment reflects the influence of brokers in the decision process—brokers have no incentives for a large number of TWs, large TW payments, or long periods of deferment, as this tends to reduce their commissions (which are entirely related to the annuity component). Additionally, a short deferment period may enable a higher initial payment to be illustrated to the potential customer.

Assessing the Menu of Retirement Products

Table 5.5 summarizes the features of each of these products, and the last rows summarize their strong and weak aspects. It is apparent that a more diversified menu of retirement products may generate welfare gains, as it meets more effectively the different needs and preferences of different retiring workers. Empirical studies that construct measures of utility or annuity-equivalent wealth based on a lifetime utility function conclude that a diversified menu is likely to generate welfare gains. Fixed and indexed annuities generally fare well among individuals with a high degree of risk aversion, whereas variable annuities are attractive to individuals with a low degree of risk aversion. Not surprisingly, the existence of a price-indexed social security benefit makes riskier products such as variable annuities attractive to a wider range of individuals.[7]

Chilean regulators seem to have reached a reasonable balance overall, considering the preferences and needs of different workers, the social protection objectives of the pension system, the absence of a front-ended social security benefit, and the need to avoid excessive recourse to the back-ended MPG. Fixed and indexed annuities provide insurance against longevity, investment, and inflation risks. Joint annuities extend this protection to spouses. Guaranteed annuities are optional and provide some room for bequests. PWs allow bequests and have been designed so as to avoid a very premature depletion of funds. Therefore, the menu of available products provides a reasonable range of choices for most workers, while limiting their exposure to risk. Higher income workers are probably more constrained than other workers, but they can also offset these constraints by managing their personal savings. The new Pension Law allows more choices to retirees, but through combined products, maintaining the obligation for retirees to buy a fixed indexed annuity providing minimum protection against inflation, longevity, and investment risks.

Table 5.5. Comparison of Retirement Product Features

	Lump sums	*PWs*	*Annuities*	*TWs*
Liquidity	Immediate control of funds.	Provides limited opportunity for deferment and advancement of payments.	None.	Provides limited opportunity for some advance payments up to 200% of ultimate deferred annuity.
Portability	Immediate control of funds	Can change to another AFP provider or opt for an annuity at a later stage.	None.	Limited relevance
Bequests	Yes	Yes	No for non-guaranteed annuities. Limited in the case of guaranteed annuities.	Limited in deferment period.
Protection against investment and longevity risks	No. (Residual protection provided by MPG)	No. (Residual protection provided by MPG)	Yes for fixed annuities. Partial for variable annuities and combinations.	Limited exposure to investment risk in the short deferment period.
Protection against bankruptcy risk	Not applicable	Limited relevance in the case of AFPs, as risk is shifted to workers and PW holders. Protection against residual risk of AFP not meeting the minimum return guarantee	Protection provided by annuity guarantee, equal to 100% up to the MPG and 75% for annuity values exceeding the MPG	Limited relevance for the TW component. For the annuity component the protection is the same as described in the annuity column.

(Continued)

Table 5.5. Comparison of Retirement Product Features *(Continued)*

	Lump sums	*PWs*	*Annuities*	*TWs*
Strong / Positive features	Full liquidity and control, allowing bequests	Some liquidity and control. Some liquidity through larger early payments. Some control through choice of AFP and type of fund, as well as bequest provision.	Longevity and investment insurance. Lower risk of falling into poverty, especially spouse. Substantive protection against bankruptcy.	Some limited liquidity/control in temporary period. Longevity insurance in annuity period. Lower risk of falling into poverty, especially spouse.
Weak / Negative features	Exposure to investment and longevity risks. Risk of rapid depletion of funds, resulting in poverty, excessive demands on MPG.	Exposure to investment and longevity risks. Limited control for emergency payments. Risk of very small balances, excessive demands on the MPG.	No liquidity or control. Locked to single provider. Some residual loss in the case of provider bankruptcy.	Same as in the annuity case. Flexibility limited when deferment period is short.

Source: Staff analysis.

Of course, this positive assessment of the menu of retirement products assumes that individuals generally behave rationally and that the market is transparent, allowing individuals to make well-informed choices. These conditions cannot be taken for granted in real life situations. In the particular case of Chile a number of relevant questions can be raised, including the question of whether individuals understand the characteristics of each product, including their time paths, and whether brokers have played a positive role. These questions will be examined in the following sections.

The Time Path of Annuities and Phased Withdrawals

PW and Annuity Paths under a Stylized Scenario

Figure 5.1 shows the time path of an annuity and a PW for a male single life annuitant aged 55 under a hypothetical scenario. The annuity and the PW are both calculated with the same mortality table—the RV-85 period table that has been applied until recently. Also, the technical interest rate of the PW and the actual rate of return on PW funds are both equal to the annuity rate, at 4.5 percent p.a. The purchase price and account balance have been assumed to be UF 2,000 and generate payout levels consistent with the average outcomes in 2003 of about UF 11 per month. In this stylized example of equal mortality tables and interest rates, the first PW and annuity payments are exactly the same. This reflects the fact that the PW formula in the first year is the same as the formula for an actuarially fair annuity. The PW then progressively falls below the annuity, reaching zero at the end of the mortality table (which is 110 years of age).

PW payments decline because the PW balance is gradually exhausted over time, while the annuity remains constant because of risk pooling—the balances of the members who die stay in the pool, generating a "mortality profit" which is shared by those who survive. In the case of the PW there is no such sharing. At the end of each year the PW balance is reduced by one year of payments, while life expectancy is reduced by less than a year, resulting in declining PW payments.[8] Figure 5.1 would seem to suggest that no one would ever select a PW under this highly stylized scenario, but this is not necessarily the case. Members who wish to leave a bequest because of short life expectancies could still prefer to take a PW.

It is intuitive to think of the PW as having declining payments because the product does not participate in the "pooling benefit" offered by annuities. Instead, the funds from those that die are bequeathed away

Figure 5.1. Hypothetical Payment Paths for PW and Annuity, 55-Year-Old Pensioner

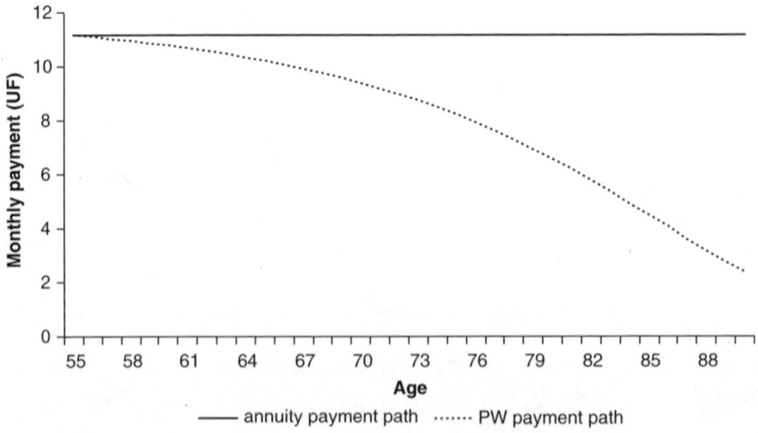

Source: Staff analysis.

to others. In the case of the annuity option, the funds could be considered to be "bequeathed" to the rest of the annuitants to provide for the maintenance of their payments. As such, the sum of the expected values of the two products will be the same in this hypothetical scenario (Figure 5.1), such that the expected present value of the annuity is equal to the expected value of the PW payments plus the expected value of the final bequest that the PW allows.

The Impact of Regulation and Age on PW and Annuity Paths

The actual time paths of PWs and annuities have been different from Figure 5.1, because the parameters driving the two paths have been different. First, annuity providers have used their own mortality tables for pricing, and these tables reflect more updated information on future mortality of annuitants. By contrast, the RV-85 which was used until recently for calculating PW payments is an outdated period table. Second, the technical interest rate used in the PW is determined through a backward-looking formula that has yielded numbers higher than the current annuity rate. Finally, the current rate of return on the PW account has also been very different, generally higher than the annuity rate and also much more volatile.

A more accurate representation of the PW and annuity payments paths is provided in Figure 5.2. The rate of return on the PW funds is assumed to be constant at 6 percent p.a., higher than the reported annuity rate of

Figure 5.2. Payment Paths for a 55-Year-Old Pensioner

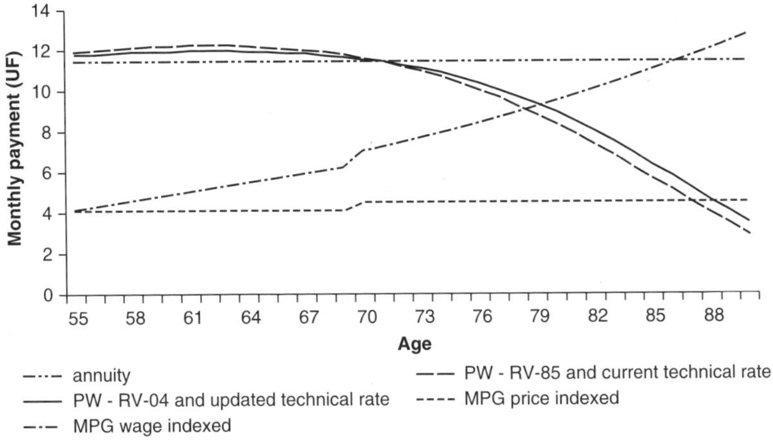

Source: Staff analysis.

4.17 percent p.a. in 2003.[9] The technical interest rate on the PW was obtained from the formula, resulting in a rate of 4.54 percent p.a., thus higher than the annuity rate. The purchase price is unchanged at UF 2,000, consistent with the observed average annuity payment of around UF 11 per month. This set of assumptions reflects general conditions in 2004.

The use of an outdated mortality table for PWs and a technical interest rate higher than the annuity rate leads the first PW payment to exceed the first annuity payment, as shown in Figure 5.2. The reason for this result is straightforward. A table with heavier mortality rates yields larger initial payments with the same initial balance, because the formula "assumes" that the PW holder will lead a shorter life. A technical interest rate computed through a backward looking formula produces a similar effect. Therefore, the regulated parameters introduced a small bias in the selection process.

After the initial PW payment is set, the path of the PW will depend to a good extent on the actual return on PW funds. Very large returns would lead the balance and the initial payments to increase sharply, while low returns could lead the PW to fall below the annuity path already in the initial years. The assumed rate of return of 6 percent p.a. in Figure 5.2 leads PW payments to increase only moderately, start declining after 7 years, and cross the annuity path after 14 years. PW payments decline rapidly after that date, reflecting the premature exhaustion of the PW balance due to inaccurate parameters.

The adoption of an updated mortality table for the PW will result in lower initial PW payments and will remove part of the bias. As shown in Figure 5.2, the adoption of the RV-04 will lead PW payments to fall below the first PW line and closer to the annuity line in the initial years. The new PW line would cross the annuity line at a slightly later date. In the final years, the decline in PW payments would be less pronounced. The differences between the two lines cancel each other on a discounted basis, as the net present value (the premium) is the same.[10] The first PW payment remains larger than the first annuity payment because the technical interest rate remains higher than the annuity rate. The regulatory authorities have already adopted an updated mortality table for the PW but have not yet introduced a new formula for the PW technical rate.

The path of PW payments also depends on the age of retirement. To illustrate the impact of the retirement age, Figure 5.3 provides the example a 65-year-old with the same annuity payment. This same annuity payment is provided with a smaller premium of UF 1,500, reflecting the fact that older retirees obtain larger annuity payouts for a given premium due to shorter life expectancies, i.e., they benefit relatively more from risk pooling. The first PW payment will again be slightly higher than the annuity payment, under the same assumptions about mortality and interest rates. (It would be exactly the same if the mortality and interest rates were the same, as discussed above.) Given the similar initial payment, the PW path will have to be steeper at older ages of retirement. This is

Figure 5.3. Payment Paths for a 65-Year-Old Pensioner

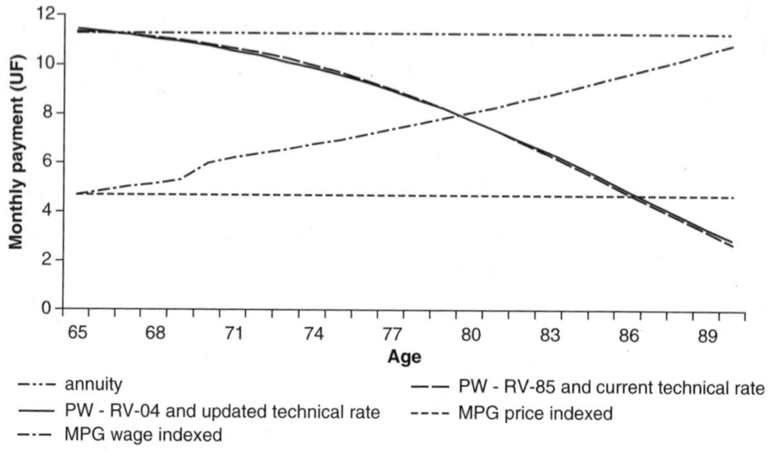

Source: Staff analysis.

because the initial PW payments as a proportion of the (lower) balance is much higher, leading to a faster payout rate of the balance, and its more rapid depletion until the same ultimate age of the mortality table.[11]

It is also noteworthy that the bias produced by outdated mortality tables and the technical interest rates is less pronounced at older ages of retirement. This reflects simply the shorter life expectancy of a 65-year-old pensioner. The impact of an excessive technical discount rate is weakened by fewer years of compounding. The impact of an outdated mortality table is weakened for the same reason.

The Selection of PWs and Annuities[12]

A straight comparison of Figures 5.2 and 5.3 could lead to the conclusion that younger retirees would tend to favor PWs while older retirees would tend to favor annuities. There would seem to be a puzzle, as exactly the reverse happens in Chile. As shown in Chapter 2, the high degree of annuitization in Chile is very closely related to early retirement. Approximately 60 percent of old age retirees (excluding the disabled and survivors) retire early. Roughly 90 percent of early retirees choose annuities, and 65 percent of normal age retirees choose PWs.

To understand the high degree of annuitization in Chile, and the selection of PWs and annuities by different classes of pensioners, other factors need to be taken into account. The most important factors are: (i) the sharp differences in the average income of early and normal age retirees; (ii) the exposure of higher income PW holders to investment and mortality risk; (iii) the rule that forces workers with small balances to buy PWs; (iv) the much greater importance of the MPG for low income workers; and (v) the influence of brokers in retirement and selection decisions.

Figures 5.2 and 5.3 are drawn for two retirees with different ages but the same level of annuity payouts. By contrast, the early and normal retirement populations, which largely correspond to the annuitant and PW populations, are very different. Early retirees have on average much higher incomes, while most normal retirement workers delay retirement precisely because they have small incomes and balances and cannot meet the conditions for early retirement. Therefore, Figure 5.3 is not representative of the typical normal age retiree. The situation of the typical normal age retiree is better reflected in Figure 5.4, which shows the PW and annuity paths for a low income 65–year-old worker.

The selection of annuities and PWs in Chile can now be examined based on the more typical situations depicted in Figures 5.2 and 5.4. The PW would first seem to be a more attractive option for a typical

Figure 5.4. Payment Paths for a Low Income 65-Year-Old Pensioner

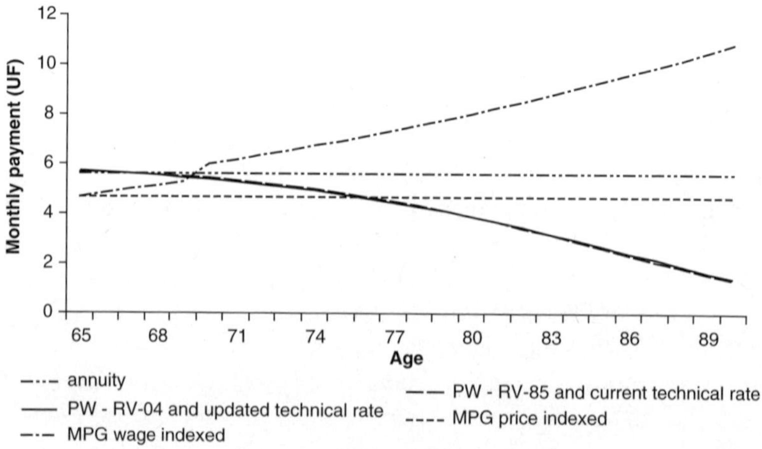

Source: Staff analysis.

55-year-old retiree, as it stays above the annuity line for a few years under reasonable interest rate assumptions. However, the early retiree that chooses a PW is subject to both investment and longevity risk. The well-behaved PW path does not reflect accurately real world situations, which can involve volatility and years of reduced retirement income due to poor investment performance. The retiree may value the stable real payments produced by the annuity, as well as the longevity insurance, especially in the absence of a front-ended first pillar benefit. A strategy of selecting a PW in the early phase of retirement and then switching to an annuity would take care of longevity risk, but would not address the exposure to investment risk.

The presence of the minimum pension guarantee probably does not affect the decision. As illustrated in Figure 5.2, the average annuity payout of early retirees is much higher than the MPG for early retirees. This is due both to their higher average income and balances, but also to the fact that early retirees suffer a discount in their MPGs.[13] Under the assumptions in Figure 5.2 the PW path crosses the MPG path only 25 years after retirement, if the MPG is wage-indexed. If the MPG is price-indexed, the PW would cross the MPG more than 30 years after retirement. If the PW is calculated with the RV-04 it crosses the MPG path even later (as mentioned before, this is the case for all PWs issued after February 2005).

It is clear that the MPG does not provide too much comfort for a PW holder in this situation. The retiree would be extremely exposed to investment risk in the first 15 years, and could suffer a decline in his benefit of up to 50 percent. A wage-indexed MPG would provide effective comfort only after 20 years, too far away to be considered in the decision of most retirees. A price-indexed MPG would provide even less comfort. The rules on the MPG constitute another source of uncertainty, as there is no formal obligation to index the MPG to wages. The conclusion is that annuities may be effectively the most attractive option for most early retirees, especially considering the absence of a first pillar benefit in Chile.

By contrast, low income workers probably find PWs a much more attractive option. As shown in Figure 5.4, if the first PW payment is close to the MPG, the exposure of the PW holder to both investment and longevity risk would be extremely small. These retirees could benefit from any upside gain caused by high investment returns while being exposed to only limited downside risk. They could also leave a bequest in the event of death. Therefore, it is not surprising to observe large numbers of normal age retirees choosing PWs, as most of these workers have lower incomes. These numbers comprise workers who simply cannot buy an annuity, and workers who have this option but find the PW more attractive due to the MPG.

The normal age retirees with higher incomes—the situation in Figure 5.3—probably find annuities a much better option, because they do not benefit nearly as much from the MPG and benefit much more from risk pooling. However, they constitute only a small share of the population retiring at the normal age.

Finally, the marketing activity of insurance brokers has also contributed significantly to the joint decision to retire early and to buy an annuity. Insurance companies market annuities aggressively, while AFPs focus on the very profitable accumulation phase of the pension business and do not have an interest to sell PWs. Therefore, marketing influences are totally one-sided. Moreover, insurance brokers have an obvious interest to concentrate their efforts in higher income workers with larger balances, as they receive larger commissions, and these are precisely the workers who can retire early. The next section examines in much more detail the regulation of marketing activities and the influence of brokers.

Marketing Regulation

The Main Elements of Marketing Regulation under the Old Law

The distribution of PWs is conducted by the AFPs themselves, while annuities are sold by employees and sales agents of life insurance companies, as well as independent brokers. In practice, active marketing only takes place in the annuity segment, as AFPs do not compete actively in the PW market—they do not maintain an active sales force for PWs and do not pay a bonus to employees when a member buys a PW. This attitude by the AFPs reflects their focus on the profitable accumulation phase of the pension business, and the administration of other tasks such as unemployment insurance. The AFPs do not generate profits in their PW business, partly because two-thirds of the population consists of older and low income retirees who are forced to buy PWs due to their small balances. The AFPs charge the same modest fee on all PW holders, and these fees are designed to just cover their marginal operating costs (the fee is around 1 percent of benefit payments).

By contrast, life insurance companies have much stronger incentives to market annuities, as this product constitutes the core of their business. Independent brokers, who play an important role in the distribution of annuities, have to pass a certification test administered by the SVS, and also have to pass a very basic test of fitness and propriety. Most applicants usually take a course on annuities that comprises a total of 120 hours. Licensed brokers are legally obligated to represent the client, and generate their income from commissions on the sale of annuities. They are not permitted to accept volume-related remuneration from insurers such as volume bonuses. In 2003 there were approximately 1,300 licensed brokers, clearly an excessive number, considering that the annuities market comprised about 22,000 new policies in that year, and that brokers accounted for 40 percent of sales.

The productivity of brokers has been low by international standards, as indicated by the large number of brokers relative to the size of the market, and anecdotal evidence that brokers only conclude 1 contract out of 10 prospects and that it takes three months to finalize a contract. The low productivity is in good part explained by the extensive work required in prospecting for affiliates that are eligible for retirement (particularly early retirement), and the need to "sell" both the retirement decision and the annuity purchase. Additionally, with respect to the bonds that affiliates may have as an entitlement from the prior retirement system (recognition bonds), the broker assists in ensuring that the entitlement is correctly calculated and accessed.

Sales agents acting for a single company account for the remainder 60 percent of sales. Companies also can distribute annuities through their own staff. Those that are paid solely through commissions are considered as "free agents" and are registered with the SVS. Company staff are not registered with the SVS, whether paid through a salary plus commissions or entirely through salaries.

The objective of marketing regulation should be to ensure well informed choices by consumers, not only in their decision to take a PW versus an annuity, but also in the selection of the annuity provider. In addition, marketing regulation should also try to avoid outside interference on an even more fundamental decision, i.e., the decision to retire or not in a particular year. Although the levels of disclosure in Chile are generally good, a number of problems may have prevented customers from always making the best choices. Curiously, some of these problems biased the choice towards PWs while others biased the choice towards annuities. The selection of providers was not always made on a well-informed basis, and the decision to retire early was possibly influenced as well.

In recent years PW regulation may have resulted in some bias towards PWs due to the use of an outdated mortality table and a backward-looking technical interest rate. As discussed above, annuity providers are free to use their own proprietary mortality tables and to adjust annuity prices in line with the most recent mortality projections. PWs, on the other hand, were determined by an outdated mortality table (the RV-85) that results in larger initial PW payments. The backward-looking formula for the technical rate, combining past AFP returns and the average annuity rate in the previous year also biased the choice towards PWs, because it has resulted in a higher technical rate and larger PW payments (this was due to the historical decline in AFP returns and, more recently, to falling annuity rates as well).

The way the PW and annuity options were presented to the consumer may also have biased the choice towards PWs. As discussed above, the time paths for PWs and annuities are clearly different, reflecting not only the different mortality tables and interest rates, but, even more fundamentally, the fact that one product provides longevity insurance while the other does not. PW payments may initially increase if returns are high, but they will inevitably follow a declining path over time, and will also inevitably fall below the level of the annuity that would have been bought with the same premium. Apparently, consumers were not aware of this basic fact, as judged by the complaints lodged in the AFPs and the SVS, revealing that the selection in these cases was made solely on a comparison between the initial values of the two products.

Whereas these factors biased the selection towards PWs, the influence of brokers possibly resulted in a stronger bias towards annuities. As discussed above, the motivation of AFPs and insurance companies in marketing their retirement products is very different, with active marketing only taking place on the side of annuities. Moreover, the bias produced by brokers towards annuities is accompanied by a bias towards early retirement as well, as the generation of annuity business also involves to a large extent convincing workers below the normal retirement age to retire. The arguments most commonly employed by brokers include the access to two sources of income and the added flexibility. Brokers have also influenced the retirement decision by offering valuable services to eligible workers, such as the identification and calculation of their recognition bonds and other paperwork.

Commission rates are built into the annuity price; so are not separately disclosed or explicitly charged to the customer. As shown in Chapter 2, during the 1990s commission rates increased substantially, from an average of 2.5 percent to about 6 percent of the premium. Although not able to be officially substantiated, this increase in commissions was apparently matched by rebates to customers by way of cash or "in kind" payments to encourage purchases and to subvert the limitations on access to lump sums. Since 2000, commission rates have declined to the levels in the early 1990s. The reason for this outcome is not entirely clear, but it seems to have been due to an informal agreement among the companies, driven by strong political pressures and the threat imposed by the submission of the new Pension Law to Congress in 2000.

Marketing regulation included the requirement for the retiring worker to obtain at least six annuity quotes in the market before making his selection. These quotes had to be presented to his/her AFP, which would not authorize the transfer of the pension balance to an insurance company unless these quotes were presented. This obligation of a minimum market search was clearly motivated by a concern with disclosure and transparency. It was also a measure to prevent AFPs from directing their members to the life insurance companies in the same financial group. The regulation was sensible, but it never worked fully as intended by regulators, because brokers frequently manipulated the process, directing the customer to the company that offered the highest commissions, not necessarily the best quotes, and failing to present the best quotes in the market.

The final outcomes in the past 15 years suggest that, on average, brokers gained the upper hand and biased the choice towards annuities. They have had a key role in identifying customers who may be eligible for early retirement and, at the same time, a motivation that is oriented directly to persuading the customer to both retire and to take an annuity. Therefore, they are at least partly responsible for the high degree of annuitization in Chile, especially among early retirees. Brokers also seem partly responsible for the low share of TWs and the short period of deferment periods. Finally, brokers may have also contributed to an excessive dispersion of annuity prices, or differences between individual MWRs and annuity rates that cannot be explained by individual annuitant characteristics, such as age, gender, and income.

Judging the quality of these outcomes is not an easy task. The high degree of annuitization in Chile can be seen positively, as it implies a high degree of protection against longevity risk, and reduces future demands on the MPG. However, the decline in the average age of retirement and the increasing share of early retirees are more questionable outcomes. Whereas many people may continue working and saving voluntarily, and simply enjoy the added flexibility, in other cases there may an anticipation of consumption, erosion of savings, and a low income at retirement. Unfortunately there has been no empirical research in Chile investigating the behavior of early retirees in the postretirement period.

The low share of TWs and the short deferment periods is also a questionable outcome, especially in the cases of people retiring close to the normal age. If a worker has accumulated a reasonable balance, the TW may be a genuine option to gain access to early payments while preserving longevity insurance. The broker's influence in this decision may be welfare reducing. The dispersion of annuity prices, whereby two annuitants with similar individual characteristics receive very different annuities just because of the broker's influence, is clearly an unfavorable outcome.

The Changes Introduced by the New Pensions Law

These problems were identified in the 1990s, prompting a debate about possible solutions. Regulators and policy makers seemed to be particularly concerned with the decline in the retirement age which, combined with the relatively low density of contributions and the historic decline in AFP returns, would lead to declining replacement ratios. Regulators were also concerned with the high commissions and the spread of illegal marketing practices such as the cash rebates. Finally, there was a general awareness that several annuitants were not selecting the best available quotes.

To address these problems, the new Pensions Law introduced the following measures: (i) stricter conditions for early retirement; (ii) the capping of the commission rate to 2.5 percent of the premium for two years, after which this price control would be reassessed; (iii) the introduction of a new electronic quotation system; (iv) the permission for banks to participate in the distribution of annuities[14]; (v) the creation of room for parametric changes in the PW formula; (vi) the expansion of the menu of retirement products; (vii) other changes affecting disability and survivorship insurance.

The stricter conditions for early retirement were discussed above, and have already contributed to an increase in the average retirement age, as shown in Table 5.4. The capping of commissions at 2.5 percent of the premium and the new quotation system are clearly aimed at reducing the influence of brokers, not only in the retirement decision, but also in the selection of retirement instruments and providers. The SVS and the SAFP have been empowered to regulate the PW formula and have already adopted the RV-04 for PWs issued after February 2005, reducing the bias. The expanded menu of retirement products has been examined above and is expected to improve consumer welfare.

The new Pension Law was only passed after an intense and long debate, revealing not only the strong lobbying power of the industry but also the lack of genuine technical consensus on some of the measures. The capping of the commission rate was subject to a fierce debate, and was only passed after a compromise solution involving a reassessment after two years. The increase in the conditions for early retirement was passed, but against the opinion of many experts and politicians that opposed the removal of flexibility for workers in general, and advocated the use of early retirement as a source of income for unemployed older workers. The quotation system was passed after modification of the original proposal that consisted of an auction system.

The new quotation system has attracted particular interest, because it represents an important innovation that has changed the role of intermediaries in the annuities market and the way the industry operates. The intention of this system, known as *Sistema de Consultas y Ofertas de Montos de Pensión* (SCOMP) is to advance the quality of information provided to customers as well as to permit them to access directly a full range of annuity quotations.

The quotation system involves essentially the following steps: (i) the retiring member goes to his/her AFP and initiates the procedures for a pension. The AFP sends the member's balance certificate with personal data to SCOMP; (ii) the member selects a participant in SCOMP to solicit quotations. Participants include AFPs, brokers, and life insurance companies; (ii) the member sends a request for annuity quotes, with or without the assistance of brokers or sales agents. Members can make up to three separate requests for each certificate issued by his/her AFP; (iii) the central information system validates the personal information of the member (e.g., age, sex, eligibility, balance), assigns a code and sends the information with the request to life insurance companies; (iv) the life insurance companies send their annuity quotes, while SCOMP itself calculates PW payments, which are regulated; (v) SCOMP sends the PW and annuity quotes to the member. The quotes are valid for 15 days; (vi) the member must either accept one of the offers, or accept another offer made outside SCOMP. These outside offers can only be made by the companies that offered quotes in the first round, and have to be better than the first quote. Alternatively, the member can request bids from at least three companies (an auction) and accept the best offer; or simply decide not to retire.

In addition to the quotation system itself, the new system also includes the elaboration by the AFPs of a list of all potential retirees, including not only those approaching the normal retirement age, but also those who are eligible for an early retirement. The objective of this list is to disseminate the information on all the potential retirees to all participants in SCOMP, brokers, AFPs and life insurance companies, eliminating the excessive influence of individual brokers or other distributors on members. The members who do not want to see their names and personal information disclosed through this list may request to have their names removed.

The new system has been well designed and should address most of the problems identified in recent years. The prospecting task of finding candidates who are eligible to retire and contacting them has been diminished. The room for the manipulation of prospective retirees by brokers has also been diminished. The broker is not able to isolate the retiring worker from other distributors, and is not able to hide good quotations either. Additionally, the provision of a full range of quotations to clients has become a more automated task. Brokers are generally aware that they will probably need to play another role, such as the provision of financial advice. The Brokers' Association has already organized workshops and training courses for brokers in order to facilitate the transition into this new role.

Preliminary data for the first year of operation indicates that the new system has been operating reasonably well and has increased transparency. As shown in Table 5.6, between August 2004 and October 2005, 41,244 retiring members made 54,090 requests for quotes through the new system, corresponding to an average of 1.3 requests per member. Each request asked on average for quotes of 4.5 different types of annuities. Brokers participated in about 38 percent of these requests, indicating a

Table 5.6. Number of Requests for Quotes, Broken Down by Type of Access, Aug. 2004–Oct. 2005

Number of Members	Number of Requests	Access to the System (% of total)			Participation of Brokers and Agents (% of total)		
		Broker	LICO	AFP	Broker	Sales Agent	Direct
41,244	54,090	37.9	26.0	36.0	37.9	23.7	38.4

Source: SVS.

reduction in their influence in the selection process. Approximately 38 percent of the requests were done directly by the member, most typically through his/her own AFP. On average, eight companies have provided quotes for members, indicating both an increase in the number of quotes and direct and easy access to the best quotes.

By October 2005, 33,867 quotes had been accepted by retiring members, of which 61 percent consisted of annuities and 39 percent of PWs (Table 5.7). Approximately 75 percent of members who were assisted by brokers or sales agents chose annuities, suggesting that the channel of access to the system may still influence the final product selection. However, a significant number of members who chose annuities operated directly and without the assistance of brokers and sales agents, indicating that the new system provides easier access to information and selection.

Although only a small fraction of participants has utilized the option to request bids from annuity providers, the final selection of the provider has been closely associated with the ranking of quotes, suggesting increased price competition. As shown in Table 5.8, approximately 64 percent of annuities contracted in this period were based on the best quote provided in the first round and 87 percent in one of the three best quotes in the first round. It seems that the typical procedure involves a separate negotiation outside the system with one of the companies providing one of the three best quotes, resulting in some improvement of the quote for the member. It is impossible to assess whether this improvement is similar to the one that would be produced by a formal bid in the second round, but the system seems to have improved market search and selection conditions for most members. The reduction in broker's commissions to about 2.2 percent of the premium provides additional evidence of increased price competition in the annuities market. Finally, there seems to have been a reduction in price dispersion, although the reduction has been moderate and the results should be seen as preliminary, based only on data for March 2005 (Annex 1).

It is interesting to note that such an improvement in transparency and price competition has been accompanied by a concentration of the

Table 5.7. Choice of Retirement Products under New Quotation System, Aug. 2004–Oct. 2005

	PWs		*Annuities*		*Total*		*% of Each*
Access into System	*Number*	*%*	*Number*	*%*	*Number*	*%*	*Participant*
Broker	3,167	24.0	10,026	76.0	13,193	100.0	38.9
LICO – Sales Agent	1,960	22.9	6,596	77.1	8,556	100.0	25.3
LICO – Direct	177	24.3	552	75.7	729	100.0	2.2
AFP	7,777	68.3	3,611	31.7	11,388	100.0	33.6
Total	13,081	38.6	20,785	61.4	33,866	100.0	100.0

Source: SVS.

Table 5.8. Acceptance of Annuity Offers by Ranking of Quotes, Aug. 2004–Oct. 2005

	Number	*% of Total*	*% Accumulated*
Best quote	13,202	63.5	63.5
Second best quote	3,258	15.7	79.2
Third best quote	1,578	7.6	86.8
Other quotes	2,747	13.2	100.0
Total	20,785	100.0	—

Source: SVS.

annuities market. The share of the three largest companies in the annuities market increased from one-third to about half, whether measured by premiums or the number of new annuity contracts (Chapter 2). It seems that increased transparency and price competition is creating difficulties for some companies to preserve their traditional market niches. This may be judged as a favorable outcome, but the increasing market concentration and its consequences will need to be closely monitored and assessed. The emphasis that the quotation system places on prices, possibly at the expense of quality of services and credit standing, is another issue that will need to be closely monitored by regulators.[15]

Conclusions and Recommendations

Chile has adopted a cautious approach to product regulation since the market for retirement products was created in the early 1980s. Access to lump sums has been severely limited. PWs have been designed in a way to avoid a very early exhaustion of funds. Only fixed and indexed annuities were initially allowed, and joint annuities have been obligatory for married couples. TWs have also been designed to limit large early payments. The role of annuities with a guaranteed term has also been significant and they represent a valuable product. The new Pensions

Law has widened the range of retirement products but preserving the careful approach, as the new products are combinations that still require a fixed and indexed annuity component designed to provide protection against investment, inflation, and longevity risk.

This approach to product regulation is well justified in the Chilean case, as the absence of a front-ended first pillar benefit implies a much greater exposure of retiring workers to investment and longevity risk than in other countries. The market still provides overall a reasonable range of options for retirees, capable of meeting most of the needs of workers with different preferences and risk profiles. The MPG provides minimum investment and longevity protection for low income workers.

Marketing regulation in the 1990s included the obligation for retiring workers to perform a minimum market search, presenting a minimum of six quotations. This regulation never achieved the level of transparency to the degree intended. Insurance brokers apparently influenced significantly the retirement decision, the choice of the product and the choice of the provider. The bias introduced by brokers towards annuities can be seen positively—the high rate of annuitization in Chile is a welcome development in the absence of a first pillar benefit, as it helps prevent poverty in old age. However, the reduction in the average age of retirement is a more questionable outcome. The influence of brokers in the choice of the provider is also questionable.

The authorities reacted to these developments by imposing stricter conditions for early retirement and strengthening marketing regulation through a 2.5 percent cap on broker's commissions and the introduction of a new and innovative quotation system. These measures seem to have produced positive outcomes, as indicated the increase in the average retirement age, the decline in broker's commissions to levels below the cap, and evidence that new annuitants are selecting their providers based on the best quotes.

The assessment of Chile's product regulation is, therefore, largely positive. However, there may be some further steps that can be taken in the future. Some additional annuity designs could be considered, which could improve further consumer welfare, the management of risk by providers, and the control of fiscal expenditures with the MPG. At the same time, there should be a greater effort to provide more information and education on the differences between fixed annuities, variable annuities, and PW options, in order to allow well-informed decisions. Some of the riskier options may not be appropriate for all consumers. The need for more information and education will increase if additional designs are introduced in the future. The new quotation system is a positive step and should increase market transparency, but it will create some challenges as well. This will require a number of specific actions, as discussed below.

First, the additional annuity designs that could be considered by regulatory authorities would include adjustable and escalating annuities. Adjustable annuities are annuities whose rates are adjusted periodically (e.g., every 3, 5, or 10 years), in line with the evolution of market interest rates and annuity rates.[16] Individuals would be able to enjoy a higher initial payout, since the provider would not be exposed to reinvestment risk. The downside for the annuitant is the risk of a decline in future annuity rates and the resulting decline in payouts. Some annuitants may prefer this option, however, since their planned consumption may be considerably stronger in the early stages of retirement.

Escalating indexed annuities would involve a predefined yearly rate of increase in real payments (e.g., 1–3 percent). This option may prove attractive to early retirees, especially those who continue working after formal retirement, do not need the pension income in the first years of retirement, and value the increase in real payments in the future, when they will be effectively retired. This design would also result in more back-loaded payments, reducing the potential number of retirees eligible to receive the MPG.

Second, the residual bias produced by the current PW formula could be removed by adopting a more forward-looking technical rate. A higher assumed return performance for PWs relative to annuities should incorporate prospective market information, not higher historic returns that would not be expected to continue. The fact that PW holders can choose between three portfolios with different expected returns creates some challenges, as the expected return would be fund-specific. One simple option would involve using simply the average yield to maturity of fixed income securities in Fund E.

Third, although the new quotation system is expected to improve transparency, retiring workers may still make decisions about PWs, fixed annuities, and variable annuities based primarily on a comparison of initial payouts, not taking into consideration future paths. The quotation system provides projections of future PW paths, but it would be difficult to project the path of variable annuities, especially when the underlying portfolio contains variable income instruments. The fact that variable annuities need to be combined with fixed indexed annuities reduces the overall exposure of consumers to investment risk, but this new instrument may still not be appropriate for all consumers, and its characteristics need to be well explained.

Fourth, the new quotation system addresses well-identified problems, but the transition to the new system will present challenges for companies, with the heightened emphasis on price in an already price competitive market. The ongoing realignment and consolidation of the market may pressure providers who are less well equipped to handle the transition and will need careful monitoring by the authorities in the interests of the policyholders and members.

Fifth, the impact of the increasing concentration of the industry on annuity pricing and the quality of services will need to be closely monitored. A certain reduction in MWRs is to be expected, given that the ratios observed in recent years are probably not sustainable. However, it is important to avoid a repetition of the experience with the pension fund sector, which is characterized by excessive concentration and high fees. It would be desirable to see MWRs decline to levels closer to one, but not to lower levels, as that could indicate the emergence of an oligopolistic market structure in the payout phase as well. The annuities market is probably more contestable than the pension fund market, as life insurance companies, which are leaving the annuities market but not other areas of the life business, could return to the market if profit margins increased significantly. While this provides room for optimism, it would still be essential to build regularly measures of market performance, including MWRs and intermediation spreads, to assess whether the market will continue to generate good outcomes for the annuitants.

Sixth, the design of the MPG is generally sound, for penalizing early retirement, and the introduction of the stricter conditions for early retirement will tend to reduce future demands on the MPG. The introduction of updated parameters for the PW will also reduce further future demands on the MPG. Projections based on a highly stylized model prepared by the Ministry of Finance before the adoption of the new Pensions Law indicate that future expenditures with the MPG would remain moderate—about 0.8 percent of GDP in 10 years, and the new Law will presumably reduce future expenditures. However, the Government should make an effort to build an actuarial model capable of producing more robust estimates for the expenditures with the MPG, and able to provide more accurate inputs for future policy formulation.[17]

Notes

1. The "density of contributions" measures the extent to which contributions are actually made during the contributory period. Density declines when there is an interruption of contributions due to unemployment, withdrawals from the labor force, or collection problems. See Ministry of Labor (2004).
2. Higher voluntary contributions above the mandatory levels can offset to some extent this effect. While it has always been possible to make additional contributions within the AFP system, the recently introduced APV (third pillar voluntary product) with more flexible rules is expected to result in higher contributions and pension savings, and therefore, earlier qualification for a benefit.
3. Australia provides an interesting contrast in system design. The Australian first pillar benefit also amounts to about 25 percent of the average wage but is provided as a horizontal rather than vertical support—i.e., not back-ended. In contrast to Chile, a large share of the retired population receives this benefit, and the related expenditures are much larger, amounting to about 3 percent of GDP. This allows much more liberal rules for lump sums. In addition, restrictions on lump sums would not have been politically acceptable in Australia, due to the original "lump sum mentality."
4. Dus, Maurer, and Mitchell (2003) propose a taxonomy that includes four classes of PWs: fixed benefit, fixed fraction, 1/T rule, and 1/E(T) rule, or life expectancy PWs. The Chilean PW belongs to the fourth class.
5. Lower PW payments in early years of retirement will mean that early retirees seeking to meet the qualification criteria may have to defer retirement slightly.
6. In the recent case of the failure of Le Mans, the ongoing liquidation of the company has yet to lead to a reduction in annuity payments, as the law permits continuing contractual payments while assets are available. In the event of an asset shortfall, and this is to be expected in the future, it is estimated that the effective payout to annuitants would be of the order of 92–95 percent of their full annuity.
7. Brown, Mitchel, and Poterba (2001); Doyle and Piggott (1998 and 1999); Bateman, Doyle, and Piggott (1999).
8. For example, life expectancy at age 60 is 75, while life expectancy at age 61 is 75.5.
9. This rate is the average *tasa de venta* in 2003, based on the RV-85 table.
10. It is assumed that the new mortality table leads to a recalculation of the historic reported annuity rates and therefore the technical rate. If the past annuity rates are not recalculated the impact of the new mortality table will be somewhat weaker.

11. This outcome reflects the *mortality drag*. As mentioned before, annuitants benefit from a cross-subsidy, or the sharing of the mortality profit, but PW holders do not. The effect of not having this subsidy is called the "mortality drag." Moreover, the impact of the mortality drag increases with age.
12. This section of the report benefited from the earlier analysis in James, Martinez, and Iglesias (2006) and from extensive discussions with the authors.
13. The formula that discounts the MPG is very complex, depending on the year of retirement, the benefit, gender, interest rate, and family situation, resulting practically in an individualized MPG.
14. Banks, while permitted to have affiliated insurance agents or broking firms, were previously prohibited from having such brokers participate in the annuities market.
15. Examples of service standards include the ability of the company to make payments accurately and in a timely manner, to maintain effective administration systems, and to provide information to customers in a form that is easy to access and understand.
16. Blake and Hudson (2001) propose adjustable annuities where the annuity rate is corrected every three years.
17. An example can be found in the Retirement Income Modeling (RIM) Task Force, part of the Department of the Treasury in Australia. Since the RIM model was established, other researchers have also developed models, generating a healthy policy debate. The elaboration and dissemination of an actuarial model by the Chilean Ministry of Finance and the SAFP could replicate this positive experience.

CHAPTER 6

The Regulation of Market Participants

Background

There are two providers of retirement products in Chile, the AFPs providing the PWs and the initial part of TWs, and the life insurance companies who provide immediate annuities and the deferred annuity part of the TW option. The AFPs were created as single-purpose institutions, and were expected to focus entirely on social security activities, including the management of mandatory individual accounts, PWs, TWs, and several tasks related to the administration of social security (such as the management of the MPG). In recent years, the AFPs have also become involved in the administration of unemployment insurance, but pensions still account for most of their business. Life insurance companies can have other lines of activity such as other life insurance and savings policies, and some of them have a relatively diversified portfolio of life products. However, annuities still account for most of the sector's business.

The provision of retirement incomes is regulated primarily by the Pension Law (Decree Law 3,500), but life insurance companies are also subject to the requirements of the Insurance Law. Both AFPs and insurance companies must also comply with the wider Company Law, except in the areas where there is a conflict with the more specific Pension and Insurance Laws. Each entity is subject to regulations on licensing, corporate governance, accounting and auditing, disclosure and financial reporting, investments, capital, and reserves. The AFPs are supervised by the *Superintendencia de Administradoras de Fondos de Pensiones* (SAFP), while the life insurance companies are supervised by the *Superintendencia de Valores y Seguros* (SVS). The SAFP is totally dedicated to the oversight of the AFPs, whereas the SVS also oversees the securities markets and both life and non–life insurance companies.[1]

This chapter examines the regulation of market intermediaries, with particular focus on the investment and capital regulations of life insurance companies. This focus is justified for three reasons. First, there is a much more extensive literature on AFPs than on life insurance companies in Chile. Second, the regulatory framework for the insurance sector in Chile is generally in line with international norms. Third, regulations on investments, capital, and technical reserves are the most critical ones for annuity providers, and a closer examination of these areas enables the identification of important lessons for other countries.

The chapter is structured as follows. The next section examines the investment regulation of AFPs and life insurance companies, with focus on the latter. The third section examines the capital regulation of AFPs and life insurance companies, with focus on the latter as well. The fourth section examines in more detail whether capital regulation has delivered its objectives. The fifth section analyzes the annuity guarantee and the resolution mechanisms in the insurance sector. Finally the last section summarizes the main findings and provides some policy recommendations.

Investment Regulation of AFPs and Life Insurance Companies

The Investment Regulation of AFPs

The investment regime for AFPs was initially very restrictive, forbidding holdings of equity and foreign assets. The investment regime was changed on several occasions over the past 20 years, allowing AFPs to increase the depth and breadth of their investments across different asset classes. In 2002 a multiple portfolio regime was introduced, allowing workers to choose among five different funds, A, B, C, D, and E.

These funds can be offered by each AFP, and are defined mainly according to the maximum share of variable income instruments that they can have, which are 80, 60, 40, 20, and 0 percent, respectively. PW holders can choose among the three less risky portfolios. Assets of AFPs are marked to market daily, based on a vector of prices which is provided by the SAFP.

As mentioned in Chapter 4, although the investment regime for AFPs has been progressively liberalized, it has not diminished in complexity, involving an intricate web of regulations imposed on instruments, classes of instruments, individual issuers, and related issuers. There are also joint limits on different combinations of variable and fixed income instruments, and sublimits depending on risk, liquidity, particular instrument characteristics, and the age of the company. As shown in the statistical annex, the investment regime for AFPs is much more complex than the regimes for pension funds in the OECD, including countries that also adopt quantitative restrictions. Moreover, the detailed investment regime is mostly defined in the Pension Law itself, and not through secondary regulation, leaving very little margin for its adaptation to changing market conditions.

A regime of quantitative restrictions on pension fund investments can be justified in the Chilean case, as the private pension system is the core of the country's social security. However, it is unlikely that the complex web of regulations deals with portfolio risk effectively. It would seem possible to simplify the regime and relax some limits, allowing more room for asset managers to operate without any meaningful increase in risk. Moreover, the investment regime also contains designs that prevent managers and participants from pursuing optimal low risk strategies. As illustrated in Chapter 4, the value at risk (VAR) estimated for Fund E (a fund chosen by several holders) has been similar to those estimated for Fund D, while the latter fund has generated higher returns. This concrete example suggests that there is room for improving the outcomes for PW holders through selective reforms to the investment regime.

The Investment Regulation of Insurance Companies

There are two regulations that influence the investments of a life insurance company offering annuities—the investment regulation itself and capital regulations. Insurance company investments are subject to detailed direct rules and supervisory oversight. However, in the case of annuity providers, capital regulations have had a more powerful influence on the portfolio composition than the investment rules themselves, as explained in this section and the next.

Investment rules are defined according to the product mix on the liability side, but without imposing a formal segregation of assets on the balance sheet. Investment rules include limits on instruments and issuers, in a similar fashion to the regulation of AFPs, but with a lower level of complexity (see Annex 3). In the case of insurance companies, the limits on instruments are expressed as a percentage of the technical reserves and solvency margins. The most restrictive rules are those that limit holdings of fixed income instruments issued by unrated companies or companies rated below investment grade to 5 percent of the technical reserve plus solvency margin. Other limits such as those on foreign assets, mutual funds, or real estate, do not impose material constraints for annuity providers, given their focus on fixed income instruments. The limits on issuers are defined as fractions of total securities issued or the total deposits in the case of a bank, but without the additional and multiple restrictions that apply to AFPs. A small number of additional limits regulate counterparty exposure and related party investments.

Valuation rules are also different from those applying to AFPs. Assets are separated between those that are essentially considered to be buy and hold and those that are traded. The first group of assets is held at book value while the second group is marked to market. The consequence of this philosophy is that life insurance companies report primarily book values while non-life companies generally report market values. There is no particular requirement, however, that designated assets valued at book are not to be traded. In fact, life insurance companies can sell and buy the same asset when they want to have an increase to market values reflected in their balance sheets.

As mentioned above, annuity providers are more constrained by capital regulations, particularly one regulation called the CALCE rule[2] that is designed to address mismatch risk. As part of that rule (examined in greater detail in the next section), assets that count for the computation of provisions are generally restricted to fixed income instruments of investment grade denominated in UFs. Instruments like mortgages and other securitized fixed income investments with prepayment risk are allowed with restrictions. Under the CALCE rule, other investments fail to count for the CALCE provisions and, therefore, require a capital increase. This provides a strong incentive for investing in high-grade fixed income assets denominated in UFs.

Capital Regulations of AFPs and Life Insurance Companies

While the investment rules of AFPs are much more complex than those of life insurance companies, their capital rules are much simpler. This relative simplicity reflects the defined contribution nature of pension funds, and the fact that most of the investment risk is borne by AFP members, both active contributors and PW holders. By contrast, life insurance companies offering fixed annuities bear entirely the investment risk. The new products introduced by the new Pension Law, such as variable annuities, will result in some risk sharing between providers and policyholders, but life insurance companies will still bear most of the investment risk on the more traditional style products and, therefore, will remain subject to more stringent capital regulations than AFPs.

Capital Regulations of AFPs

In the case of AFPs, the first feature to note is the asset segregation rule, i.e., the separation of the assets of the pension fund from the assets of the AFP. AFPs are constituted as joint stock companies with the sole purpose of managing a pension fund, and their capital is not affected by changes in the value of the pension fund assets, unless they are caused by theft and fraud or by very weak returns relative to the market, as explained below.

AFPs entering the market are subject to a minimum capital requirement of UF5,000, or about US$130,000. Minimum capital requirements increase with the size of membership, but the maximum level is only UF20,000, or about US$500,000, for a membership exceeding 10,000. Therefore, minimum capital requirements are modest and hardly a deterrent to entry. A more stringent regulation is the minimum obligatory reserve (*encaje*) of 1 percent of the assets of the pension fund, which is designed to back the minimum relative return guarantee. Any company contemplating entry into the Chilean pension sector and targeting an initial market share of 1 percent of assets would need to build approximately US$500 million in reserves from its own resources.[3]

The minimum relative return guarantee specifies that the average rate of return of any fund over the past 36 months cannot be lower than a percentage of the industry's average over the same period. Such a percentage varies by type of fund, with greater differences being allowed for the riskier Funds A and B. The obligatory reserve has to be invested in units of the pension fund. This guarantee has never been called, as pension funds tend to herd and hold similar portfolios.

Capital Regulations of Life Insurance Companies

The capital regulations of life insurance companies can be more easily understood making reference to the consolidated balance sheet of the life insurance sector. As shown in Figure 6.1, total assets and liabilities of the life insurance sector amounted to approximately UF695 million in September 2005, or roughly 20 percent of GDP. Technical reserves on annuities (reflecting the expected present value of future annuity payments) amounted to UF523 million, the equivalent of almost 90 percent of total technical reserves. This high share reflects the predominance of annuities in the life insurance business in Chile.

The total net worth of life insurance companies amounted to UF82 millions in September 2005, the bulk of which consisted of shareholders' capital and retained earnings (UF62.7 millions) and the CALCE reserves (UF16.7 millions). These are special reserves that reflect the duration mismatch of life insurance companies (and the resulting reinvestment risk) as explained further below. The average leverage or "gearing ratio" (defined as technical reserves over capital and retained earnings) amounted to 7.2. Portfolio investments amounted to 95 percent of total assets, the bulk of which consisting of financial investments. Moreover, fixed income assets accounted for the bulk of financial investments, as discussed in previous chapters.

Figure 6.1. Consolidated Balance Sheet of Life Insurance Companies (UF millions), Sept. 2005

ASSETS		*LIABILITIES*	
1. Investments	663.2	**1. Technical Reserves (TR)**	588.2
Financial	592.7	TR on Social Security Products	539.3
Real Estate	51.2	**Annuities**	**522.5**
Dedicated Account (CUI)	19.3	Disability	16.8
		TR on Other Life Products	46.9
2. Amounts due from Policyholders	4.7	Other Technical Reserves	2.0
3. Amounts due from Reinsurers	0.9	**2. Other Liabilities**	24.8
4. Other Assets	26.4	**3. Net Worth**	82.2
		Legal Reserves	2.6
		Regulatory Reserves	16.9
		CALCE Reserves	**16.7**
		Other Reserves	0.2
		Shareholders' Capital	43.7
		Retained Earnings	19.0
Total	**695.2**	**Total**	**695.2**

Source: SVS.

For life insurance companies, the minimum initial capital is specified at UF 90,000, or the equivalent of US$2.4 million, which is considerably higher than the minimum capital required from an AFP. Until recently, life insurance companies were also subject to a maximum gearing ratio of 15, which defines the minimum build-up of additional capital required to support the growth of their annuity and other life business. This gearing ratio is equivalent to a solvency margin of 1/15, or 6.67%.[4] The gearing ratio was modified in 2005 in the context of other changes in capital rules that included the adoption of an updated mortality table and an asset sufficiency test, as explained further below.

The SVS imposes liability valuation rules for the establishment of technical reserves after the product is sold. This approach is consistent with international standards,[5] leading to comparable technical reserves between companies and providing a base for the other elements of the capital regime. In addition to the gearing ratio, another critical element of the capital regime is the CALCE rule, which addresses asset-liability mismatch risks. The rule was introduced in 1990 and represents one of the earliest attempts around the world to quantify and elaborate a capital charge for asset-liability mismatch risks.

To understand the CALCE rule it is necessary to understand how critical elements are valued starting with the valuation of annuities. The fundamental equation of value for an annuity is the expected present value of the respective cash flows under the contract. The annuity cash flows themselves are subject to probabilities that they will be paid, which will depend on the terms of the contract and on the survivorship of the annuitant and their dependents. The future cash flows at time t can be considered algebraically (in the joint annuity case) as follows:

$$FP_t = P_t \; p_x + (1 - {}_tp_x) \sum_n {}^nP_t \; {}_t^np_y \tag{6.1}$$

Where:

FP_t is the future pension payment at time t adjusted for the assumed probability that it will be payable;

P_t is the level of the pension payable to the annuitant, assuming that they are alive at time t;

${}_tp_x$ is the assumed probability that the annuitant, aged x at the commencement of the annuity contract, is alive at time t;

${}^nP_t$ is the level of pension payable to beneficiary n at time t in the event that the annuitant is not alive at that time; and

${}^{n}_{t}p_y$ is the probability that the beneficiary n who was aged y at the time the commencement of the annuity contract, is alive at time t.

The probabilities in equation (6.1) are regulated by the SVS for the purposes of computing the technical reserves and the CALCE reserves. In the case of annuities offered with a guaranteed term and life thereafter, some of these probabilities will be taken to be 1, where t is less than the guaranteed term. Until 2005 the CALCE rule employed the RV-85 mortality tables, which differentiated between those that apply to retirement annuities, survivorship beneficiaries, and disability beneficiaries and, in each case, between rates for males and females. This differentiation is based on the classification at the point the annuity is issued. The RV-85 tables were developed by the SVS in the 1980s, when the rule was originally developed. In 2005 a new table was introduced, the RV-04. This table maintains the distinctions between types of annuitants and has separate mortality rates for males and females. It has the advantage of having been developed with reference to the actual experience of Chilean annuitants since the system commenced. The new table applies fully to all new annuities issued from March 2005 and to the whole stock of annuities from September 2005, with a transition period over five years being allowed.[6]

A simplified equation of values for the annuity payment stream can be established and this formula is used to establish key parameters for the system.

$$Premium = \sum_{t=0}^{T} \frac{FP_t}{(1+i_v)^t} \tag{6.2}$$

where i_v is the rate of interest that equates the annuity payments with the premium on the basis of the regulated mortality table, i.e., the reported annuity rate, or still the *tasa de venta*.

Before proceeding to the actual reserve calculations, it is also necessary to consider one special feature of the CALCE rule. Eligible asset and liability cash flows are identified in a series of term "brackets" for the whole book of business. The 10 brackets are defined as shown in the first two columns of Table 6.1. Within each bracket, asset cash flows are added together to determine a value A_k taking account of eligible assets only and deducting non–policy-related financial liabilities. Liability cash flows are also added together within each bracket after deducting any recoveries from reinsurance policies to determine B_k. Within each bracket a factor,

Table 6.1. CP_k Factors Used in the CALCE Rule

Bracket number "k"	*Flows during periods (years)*	*Average CP_k value*
1	1 and 2	0.995
2	3 and 4	1.000
3	5 and 6	0.996
4	7 and 8	1.000
5	9 and 10	1.000
6	11, 12, and 13	1.000
7	14, 15, and 16	0.992
8	17, 18, 19, 20, and 21	0.883
9	22, 23, 24, 25, 26, 27, and 28	0.396
10	29 and over	0.203

CP_k is determined according to equation (6.3). This formula has the effect of generating a value bounded between 0 and 1. These values are determined by each company and reported to the SVS monthly. It can be seen that, where a company has asset cash flows in excess of the liability flows in a given "bracket," this has no effect on the value of CP_k and the consequent determination of further values. However, asset cash flows that are not able to cover net liability cash flows (i.e., mismatches) result in CP_k values lower than one. It is clear from Table 6.2 (see p. 127) that the mismatch problem is concentrated in the two last brackets.

$$CP_k = Min\left[\frac{Max(0, A_k)}{B_k}, 1\right] \tag{6.3}$$

Having determined the matching position as measured by the vector of CP_k factors, it is useful to explain the Basic Financial Reserve (BFR). Its value appears on the balance sheet as technical reserves, and is determined using equation (6.4). The SVS computes i_m, the market interest rate, defined by the average interest rate of Government and Central Bank bonds with maturities of eight years and longer. The effect of the formula is that, when the CP_k factor is equal to one in a given "bracket," the corresponding projected cash flows are discounted at the market rate i_m, whereas when the value of CP_k falls below one, the discounting at the 3 percent technical rate gets a greater weight. Therefore, the worse the matching position, the higher the *BFR*. During the life of the annuity contract values of CP_k will vary, as well as the mortality experience of annuitants. If matching deteriorates for any given i_m, the *BFR* will increase. Moreover, the impact of any measured mismatch on *BFR* is stronger the higher the difference between i_m and the technical interest rate of 3 percent.

$$BFR = \sum_{t=0}^{T} \frac{FP_t(CP_{k,t})}{(1+i_m)^t} + \sum_{t=0}^{T} \frac{FP_t(1-CP_{k,t})}{(1.03)^t} \tag{6.4}$$

The *Basic Technical Reserve (BTR)* is also defined in the CALCE rule and has the effect of separating the effects of the normal maturation of the annuities from the market and matching parameters. This reserve does not appear on the balance sheet, and is determined based on parameters established for each annuity contract *at the time of issue* as follows. The *BFR at the time of issue* can be determined using the matching position of the company and the market rate prevailing at the time. It is then possible, in the case of each annuity at its issue date, to determine the rate of discount that would equate this reserve to the present value of the future payments, as shown in equation 6.5. This rate, i_c, is recorded for each annuity issued and is unique to that contract. In addition, if the rate determined by equation 6.5. is greater than the *tasa de venta*, then that rate is substituted to ensure that the initial *BFR* is not lower than the actual premium at the point of issue, i.e, the company would not book an immediate profit but, rather, such a profit would emerge over the life of the contract. In the normal course, given the market conditions and practices, the *BFR* at inception will exceed the premium and i_c determined under equation (6.5) will be less than the *tasa de venta*.

$$BFR_0 = \sum_{t=0}^{T} \frac{FP_t}{(1+i_c)^t} \tag{6.5}$$

For valuations of the annuity stock, the *BTR* is determined using equation (6.6) calculated for each contract using that contract's unique value of i_c. The balance sheet items are then defined in full. The *BFR* is shown as the technical reserve for the annuities and the CALCE reserve is recorded as the *BTR* minus the *BFR*.

$$BTR = \sum_{t=0}^{T} \frac{FP_t}{(1+i_c)^t} \tag{6.6}$$

As each contract issued has a specific value for i_c, *BTR* will be relatively stable over time relative to *BFR*, which will reflect the changes in the matching position, as measured by changes in the CP_k parameters. A deterioration of the mismatch position will increase *BFR* and reduce the

CALCE reserve on the balance sheet. These movements will imply a deterioration of the company's net worth and an increase in the gearing ratio (or a decrease in the solvency margin). If the gearing ratio was already high, the company could be forced to put fresh capital or abstain from distributing profits from retained earnings. Likewise, an improvement in the matching position will be reflected in lower technical reserves and larger CALCE reserves, implying an increase in net worth and in the solvency margin.

Note that neither the basic technical reserve nor the basic financial reserve is affected by changes in market rates. The market rates used for their computation are those prevailing at the time the contracts were issued. The major difference lies in the fact that the basic financial reserve is affected by changes in the CP_k while the basic technical reserve is not. Technical reserves do not need to reflect movements in market rates because companies do not have to mark their assets to market.[7]

As noted above, the CALCE rule has a constraint on asset mixes that is most relevant to annuity companies in Chile. Excess assets in "brackets" where the matching factor is already subject to the maximum value will not change the CALCE outcome. Similarly, assets that do not meet the eligibility criteria are of little use to the company. However, the absence of assets of very long maturities and durations to match the tail end of annuity payments (which can extend for 30 years or longer), leads to much lower values in the very last "brackets" (Table 6.1). As mentioned before, companies tend to have sufficient or excess assets to meet the liability cash flows in the "brackets" up to number 7 and then have difficulty with the longer-term brackets, where asset flows tend to be lower than liability flows. Several companies have zero values in the last bracket. Not all assets are considered in the determination of A_k. To be eligible for inclusion, an asset needs to meet certain conditions, namely: (1) it must be denominated in UF or be adjusted by the variation in the CPI[8]; (2) it must offer a fixed interest rate; (3) it must not be prepayable to be fully considered. Prepayable securities such as mortgage bonds and callable corporate bonds are accepted only for the first eight "brackets," which makes them less attractive for consideration under the CALCE rule.

Equally, the allowance for reinsurance is limited by specifying the extent to which the values for the liability cash flows can be reduced through reinsurance. Permissible reinsurance has, hitherto, effectively been restricted to locally licensed insurers through the effects of asset localization rules[9]. This reflects a concern that annuities are part of the social security system and also avoids arbitrage. Reinsurance is limited in use in any event. A relaxation of the localization requirement would, according to industry practitioners, lead to a greater use of reinsurance, and the SVS has been preparing changes in reinsurance regulation.

In summary, the *Base Technical Reserve* represents the liability to the annuitants reflecting all the conditions at the time of writing each contract by establishing parameters at the point of issue, and then applying them through the life of the contract. The *BTR* is conservatively calculated, largely through the use of an average discount rate that is lower than the market rate, imposing a capital charge (loss) at the time the contract is issued that is returned through a profit over the life of the contracts. The *Base Financial Reserve* appears on the balance sheet and reflects variations in the mismatch position of the contracts. The CALCE reserves in the balance sheet are calculated as the difference between the *BTR* and the *BFR*. Equations (6.1) through (6.6) show that the CALCE rule penalizes companies that are exposed to larger mismatches of assets and liabilities. A deterioration of the mismatch position at any point in time leads to larger technical reserves, smaller CALCE reserves, and a reduction in the solvency margin (an increase in the gearing ratio).

Evaluation of Capital Rules for Annuity Providers

Is the Approach Reasonable?

For life insurance companies, the rule-based investment regime is less detailed and restrictive than for AFPs. Combined, however, with the asset restrictions in the CALCE rule, they operate to limit the risks associated with the investments, limit credit risk, limit and make provision for residual market risk in a way that was particularly innovative at the time it was introduced, address prepayment risk, and ensure currency matching with liabilities.

This comprehensive approach to capital regulation was well conceived and contributed to the sound development of the industry in its early stages, but may have also produced some adverse consequences over time. In the event that a company and its management focus excessively on the operation of the rules and simply optimize performance against them, it may not pay due attention to the underlying economic risks. Two concrete examples may illustrate how the rule may hinder more effective asset-liability management by providers.

First, an insurance company may be motivated to exchange assets in CALCE-defined "brackets" where it has excess, for assets in "brackets" where it does not have an excess, or will seek to reduce the liability in those "brackets." Companies report that they actively seek these opportunities in an effort to influence the effect of the CALCE rule through the CP factors. Under the current rule-based system, the company's result may be improved in an accounting sense by selling a higher yielding asset to purchase a lower yielding one of a longer duration. Such decisions may have merit, but would require both an economic and an accounting assessment. The economic assessment would consider the actual reduction in mismatch risk compared to the capital reduction that results from a portfolio with lower returns.[10]

Second, the CALCE rule has also led to an unusual form of reinsurance where some companies have reinsured out to other insurers the liabilities in the last CALCE "brackets." While this form of reinsurance is not common, interest in it is a direct consequence of the rule. In part, the limited number of contracts seen to date is explained by the localization effects of the rules to allow outward reinsurance to be taken as a credit for the company taking the reinsurance, and because the receiving company would have an increase in their *L* values in that "bracket."

More generally, the rule has hindered the development of an economic analysis of mismatch risk within companies. The opportunity exists to reform the rule and move toward a more risk-based approach. The need to reform the rule exists in any event, as a result of the changes in underlying risks and the introduction of new products such as variable annuities. For example, prepayment risk concerns have arisen due to the recent decline in interest rates on instruments where they were, previously, thought to be less material. New products will transfer some of the investment risk to the annuitant, reducing exposure to mismatch risk and increasing the scope for lower credit rating investment. New products will also permit liabilities in other currencies, raising the need to handle currency risk more explicitly.

It will, however, take time and require considerable effort to move to a risk-based approach to asset-liability matching in the Chilean life insurance market, both from the side of market participants and the supervisor. The implementation of a risk-based system will take several interactions with the industry, in line with the approach being taken by the SVS toward industry consultation with respect to other reform initiatives. The implementation of a risk-based system that encourages economically driven investments in an asset-liability management context will also require further securities market development, including the development of risk management instruments such as currency and interest rate swaps and options.

Have Capital Rules Provided Effective Protection?

As noted before, the actual calculation of technical reserves and CALCE reserves involves the utilization of key regulated parameters, including a mortality table and a discount rate. The values for the probabilities of survivorship were until recently based on the RV-85 tables, which became progressively out of date, as explained in more detail in Annex 1. In the absence of other offsetting factors, the use of an outdated mortality table would imply a progressive mismeasurement of the true liabilities, i.e., understated technical reserves.

At the same time, the technical reserves have been computed on a technical discount rate of 3 percent per annum, well below the historic level of market interest rates, which tends to overstate technical reserves. During the 1990s the low discount rate possibly outweighed the impact of the generous mortality table, resulting ultimately in conservative provisions.

Since the late 1990s interest rates have fallen, however, and in more recent years the decline has been more pronounced, including the rates at longer durations. Discussions with actuaries suggest that the discount rate used in the rule is not conservative any longer. Therefore, the predominant effect of a low discount rate may have been dissipated in recent years, raising the question of whether the level of reserves remained adequate. Addressing this question requires computing the required level of reserves under the rule with three adjustments, namely: (i) an updated mortality table; (ii) market interest rates; and (iii) market valuation of assets.

As discussed in more detail in Annex 1, the most up-to-date mortality table for annuitants in Chile is the recently completed RV-04. The table has been published and exists in two forms, first a table that is representative of the actual data and experience, and another table that is made more conservative by including adjustments based on the standard deviation of mortality rates. The first and more representative table was used in this analysis to avoid the deliberate bias introduced by the conservative margin. For discount rates we used the risk-free yield curve in March 2004.

As shown in Tables 6.2 and 6.3, updating the table and making an allowance for future mortality improvements leads to a significant increase in the base liability, showing that the CALCE rule understated the true liability for given discount rates. Columns (2) and (3) show that this increment can be separated in two components of similar magnitude, the first resulting from the updating of the table and the second from allowing for future improvements in mortality. The increase varies by age, implying that the impact of these changes varies across companies

Table 6.2. Liability Impact of Updating Mortality and Discount Rates—Male Annuitants

Mortality table	*RV-85*	*RV-04*	*RV-04*	*RV-04*	*Change in liability*
Improvement	*No*	*No*	*Yes, population*	*Yes, population*	
Discount rate	*3%*	*3%*	*3%*	*2004 risk-free yield curve*	
Age of annuitant	*(1)*	*(2)*	*(3)*	*(4)*	*(5) = (4)/(1) * 100*
50	18.319	19.586	20.769	18.148	99.1
55	16.460	17.782	18.869	16.789	102.0
60	14.515	15.822	16.783	15.224	104.9
65	12.526	13.764	14.577	13.492	107.7
70	10.543	11.641	12.292	11.617	110.2
75	8.629	9.529	10.019	9.664	112.0

Source: Staff analysis.

Table 6.3. Liability Impact of Updating Mortality and Discount Rates—Female Annuitants

Mortality table	*RV-85*	*RV-04*	*RV-04*	*RV-04*	*Change in liability*
Improvement	*No*	*No*	*Yes, population*	*Yes, population*	
Discount rate	*3%*	*3%*	*3%*	*2004 risk-free yield curve*	
Age of annuitant	*(1)*	*(2)*	*(3)*	*(4)*	*(5) = (4)/(1) * 100*
50	20.370	22.393	23.420	20.011	98.2
55	18.572	20.776	21.767	18.915	101.8
60	16.629	18.982	19.913	17.624	106.0
65	14.568	16.988	17.835	16.102	110.5
70	12.428	14.768	15.505	14.302	115.1
75	10.273	12.351	12.959	12.224	119.0

Source: Staff analysis.

depending on their clientele and product mix. Column (4) shows the effect of discounting liabilities according to the risk-free rate profile as of March 2004. The final column (5) shows the overall effect of the changes and the variation depending on the age of the annuitant and based on the assumptions stated.

These calculations suggest that a valuation of reserves with updated parameters would lead to an increase in the overall level of reserves of about 7.5 percent. Not all annuity providers would be able to absorb such a change in the accounting value of provisions and the resulting change in the accounting value of equity without a change in the value of the

Figure 6.2. Annuity Company Capacity to Absorb Provisioning Increases

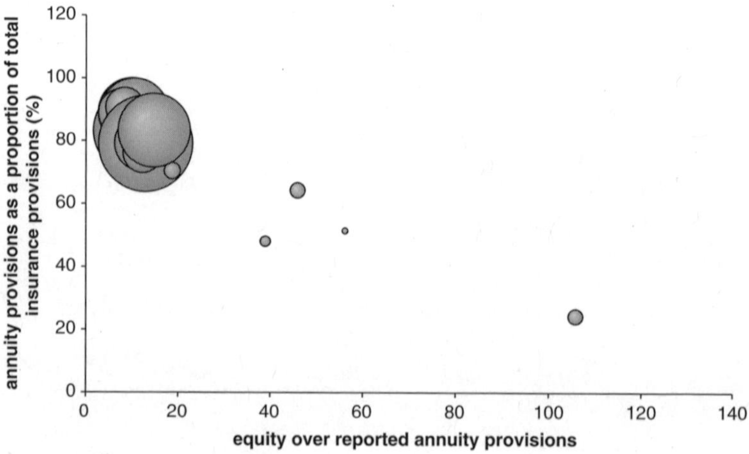

Source: Staff analysis.

assets—it must be remembered that these values represent book values so they do not take into account the margin between the book value and the market value.

Figure 6.2 shows the capital in excess of provisions available as a percentage of the company annuity provision on the x-axis and represents the extent to which annuity provisions could be increased before all available reported equity would be absorbed. The y-axis shows the relative importance of annuities in the balance sheet of the company. The size of each circle reflects the company share of the annuity provisions of the whole sector. Not surprisingly, the larger companies are most affected by this effect but it is notable that these companies also tend to be predominantly annuity companies rather than more diversified in their product mix.

Figure 6.3 focuses on this quadrant and includes an additional vertical line at the level of the 7.5 percent absorption of capital/increase in provision. Increasing the provision reduces the equity reported by an equivalent amount, all other things constant. The result, moving the origin to the dotted line shown, would still entail assets in excess of total liabilities for all companies. At the same time, the increase would increase the reported leverage ratio in the absence of a change in the value of the assets to reflect market value rather than the historic book values.

Figure 6.3. Annuity Company Capacity to Absorb Increases (Detail)

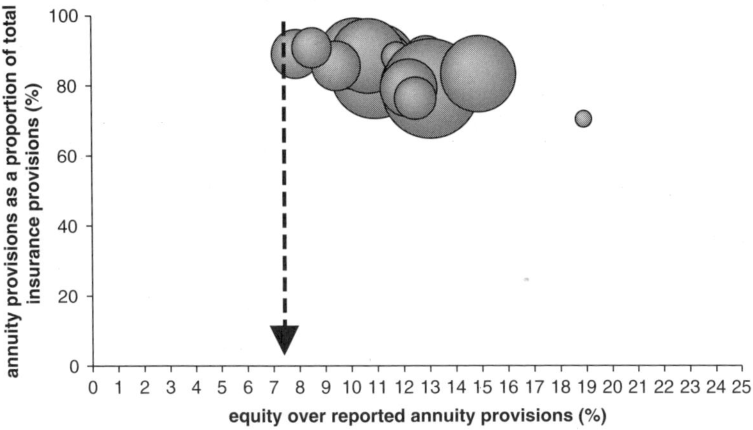

Source: Staff analysis.
Note: To increase provisions by 7.5%, reported equity would reduce accordingly, but all companies would continue to be solvent.

We do not have sufficient information to estimate numerically the impact of marked-to-market valuation of assets. Discussions with the industry suggest that this last adjustment would bring leverage ratios closer to their current reported level. Therefore, the net and final impact of the three adjustments would probably entail some increase in technical reserves and leverage ratios, but not a large amount. However, there could be significant differences across companies.

Relating this result with the analysis of previous chapters, it is apparent that the economic reserves accumulated during the 1990s provided a buffer sufficiently strong to absorb the losses that at least some companies experienced with the annuities issued in the past three years. The analysis also suggests that the excess buffer that was built in the 1990s has probably been partly eroded, and that a continuation of aggressive annuity pricing could lead some companies to experience a sharper erosion of capital.

Regulatory Response by the SVS

In 2005 the SVS responded by strengthening capital rules. The changes that have been introduced include the adoption of a much improved mortality table, the RV-04, and the adoption of a new rule—the asset sufficiency test. The new mortality table has been applied fully to all new annuities issued after March 2005 and over a period of five years to the stock of previously issued annuities, with this adjustment starting in September 2005. This adjustment should lead to a significant increase in the stock of technical reserves. Under certain conditions the period of adjustment could be extended to 10 years.

The new asset sufficiency test involves the explicit estimation of the projected flows of assets and liabilities, incorporating relevant credit and prepayment risks, and the computation of the reinvestment rate that would equalize the flows of assets (with shorter duration) with the flows of liabilities. This reinvestment rate would be disclosed in a footnote to the financial statements, providing more solid information for the assessment of the financial situation of the company by private analysts. This test is seen as an important complement to the new rules on technical reserves and an important step towards the adoption of a risk-based approach to supervision.

At the same time, the SVS has also increased the maximum leverage ratio from 15 to 20, or the equivalent of a solvency margin of 5 percent. This solvency margin is slightly lower than the one observed in the EU and other jurisdictions, but the SVS considers that the adoption of an aggressive mortality table, the maintenance of a technical rate of 3 percent p.a. and the new asset sufficiency test should lead to a substantial strengthening of the amount of capital backing the stock of annuities.

The Annuity Guarantee and Resolution Mechanisms

As mentioned in several parts of this report, the Government provides an additional guarantee to all annuitants, over and above the MPG, to protect them in the event of the failure of an annuity provider. This guarantee provides coverage of 100 percent up to the MPG level and 75 percent for annuity values above the MPG, up to a maximum annuity value of UF45 per month. This maximum value of protection amounts to roughly 2.3 times the average wage. This guarantee is not funded by contributions from annuity providers, being backed entirely by general tax revenues.

The potential fiscal costs of this guarantee will depend on many factors, including the average age of retirement, the design of retirement products, and the quality of the regulatory and supervisory framework. An effective regulatory and supervisory framework contains potential fiscal costs of a guarantee by minimizing the occurrence of bankruptcies and dealing effectively with failed companies. Efficient resolution mechanisms are an important component of the regulatory framework and its last line of defense, so to speak, not only because they reduce the ultimate cost to the Government but also because they ensure other desirable outcomes. An efficient resolution system minimizes market disruptions, protects all policyholders by maximizing the residual value of the company's assets, and avoids unfair redistribution of income across different types of stakeholders. Key principles for efficient resolution mechanism are set out in the IAIS Insurance Core Principles.[11] These include the following:

- a clear determination of the point at which it is no longer permissible for an insurer to continue its business;
- procedures for dealing with insolvency and the winding-up of the insurer that are clearly set out in the law;
- a high legal priority given to the protection of the rights of policyholders and other policy beneficiaries in the event of an insurer becoming insolvent; and
- limited disruption to the provision of benefits to policyholders.

During 2003 Chilean regulators handled the first case of bankruptcy of an annuity provider—the small life insurance company Le Mans, associated with the larger Inverlink financial group. The experience of handling the failure of this small insurance company revealed a number of possible gaps in regulation that should be addressed.

Once the SVS determined that the Le Mans company was likely to be insolvent, it was able to arrange for the appointment of an administrator. This administrator is in effect an official appointment under the bankruptcy law, who acts in the interests of the creditors, most of whom are policyholders. The definition of insolvency was tested through this process. Whilst the company was found to be insolvent on a present value basis, it is an unusual case because it holds some of the "tail" reinsurance purchased from another company. Therefore, if it gets to the point where the reinsurance commences to pay, it has the potential to become a solvent company again on any assessment.

The system in place allows the company to meet its current payment obligations in full, regardless of which type of policy creates the obligation. This is unusual compared to international practice. As there is no segregation between annuities and other life policies, and the assets backing each, this presents a risk to annuitants, because in practice some life policies can be surrendered earlier while annuities cannot (annuities are irrevocable contracts). In most countries, the company would pay only limited claims or none at all for all contracts, whilst an assessment of the situation is carried out so as to avoid prejudicing any group of creditors over another. In the Chilean case, it could be assumed under such an alternative that contractual payments for annuities and death and disability claims would be the limited claims that may get attention.[12]

In the Le Mans case, it can be currently expected that the company will run out of assets to make claims payments before the annuities become the responsibility of the reinsurance contract. In that case, the annuity guarantee will be called. The effect of the guarantee on the annuitants depends on the future level of the MPG, and any real increases will further insulate the annuitants. However, the guarantee is not total, implying that there could be some reduction in payment levels for a proportion of the annuitants. Moreover, the fact that some non-annuity policyholders are able to redeem their policies implies a reduction in the residual value of the company's assets and larger losses for annuitants. It also implies larger fiscal costs for the Government.

The definition of the point of intervention is also an area of regulation that requires review. As noted before, provisioning rules can be considered to be adequate if leverage is measured taking into account the margins on the asset side of the balance sheet. A company that is experiencing financial difficulties is able to reduce these margins by realizing these gains to prop up falling equity levels. Management may take such action to avert the less palatable option of a capital injection or closure of the firm. Consequently, as there is no law requiring a minimum margin on the asset side, then the likely condition of a company that reaches the point of failure is that it will have exhausted the asset margin before this point.

There are two possible alternative solutions to deal with this problem. The first is to maintain current provisioning and intervention rules, but mandate a minimum asset margin buffer. An alternative solution entails the introduction of a leverage test for intervention which uses economic values to replace the current book-value-based trigger, that is, recognizing the value of the provisions at an adequate level and the value of the resources to meet them—or to alter the provisioning and related liability rules to reflect current economic circumstances. This would make the resolution mechanism more robust and reduce the potential fiscal cost of the annuity guarantee.

Finally, the question arises as to whether changes in the design of the guarantee are justified and feasible. The guarantee itself is justified, as participation in the private pension system is mandatory—there is little sense to force workers to accumulate pension savings during their lifetimes but withdraw protection in the retirement stage. However, the question is whether some changes in the scope and financing of the guarantee are warranted.

The scope for reducing coverage or increasing coinsurance seems limited. The current reduction in coverage to 75 percent of annuity values above the MPG (or a co-insurance of 25 percent above these levels) seems reasonable, especially for a mandatory system, and the aggregate cap for the insured level of benefit also limits the benefit for very high income annuitants. Retirees receiving a pension equal to 50 percent of the average wage would suffer a reduction of 12 percent in their pensions, and those receiving a pension equal to the average wage would suffer a reduction of 18 percent. High income pensioners receiving a pension equal to 4 times above the average wage would suffer a reduction of almost 25 percent.

The financing of the annuity guarantee also involves difficult policy issues. Maintaining the guarantee totally unfunded and imposing the occasional cost entirely on taxpayers may not be efficient or equitable. It may lead to a loss of market discipline, as annuitants may not care sufficiently about the quality of the provider and managers may have more room to take excessive risk. It is also regressive, as it involves taxing the uncovered population, which has a lower average income than the covered population.

Attempting to fully fund the guarantee through the imposition of contributions on intermediaries may not be efficient or equitable either. The analogy with a deposit insurance scheme or a pension benefit guarantee scheme (in defined benefit pension systems) is questionable, because these are schemes that protect voluntary savings. Imposing full contributions in mandatory system involves harder issues. First, the providers could pass most of the contribution to annuitants in terms of low annuity rates. It is difficult to justify the imposition of this burden on forced savings. Second, it would be difficult to quantify the cost with any precision. The accumulation of a large fund with an uncertain future use can be inefficient and lead to other problems.

However, there might be scope for a small fund, built from modest contributions, or postfunded. This would permit the administrator of a failed company to make up any shortfall and achieve a transfer of obligations, maintaining stability for the annuitants. Given that the Government is already providing a guarantee, then the partial funding to facilitate transfer as a separate mechanism would provide an additional tool to the administrator.

Conclusions and Recommendations

Overall, the oversight and regulation of AFPs and life insurance companies has developed well in Chile. Comprehensive and well-designed regulations have been in place and are enforced by active supervisors. Licensing, incorporation, corporate governance, and minimum capital rules are in place supported by asset valuation and investment rules and rules for the provisioning for obligations. Limitations on other activities and related party transactions assist to keep the supervised entities focused on their key obligations.

The investment regulations have generally served the sector well as a tool of oversight, especially in the early stages of market development. However, in the case of the AFPs, there is room for removing several limits and generally simplifying the rules. The regulation of Fund E should be reviewed, probably allowing a small share of equity in this fund. The authorities should also explore whether there is scope for introducing a fund with longer duration to protect retiring workers against annuity rate risk.[13]

The far more critical rule for the life insurance companies is not the investment rule, but the CALCE rule. As shown above, capital rules have been recently improved, addressing most of the problems identified in this report. A further step that could be considered would be the computation of the economic value of both assets and liabilities, reflected in a supplement to the financial accounts. Resolution and intervention rules should recognize both the accounting values and the economic values. The merit of creating a small stabilization fund to deal with troubled companies would be worth investigation, whether or not it is pre- or postfunded.

The new products introduced by the new Pension Law will change providers' exposure to risk and also require a revision of the investment and capital regimes for life insurance companies. For example, annuities denominated in U.S. dollars will require currency matching rules, while variables annuities may open room for a relaxation of some of the rules.

In the longer term, the move to a risk-based approach that is being initiated by the SVS will be of benefit. The CALCE rule has served the sector well in its early stages of development and represented an innovative approach to the mismatch problem when it was introduced. Few countries had successfully addressed the challenge of establishing a specific capital charge for mismatch risk at the time. However, the rule has reduced the incentive for companies to refine management of the mismatch risk and may have resulted in some inefficient outcomes. A more risk-based approach would encourage all companies to consider economic risk to a greater extent, probably enabling gains in efficiency and financial stability.

Notes

1. The two supervisory agencies have their own "organic" laws, which establish their operations and provide some of the powers necessary for supervision.
2. The description of the CALCE rule in this chapter is based on the updated version of Circular 1512, issued by the SVS in April 2005. It modified substantially a previous version of the same circular.
3. There has been a debate as to whether AFP *encajes* are indeed backed by equity. AFPs which are part of a financial conglomerate can receive an equity infusion from the group backed by the issue of subordinated debt by the group, indicating that the levels of equity backing the *encaje* can be much smaller when measured on a consolidated basis.
4. This level is broadly consistent with the existing EU solvency rules in the life insurance directives. Solvency II, the current EU project, is more likely to produce a more additive risk-based solvency margin structure—something not so readily adopted in a gearing ratio paradigm (Thorburn [2004]).
5. IAIS Insurance Core Principles and Methodology—October 2003, Core Principle 20 and IAIS Principles on Capital Adequacy and Solvency January 2002 Principle 1.
6. Annex 1 provides a more detailed discussion of mortality tables.
7. This approach is consistent with a buy and hold approach, which is adopted by most companies in Chile. However, there are no regulatory restrictions on asset trading, which opens room for some companies to increase the value of their assets (when market values are higher than book values) while not being forced to value their liabilities at economic values. This issue is addressed again in the fifth section.
8. As the annuities themselves must be denominated in UF, this requirement ensures that the assets that qualify for inclusion present no currency risk. (The only class of assets that is not formally denominated in UF but is also adjusted to the CPI involves "recognition bonds.") The changes introduced by the new Pensions Law permitting the introduction of annuities in other than UF will imply that this feature will need to be revisited.
9. It is legally permissible to reinsure with foreign organizations but there are associated provisions that have the effect of localizing assets. The SVS is reviewing this rule.

10. The economic assessment would need to consider the risk and return characteristics of various instruments and the possibility of extracting an increase in risk-adjusted returns by shifting from Government bonds to other less liquid instruments such as corporate and infrastructure bonds.
11. IAIS Principle number 16.
12. In the case of the failure of the Regal and Occidental insurance companies in Australia in the 1980s, all claims were frozen initially and, after a short period for assessment, death and disability claims only were considered.
13. As indicated in Chapter 5, annuity rate risk could be addressed through additional annuity designs such as adjustable interest rate annuities. The SVS has been examining the scope for introducing this and other types of annuities.

CHAPTER 7

Conclusions, Recommendations, and Lessons for Other Countries

Main Findings and Conclusions

Chile's market for retirement products has grown substantially in the past 20 years. The number of PW and annuity contracts increased from practically zero in the mid-1980s to about 520,000 in 2004, and premiums for the two products have increased to more than 2 percent of GDP. Annuities account for 60 percent of total contracts and for more than 70 percent of the premium, revealing one of the highest rates of annuitization in the world. The assets of life insurance companies have grown from 5 percent to more than 20 percent of GDP in the same period. Thirty-two life insurance companies operate in the insurance market, 17 of which provide annuities.

The rapid growth of the market for retirement products has its origins in the well-known pension reform implemented in 1981. However, the pension reform was a necessary but not sufficient condition for the development of this market. Other countries (e.g., Australia) have also introduced a private mandatory pension pillar, but have not experienced such an increase in the number of PW and annuity contracts, especially the latter. The high rate of annuitization is particularly impressive, given the thinness of annuity markets in most countries caused, inter alia, by adverse selection, bequest motives, and risk-sharing within families.

The outcomes in Chile reflect a number of additional factors, including restrictions on lump sums, the absence of a front-ended first pillar benefit, the low level of the back-ended MPG, and the influence of brokers and sales agents. The restrictions on lump sums have increased the demand for all retirement products, including annuities. The absence of a front-ended first pillar benefit and the low level of protection provided by the MPG have led most middle and higher income workers to prefer annuities. PWs are primarily held by lower income workers, because these workers benefit relatively more from the MPG, and also because some of these workers have to take PWs due to their small balances. Finally, insurance brokers have focused their selling efforts to middle and higher income workers, as their commissions are related to the size of the premium, and have induced these workers to retire early and to annuitize.

It is difficult to replicate in Chile the typical tests for adverse selection performed for other countries, which involve comparisons of MWRs for the general and annuitant populations. This is due to the lack of an updated mortality table for the general population in Chile—there has been an effort to build current tables for the annuitant population but not for the general population. Moreover, even if such tables were available and MWRs could be compared, the difference would not necessarily reflect adverse selection, because a large share of the Chilean population is not covered by the pension system. This is the informal segment of the labor force with the lowest incomes and life expectancies, and the computation of MWRs reflecting the mortality experience of this population would tend to overestimate adverse selection.

A more relevant test of adverse selection would involve a comparison of MWRs using the mortality tables for the PW and annuitant populations, but there is no information to perform this exercise either. In any case, the high degree of annuitization in Chile and the pattern of demand for PWs and annuities suggest that, if adverse selection is present, it has not been strong enough to disrupt the development of the Chilean annuities market.

Chilean annuitants have generally got a good value for their premiums, as indicated by average money's worth ratios on their indexed annuities around 1.04–1.06 in recent years, which are significantly higher than the unitary value considered as an actuarially fair annuity. Money's worth ratios increase with age, and are lower for joint annuities and guaranteed annuities. These results generally reflect the exposure of the provider to mortality and reinvestment risk, the higher risks in contracts with longer duration, and the imposition of a load to cover these risks.

Average money's worth ratios in Chile have been high by international comparison. In most other countries, money's worth ratios range from 0.9 to 1 for nominal annuities, and from 0.8 to 0.85 for indexed annuities, in the few countries that offer inflation protection, such as the United Kingdom. The higher money's worth ratios of indexed annuities in Chile are in part due to the availability of a larger supply of financial assets indexed to prices, including higher yield assets such as mortgage, corporate, and infrastructure bonds. This has allowed annuity providers to hedge inflation risk efficiently while also extracting higher real returns. Moreover, providers have been able to extract an increase in risk-adjusted returns from these higher yield and riskier instruments, as they are much less liquid than Government and Central Bank bonds and therefore contain a liquidity premium that investors with long horizons can extract. An econometric analysis of the annuity rate suggests that providers have partly shared the higher returns with annuitants.

The high money's worth ratios are also due to a very competitive annuities market. Quite in contrast with the pensions market, which became extremely concentrated during the 1990s, the Chilean annuities market became very competitive in the same period, due to the entry of several life insurance companies. In more recent years providers seem to have engaged in aggressive pricing strategies, as indicated not only by the high money's worth ratios but also the very thin intermediation spreads. Some life insurance companies have decided to leave the market in recent years as a result of the strong competitive pressures, the thin spreads, and the low returns on equity.

The high money's worth ratios of the recent years probably cannot be sustained for a longer period, however, as they indicate very low spreads and profit margins and possibly losses in the annuity business for at least some companies in this period. The industry could absorb these losses, because of the strong capital buffer accumulated in the 1990s, and which was due to the introduction of a strict capital regulation early in that decade. However, the continuation of aggressive pricing strategies could lead to further erosion of capital. Therefore, some market adjustments should be expected, leading to some decline in money's worth ratios. The implementation of a new quotation system in 2004 has enhanced price competition and led to further consolidation of the industry, suggesting that these adjustments may be taking place.

Although an adjustment in MWRs is likely, it is also likely that these ratios will probably remain attractive by international comparison, especially by comparison with MWRs of indexed annuities in other countries. This is because Chilean providers will retain an advantage over providers in other countries—their access to a diversified supply of indexed financial instruments. If this scenario materializes, market performance would still be judged as satisfactory for both consumers and providers.

The regulatory framework for the annuities market is reasonable and has evolved positively over the past 20 years. Product regulation has prevented an early exhaustion of real incomes at retirement. Annuities have been fixed and indexed, and married males need to buy joint annuities. These features imply relatively lower payments in the early stages of retirement but ensure adequate payments for beneficiaries in later stages. The PW formula follows the same approach, by preventing a depletion of the balance in a finite period of time and distributing payments according to life expectancy. The recently passed Pension Law has introduced new products, but these are combinations that always include a minimum fixed and indexed annuity, thus ensuring minimum insurance against investment and longevity risk.

Marketing regulation allowed some questionable selling practices during the 1990s, but has been tightened with the passage of the new Pension Law. Broker's commissions have been capped for two years at 2.5 percent of the premium. More importantly, an innovative electronic quotation system for annuities and PWs has been introduced. The new system has improved market transparency and seems to be producing positive outcomes—retiring workers have selected annuities based on the best quotes and broker's commissions have declined further to levels below the cap.

The regulation of providers has supported a sound development of the market in the past 20 years. In particular, strict capital rules introduced in the early 1990s penalized mismatches of assets and liabilities and provided a capital buffer that has proved essential to the stability of the industry. The capital buffer weakened over time due to the failure to account for the improvements in mortality rates in the past 15 years. This affected not only capital regulation but product regulation as well. This regulatory failure was addressed in 2005 through the adoption of an updated mortality table and an asset sufficiency test that should enhance transparency and market discipline.

Overall, the annuities market has had a good performance, and the regulatory framework has addressed reasonably well the risks identified in Chapter 3. The menu of retirement products is reasonable, capable of meeting most of the needs of retirees with different preferences and risk profiles. The restrictions that still exist are largely justified in the Chilean case. Providers have access to a large supply of indexed instruments with relatively long durations for asset-liability management that reduces their exposure to reinvestment risk.

The Government provides guarantees to retirees, but the regulatory framework contains elements that should prevent excessive recourse to these guarantees. The recent introduction of stricter conditions for early retirement will tend to raise average retirement incomes and reduce the potential number of retirees eligible for the MPG. The new combined products may expose consumers to more investment and longevity risk, but still require a fixed annuity that provides minimum insurance. The adoption of an updated mortality table in the PW formula should also delay access of PW holders to the MPG. The MPG itself is not formally indexed to wages, which allows some margin for maneuvering. The annuity guarantee has an element of co-insurance that seems reasonable, especially considering that the private pension system is mandatory.

At the same time, the report has also identified some weaknesses that would need to be addressed in the future. The separation of the accumulation and retirement phases implies that neither pension funds nor annuity providers are effectively maximizing the individuals' pension wealth over the entire lifecycle. In particular, workers in the preretirement phase are subject to some risks such as annuity rate risk that have not been properly addressed. Management of longevity risk by annuity providers remains a challenge in Chile, as it is in other countries. In addition, although annuity providers in Chile have access to a wider range of financial instruments than providers in other emerging countries to manage market or investment risk, they still face a duration mismatch problem that needs to be continuously addressed. Providers also lack access to a wider range of risk management tools such as derivatives and reinsurance.

Product regulation is generally satisfactory, but the regulation of PWs still produces a bias in selection, and additional annuity designs could be considered. Marketing regulation has evolved significantly, but there are still challenges to be faced, particularly regarding the riskier products. Investment and capital regulations have not yet been revised to accommodate the introduction of new products and the changes in risk patterns. Finally, the experience in handling the first bankruptcy case has revealed some gaps in resolution rules that should be addressed.

Main Recommendations

The investment regime for pension funds should be reviewed, as it has remained unnecessarily complex and probably ineffective in addressing several types of risk. A judicious relaxation of several quantitative restrictions could open more room for asset managers to operate without any meaningful increases in risk, benefiting both active workers and PW holders. Allowing a small share of equity in Fund E would probably improve its efficiency. Reducing the exposure of retiring workers to annuity rate risk would require an increase in average portfolio duration. This might be difficult to achieve through regulatory tools, but policy makers may consider allowing a special fund more tailored to the needs of workers in the preretirement phase.

Chile has achieved considerable progress in developing its capital market, but annuity providers still lack access to sufficient tools for risk management, especially longevity and market risk. The introduction of special arrangements to share longevity risk (such as those adopted by companies in Denmark or the TIIA-CREF fund in the United States) does not seem feasible in the Chilean context. However, regulators should examine the recent efforts to issue longevity bonds in the United Kingdom and assess the possibility for developing this instrument in Chile.

Management of market or investment risk could be seriously complicated by an excessive de-indexation of the stock of financial instruments resulting from aggressive new issues of peso- or U.S. dollar-denominated instruments. The critical role of indexed financial instruments in the asset-liability management of annuity providers cannot be sufficiently emphasized. Annuity providers must retain access to a substantial volume of long-term indexed instruments, and would also benefit from access to a more developed derivatives market. The development of instruments such as interest options and swaps, and bond futures could prove important tools for more effective management of investment risk by providers.

Policy makers may consider the introduction of additional annuity designs, such as adjustable annuities and escalating annuities. Adjustable indexed annuities would allow retirees to enjoy higher initial payouts, as the provider would be less exposed to reinvestment risk. The annuitant would be exposed to the risk of a fall in future annuity rates, but several annuitants might prefer this option to a pure fixed indexed annuity, given their planned consumption paths at retirement. If this option is allowed, however, it should probably be combined with a minimum fixed indexed annuity providing minimum protection against investment risk, in line with the combinations allowed by the new Pension Law. Escalating annuities would involve a predefined yearly rate of increase in indexed payments and would therefore entail lower initial payouts relative to regular indexed annuities. They might be an attractive option for early retirees that continue working and could also contribute to lower future expenditures with the MPG.

The updating of the parameters used in the PW formula should be completed in order to remove the residual bias that still exists in selection. The technical rate should be forward-looking, and possibly consist of the yield of a mix of fixed income instruments in Funds D and E.

The new quotation system is expected to improve market transparency, but some retirees may still select instruments based on a comparison of initial payouts only, without proper knowledge of the risks involved. For example, an excessive emphasis on initial payouts may lead some retirees to choose variable annuities, without proper knowledge of the risks involved in this instrument. Information on risks cannot be easily inserted in the quotation system, but participants in the new system should be required to provide brochures highlighting the basic aspects of each retirement instrument.

The investment and capital regimes for insurance companies may need to be reviewed to accommodate the introduction of the new products, especially the products that introduce more risk sharing between the provider and the annuitant. The move from a rules-based approach to a risk-based approach should be completed, as it is likely to generate gains in efficiency and stability.

Some improvements in resolution rules may also be needed. Intervention triggers could be improved by introducing a leverage test that uses economic values rather than book values. An alternative solution would entail maintaining the current provisioning rules and intervention triggers but mandating a minimum asset margin buffer. Intervention and administration rules should be reviewed to ensure a level playing field for all policyholders. The merit of creating a small resolution fund would be worth investigation in this context, whether or not it is pre- or postfunded.

As mentioned before, longevity risk remains one of the most difficult issues to be addressed by regulators and participants in annuities markets, requiring a constant effort to track mortality improvements and reflect these improvements in capital and product regulation. In preparing the RV-2004 table, the SVS has sought to deal with the problem of lack of data at later ages because the system is still not yet mature, by using additional data from the previous social security system. In the absence of any other data, this remains a reasonable approach, but the continuing study of mortality using the extensively available public data is to be encouraged as it remains a most significant element of annuity value estimation.

Finally, the Government should make an effort to build an actuarial model capable of producing more robust estimates for the expenditures with the MPG, and able to provide more accurate inputs for future policy formulation.

Lessons for Other Countries

One of the most important lessons that can be extracted from the Chilean experience is the feasibility of developing a market for retirement products from a low initial base. As indicated in the report, when Chile implemented its 1981 pension reform the market for retirement products did not exist. Twenty years later Chile had a well-developed and rapidly growing market for PWs and annuities, judged by the number of PW and annuity policies, the size of the PW and annuity premiums, the assets of life insurance companies, and the number of market participants.

The provision of PWs and annuities to disabled workers and survivors enabled an early and rapid start of the market for retirement products in Chile, attracting new providers into the market. Countries that have introduced a second, private pillar as part of their pension reform, and that have shifted disability and survivorship insurance to the new pillar, either partly or totally, may also experience this rapid growth or "jump-starting" effect.

Some reforming countries in Central and Eastern Europe have decided to maintain disability insurance in the first, public pillar, because of concerns about the capacity of the insurance industry to deliver this benefit efficiently, and because of the perception that disability and other programs such as health and sick pay can only be well integrated in the public sector. These concerns may be legitimate and may justify keeping disability in the first pillar in several countries. However, this policy will also imply a slower growth of the market for retirement products.

The Chilean approach to product regulation is appropriate for countries that expect the new second pillar to play a major role in retirement provision and social protection. The restrictions on lump sums that Chile implemented increase the potential demand for all retirement products, including annuities. A PW formula that is based on life expectancy prevents a very premature exhaustion of funds. The imposition of fixed annuities indexed to inflation, and joint annuities for married couples all contribute to prevent an early exhaustion of funds and poverty in old age. The introduction of new products such as variable and adjustable annuities should require a minimum fixed annuity component providing investment and longevity insurance. Provided that these minimum safety features are included, these combined products could be introduced earlier than Chile did.

Countries that have preserved a large first pillar and introduced only a modest second pillar can adopt a more liberal product regulation, as in these cases the exposure of retiring workers to investment and longevity risk is more limited. However, very liberal rules for lump sums can hinder significantly the development of the market for retirement products, especially annuities markets. The appropriate policies in this area will vary significantly from country to country. In some cases it may be appropriate to continue restricting lump sums, but adopt a more liberal approach to the design of retirement products. For example, the regulation of PWs may be more liberal, allowing designs that enable a faster withdrawal of funds. Likewise, variable and adjustable annuities may be introduced without the obligation of a fixed annuity component.

The high money's worth ratios for indexed annuities in Chile is due in good part to the existence of a large supply of indexed financial instruments, not only public sector bonds, but also other higher yield instruments issued by the private sector such as mortgage bonds, mortgage-backed instruments, corporate bonds, and infrastructure bonds. The report presents evidence that Chilean providers operating in a competitive environment have shared the higher real yield of these instruments with annuitants, in terms of higher annuity rates. Other researchers have estimated money's worth ratios for the United Kingdom—the only country that has developed markets for both nominal and indexed annuities—showing that inflation protection can cost 5 percent of the annuity premium.

Several developed countries are also making efforts to develop indexed financial instruments in order to allow domestic institutional investors (defined-benefit pension funds and insurance companies) to hedge the inflation risk associated with indexed pensions and annuities. The stock of indexed Government securities has increased in several countries, but there is not enough evidence that this effort is also leading to issues of indexed instruments by the private sector. In countries where indexation is required but providers cannot properly hedge the inflation risk, or only have access to lower yield indexed instruments, the result will be lower rates of return for indexed annuities. The development of a benchmark yield curve for Government indexed debt may be a necessary but not sufficient condition for the development of private indexed debt. It would seem important to ensure that there are no regulatory obstacles to the issue of indexed instruments by the private sector.

The computation of money's worth ratios for different classes of annuitants shows that providers in Chile price the higher risk involved in annuities with longer expected duration. This indicates the importance of developing long-term instruments, in order to reduce providers' exposure to reinvestment risk and enable them to offer better annuity rates to all classes of annuitants. Institutional investors increase the potential demand for long-term instruments, but the actual development of these instruments frequently requires a proactive approach from the side of policy makers and regulators.

Product regulation can introduce unintended biases and influence the selection process. Annuity providers should be able to price their annuities freely, developing the mortality tables most appropriate for their own clientele. However, PW payments are typically determined by formulas with regulated parameters. These parameters must be as up-to-date and market related as possible, in order to minimize biases in selection. Chile segmented the provision of the two major classes of retirement products, with pension funds providing PWs and life insurance companies providing annuities, but this segmentation does not have any obvious justification. Therefore, in designing a market for retirement products, regulators could allow life insurance companies to offer PWs as well, as is the case in most OECD countries.

The Chilean experience with marketing regulation also provides important lessons for other countries. Brokers and sales agents can influence significantly the selection of products and providers, and in the case of Chile this influence has produced mixed outcomes. The new electronic quotation system has improved transparency in the market for retirement products, and has ensured that retirees effectively get the best quotes. This is an innovative and promising reform, whose results should be closely monitored by regulators in other countries. The recent introduction of caps on broker commissions proved controversial but is another experience that merits close monitoring as well.

Chilean regulators have addressed reinvestment and mortality risks by imposing strict capital regulations on providers. The capital rules introduced in 1990 were innovative, being based in a formula that links the level of reserves to the extension of the duration mismatch, and that also uses a low discount rate for valuing liabilities. This approach to capital regulation enabled the early buildup of a strong capital buffer that has proved very important for the sound development of the industry. In other countries, providers are probably subject to even more severe mismatches and reinvestment risk than is currently the case in Chile. A capital regulation that penalizes mismatches can not only strengthen the capital buffer but also promote the adoption of appropriate asset-liability management strategies in the early stages of market development.

At the same time, the Chilean experience indicates the need to make an early effort to produce appropriate mortality tables that will be used for regulatory purposes, including the regulation of PWs and the computation of technical reserves and capital. The Chilean PW design is attractive because it incorporates life expectancy, but it has been weakened in practice by the prolonged use of an outdated mortality table. Likewise, capital regulations were innovative in many aspects but their power was eroded by the use of outdated mortality tables for many years. This problem may be avoided through efforts to review mortality experience and update mortality tables regularly.

Intervention and bankruptcy rules should prevent an early depletion of provider assets by life insurance policyholders in a bankruptcy scenario, as this will reduce the residual value of assets left to honor annuity payments, and will increase the cost of any guarantee that the Government may provide. In a system of mandatory savings, annuitants may deserve a preferential treatment over other life insurance policyholders, but, at the very least, should not be less favorably treated than other policyholders.

Countries that have introduced a mandatory second pillar may have to introduce an annuity guarantee as Chile did, as it does not make sense to force the accumulation of pension savings and remove protection in the last phase of the life cycle, when the benefits are expected to be enjoyed and the opportunity to change providers (exercising market pressure) is not available. As in Chile, the guarantee should not be total, including a reasonable amount of coinsurance by annuitants in order to minimize the possible loss of market discipline at the point of purchase. In Chile this guarantee is backed entirely by budgetary resources, but other countries may consider the introduction of a small fund financed by the industry.

ANNEX 1

An Analysis of Money's Worth Ratios in Chile*

Introduction

This annex provides a detailed examination of money's worth ratios (MWRs) in Chile during the 1999–2005 period. The existence of extensive data on individual annuity policies, including information on individual annuitant characteristics, allows not only the computation of a large number of MWRs, but also an analysis of their determinants. This analysis provides important insights on the performance of the annuities market and inputs to the formulation of appropriate policies in this area.

The annex is structured as follows. The next section discusses a number of methodological issues that arise in the computation of MWRs, including formulas, mortality tables, and discount rates. The third examines the data used for the computation of MWRs, stressing the use of data on actual annuity sales rather than quoted annuities. The fourth section presents the results, which include an examination of average MWRs across main classes of annuities, as well as a discussion of regressions of these ratios against individual annuitant characteristics such as age, gender,

*Marco Morales and Gregorio Impavido contributed to this annex.

and premiums. The fifth section compares MWRs for Chile with those produced by other researchers for Chile and other countries. Finally, the sixth section summarizes the main findings and discusses some policy implications.

Methodology

MWR Formulas

The money's worth ratio is an indication of the value provided to the customer in an annuity product. It is defined as the ratio of the expected value of the benefits payable under the contract to the premium paid. A mortality table and an interest rate yield curve are required to determine the value of the benefits for this process.

The calculation of the value of the payment streams in Chile requires that the features of the products be reflected. In particular, it is necessary to allow for the fact that annuities are issued as either joint or single life, that some are issued with a period of initial deferment, and that some are issued with the payment guaranteed for a defined period regardless of survivorship. A small funeral benefit of UF15 is provided as part of the annuity purchase and is also considered in the calculations. Benefits for dependent children have not been considered, because it is not possible to identify from the data the cases where these benefits would be payable. However, the effect of ignoring these dependent benefits is small, not affecting the conclusions or international comparisons.

As a result of these characteristics, the MWR formula for a single life annuity issued to a person aged x is as set out in equation (1):

$$MWR = \frac{\left(A \sum_{t=d+1}^{12(\omega-x)} \frac{{}_{t}p_{x}}{(1+i_{t})^{t}} \right) + V}{P} \qquad (1)$$

where:

- MWR is the Money's Worth Ratio;
- A is the monthly annuity payment in UF;
- W is the ultimate age in the mortality table, the oldest age assumed where no survivors remain;
- ${}_{t}p_{x}$ is the probability that a life aged x at commencement is still alive at time t, that is after t months in this case, at age

$x+(t/12)$. Note that, in the case of a guaranteed period then ${}_tp_x$ is set equal to 1 for the period that the guarantee is in force;

d is the number of months deferment in the case of a deferred annuity;

i_t is the interest rate used to discount payments at time t, obtained from the term structure of interest rates;

V is the value of the funeral benefit; and

P is the single premium payment made for the contract.

The first term between parentheses in the numerator is the expected present value of future annuity payments. The division of this term by the premium is the MWR formula usually used in empirical research in other countries. Equation (1) also includes the expected present value of the small funeral benefit V because it is part of the annuity benefit in the Chilean case.

The joint life formula contains the reversion of the annuity to the second beneficiary (typically the spouse) at the lower level (60 percent), and the survivorship of two lives determining the annuity payment. If the principal beneficiary is noted with symbols as above, and the reversionary beneficiary is noted with the same symbols but with a '^' mark and is aged y at commencement of the annuity, then the formula is as set out in equation (2). Note that the probability term in the numerator would be set to 1 during the period where annuity payments are guaranteed.

$$MWR = \frac{\left(A \sum_{t=d+1}^{12(\omega-x)} \frac{{}_tp_x + 0.6((1-{}_tp_x)\,{}_t\hat{p}_y)}{(1+i_t)^t} \right) + V}{P} \qquad (2)$$

Note that all annuities in Chile are quoted in UF, which means that they are indexed to consumer prices. In this analysis all values are expressed in UF and should be interpreted accordingly when making comparisons with other countries.[1]

Mortality Tables

Most empirical studies estimate MWRs with two mortality tables, one reflecting the mortality of the general population and the other reflecting the mortality of the smaller annuitant population. These are usually cohort tables, constructed either by incorporating existing projections of future mortality for each cohort, or by estimating future mortality improvements and applying them to period tables.[2] In some cases, the annuitant table is constructed less accurately because of the absence of reliable data. The difference between the estimated MWRs using the general and the annuitant population assumptions is frequently interpreted as the effect of adverse selection.

In the case of Chile, there is no mortality table for the population that is updated and reliable, but three tables have been constructed for the annuities market. The first of these tables, known as RV-85, is a period table that was developed when the annuity system started and there were few annuities in force. The table purports to represent the period experience of annuitant mortality at the time it was developed, but was partly constructed by making adjustments to mortality data from other countries. The RV-85 was developed for regulatory purposes, and served until recently as the basis for the determination of programmed withdrawal (PW) payments and the calculation of technical reserves for annuity providers.

The second table, referred to as RV-98, is a period table based on more extensive Chilean annuitant mortality data collected between 1995 and 1997. The table represents an improvement over the RV-85, by including more information on the mortality of the Chilean annuitant population. However, while the male tables were mostly determined from the data, the female tables largely impute the observed rate of change between the RV-85 and RV-98 tables for males, to the RV-85 table for females. As a result, the rate of mortality improvement is essentially the same for both sexes.

Finally, the third table, referred to as RV-04, is a period table based on Chilean annuitant mortality data collected between 1995 and 2003. The RV-04 is more representative of the Chilean annuitant population than its two predecessors and has recently been adopted for all regulatory purposes. Among several of its positive features, both male and female tables were developed separately, and the "representative" version of the table passed all the standard consistency tests comfortably.[3]

However, these more updated and constructed tables still have some shortcomings that need to be considered in empirical analysis. Due to the continuing maturing of the system, there are fewer annuitants at older ages, so data was included from the previous scheme. This implies that the mortality rates at older ages may not be as representative of annuitants as the earlier ages, and rather reflect the mortality of different group of retirees under the old system. Rates were updated to 2004 using the national statistical agency's assumed age-specific improvement rates for the population. In addition, in the construction of the published table, a bias for conservatism was added.

The RV-04 table was selected for the computation of MWRs because it is the most representative of the current annuity population. The table was adjusted to the relevant year using the same approach adopted in the official table and the same rates. However, the bias for conservatism has *not* been adopted.

As shown in Table A1.1, there are significant differences in the shape of the three mortality tables. Mortality rates in the RV-98 and RV-04 are systematically and substantially lower than those in the RV-85. Male mortality rates in the RV-04 are lower than those in RV-98 for intermediate ages, but higher at some younger and older ages. Female mortality rates, however, are substantially lower in the RV-04. As noted above, the earlier (RV-85 and RV-98) tables for females are constructed more subjectively than the RV-04 tables for both sexes and the RV-98 table for males. While the shape and level of the mortality tables is still a matter for some debate in Chile, the RV-04 table seems to be the most scientific and robust for both sexes yet produced.

Each of these three tables is published as a period table, requiring adjustments in order to convert them into cohort tables. Cohort results were initially developed using two alternatives, namely, national population projection rates, and the rates of improvement between the RV-85 and the RV-04 tables. The first method was ultimately judged as superior and has been adopted here. The basic reason was the high degree of arbitrariness involved in the construction of the RV-85 table. In particular, it is clear that the female improvement rates derived from these tables continue to be open to greater uncertainty and are well above the observed and assumed population estimates.

Discount Rates

In line with most other studies, the computation of MWRs is performed with two alternative discount rates, the interest rate on Government or Central Bank bonds and the interest rate on corporate bonds. The MWR computed with the first rate is frequently considered to be the most meaningful to the average customer, as it excludes risk and reflects its opportunity cost more accurately. It is also used to facilitate comparisons across countries. The alternative discount rate is also computed as it may reflect more appropriately the opportunity cost for some consumers, and because it is more relevant from the point of view of the provider.

Table A1.1. Levels and Changes in Mortality Rates

Age	Male					Female				
	Period Tables			Improvement Rates for Cohort Tables		Period Tables			Improvement Rates for Cohort Tables	
	RV85	*RV98*	*RV04 unbiased*	*Pop. projection*	*RV04/ RV85*	*RV85*	*RV98*	*RV04/ unbiased*	*Pop. projection*	*RV04 RV85*
50	0.0054	0.0044	0.0044	1.40%	1.44%	0.0027	0.0022	0.0015	1.40%	3.91%
55	0.0082	0.0059	0.0058	1.40%	2.39%	0.0042	0.0030	0.0024	1.50%	4.04%
60	0.0124	0.0089	0.0091	1.50%	2.23%	0.0066	0.0047	0.0035	1.40%	4.46%
65	0.0189	0.0146	0.0139	1.50%	2.16%	0.0104	0.0080	0.0049	1.40%	5.22%
70	0.0288	0.0239	0.0219	1.50%	1.94%	0.0165	0.0137	0.0072	1.50%	5.76%
75	0.0447	0.0384	0.0356	1.50%	1.61%	0.0272	0.0237	0.0127	1.30%	5.30%
80	0.0693	0.0624	0.0593	1.40%	1.11%	0.0451	0.0401	0.0261	1.20%	3.84%
85	0.1070	0.0963	0.0971	1.20%	0.69%	0.0750	0.0680	0.0523	1.20%	2.54%
90	0.1636	0.1472	0.1511	1.20%	0.56%	0.1238	0.1115	0.0942	1.20%	1.94%
95	0.2459	0.2213	0.2219	1.20%	0.73%	0.2013	0.1812	0.1527	1.20%	1.95%
100	0.3600	0.3240	0.3097	1.20%	1.07%	0.3180	0.2862	0.2283	1.20%	2.34%
105	0.5064	0.4557	0.4261	1.20%	1.23%	0.4792	0.4313	0.3328	1.20%	2.57%
110	1.0000	1.0000	1.0000	1.20%	0.00%	1.0000	1.0000	1.0000	1.20%	0.00%

Source: SVS and staff calculations.
Note: The values for the RV-04 tables shown here are not updated to any particular year, i.e., are representative of mortality centered around 1999.

The risk-free discount rates were obtained by the yield curve of 20-year indexed Central Bank bonds (the PRC-20) in March of 1999, 2002, 2003, 2004, and 2005—as indicated below, the annuity sample consists of all annuities sold in those five months. The yield curve for those five months was provided by the Central Bank of Chile, consisting of daily estimates of the zero coupon yield curve for maturities ranging from one month to 20 years. These curves are originally generated using interpolation and smoothing approaches developed by RiskAmerica, drawing on what is usually a limited number of trades on any given day in the PRC-20. The Central Bank of Chile makes some additional adjustments, based on the transactions of similar debt instruments. The yield curve utilized in the MWR computations was the average of the daily yield curves in March of each of those five years.[4]

The second technical limitation that had to be addressed was the absence of debt instruments with sufficiently long duration. Although Chile has had more success in lengthening the maturities of debt instruments than most other emerging countries, the yield curve still does not cover the possible life of annuity payments. Consistent with the approach taken by James et al. (2004a), the yield curve was assumed to be flat after 20 years. This solution seems reasonable, as the yield curve in the months examined is essentially flat in the durations from 15 to 20 years. Finally, the alternative discount rate was constructed by adding the actual spread of corporate bonds over the PRC-20 for each of the periods 2002–2004. In March of 2002, 2003, and 2004, these spreads were 1.7, 2.5, and 1.4 percent, respectively.

Data

Most empirical studies are based on reported annuity quotations, and generally involve the collection of several annuity quotations, the computation of averages for different categories, and the calculation of MWRs for these categories (e.g., single annuities by sex and age, joint annuities, guaranteed annuities). The high level of disclosure in Chile includes information on every individual annuity sold. As a result, it is possible to compute MWRs for all these categories using actual sales.

The access to actual annuity sales represents a significant improvement over other studies, because the computed MWRs are more consistent with the value actually provided to customers. Another advantage of the study is the much larger size of the sample and the wider range of data points generated. This allows more robust estimates of the averages of different categories, the econometric analysis of some of the main determinants of

MWRs, and a more robust analysis of dispersion of annuity prices and transparency of the annuities market.

At the same time, it is important to recognize the possible problems of comparability with other studies. The use of actual annuity sales may lead to higher MWRs than those computed with quotations, even in cases where there are no real differences. This is because customers receive a number of quotes and typically exercise preference for one of the better quotes. Therefore, data based on actual annuity sales will typically capture the better quotes, while data based on quotations will typically reflect the average of several quotes. As a result, MWRs produced with actual sales will tend to be higher.[5] The much larger sample used in this study may also be a source of differences. If the quotations collected in other studies are not representative of the universe of annuity sales, the results and comparisons may be biased.

The dataset used in this study comprises 937 annuities issued in March of 1999, 1,517 annuities issued in March of 2002, 1,193 annuities issued in March of 2003, 1,490 annuities issued in March of 2004, and 1,391 annuities issued in March of 2005. These 5,137 annuities only include normal old-age retirement and early retirement annuities, and exclude disability and survivorship annuities. Table A1.2 provides summary statistics for the whole dataset, while Table A1.3 provides information for separate subgroups.

As shown in Table A1.2, until 2004 the average age of retiring males and females was about 58 and 56, respectively, well below the normal retirement age of 65 and 60, and reflecting the large numbers of early retirees. The average age of retirement increased significantly in 2005, reflecting the introduction of stricter rules for early retirement. The share of deferred annuities (i.e., a TW combined with a subsequent annuity) increased from 20 to 30 percent of the total, but the period of deferment remained short—roughly 80 percent of deferred annuities were only deferred for a year, and only 3 percent or less were deferred for 3 years or more. These patterns of selection reflect at least to some extent the influence of annuity brokers—since commissions are determined by the size of the annuity premium, brokers do not have incentives to recommend TWs paired with long periods of deferment.

While only 30 percent of annuities issued were deferred, close to 80 percent had payments guaranteed for a certain period of time independent of survivorship. The length of the guaranteed period is also relatively high—roughly 60 percent of all guaranteed annuities had a 10-year guarantee, and 90 percent were guaranteed for 10 or 15 years. The choice of guaranteed versus non-guaranteed annuities is not prescribed or influenced by broker

Table A1.2. Summary Statistics of the Dataset

	1999	*2002*	*2003*	*2004*	*2005*
All Cases					
Number	937	1,517	1,193	1,490	1,391
Average Age of Males	57.83	56.98	57.77	57.70	59.46
Average Age of Females	55.76	54.85	55.55	56.02	58.46
Average Purchase Price (UF)	1,971.66	1,859.65	2,116.94	2,098.79	2,454.9
Cases with deferment	21.2%	21.8%	25.7%	27.5%	30.1%
Of which:					
- 12 months	164	275	238	322	315
- 24 months	32	54	60	75	91
- 36 months	2	2	8	10	9
- 48 months	1	0	1	2	3
Number of cases with a guaranteed term	708 (75.6%)	1,191 (78.5%)	948 (79.5%)	1,153 (77.4%)	1,093 (78.6%)
Of which:					
- 5 years	11	19	17	18	23
- 10 years	422	701	511	636	559
- 15 years	244	387	335	380	353
- 20 years	18	64	63	93	124
- other	13	20	22	26	34

Source: SVS and staff analysis.

activity, as the commission does not depend on whether the annuity is guaranteed or not. The preference for guaranteed payments probably reflects a decision to smooth retirement income within the family unit, as well as a bequest motive.

Table A1.3 provides more detailed information, showing that joint life annuities accounted for approximately 70 percent of all annuities issued in the sample months. Single female and single male annuities accounted for around 20 and 10 percent of the total, respectively. The large share of joint annuities is an important feature of the Chilean pension system, as it ensures retirement income for surviving spouses and helps prevent a large number of old people (mostly women) from falling into poverty, or having to access the minimum pension guarantee. The large share of joint annuities is to a large extent due to product regulation—retiring married males can only buy joint annuities. However, the large share of guaranteed joint annuities reveals an element of voluntary transfers within the family unit—the main beneficiary accepts voluntarily a discounted annuity in exchange for a higher annuity for his spouse during the guaranteed period (higher than the standard 60 percent reversionary payment), in the event of his death during this period.

Table A1.3. Summary Statistics of the Dataset by Subgroups

	1999	*2002*	*2003*	*2004*	*2005*
Single Life – Males					
Number	82	139	114	144	108
Average Age of Males	59.22	57.49	57.81	58.13	59.74
Average Purchase Price (UF)	1,475.85	1678.00	1,544.60	1,631.88	1973.34
Number of cases with deferment	7 (8.5%)	22 (15.8%)	14 (12.3%)	22 (15.3%)	25 (23.1%)
O/w: - 12 months	6	16	12	17	22
- 24 months	1	6	1	5	2
- 36 months and longer	0	0	1	0	1
Number of cases with a guaranteed term	52 (63.4%)	102 (73.4%)	85 (74.6%)	101 (70.1%)	75 (69.4%)
O/w: - 5 years	0	5	4	7	7
- 10 years	39	68	56	52	41
- 15 years	10	19	18	27	17
- 20 years and longer	1	10	7	15	8
Single Life – Females					
Number	185	309	256	373	520
Average Age of Females	57.89	56.46	57.51	58.66	60.99
Average Purchase Price (UF)	1,779.28	1,619.47	1,984.87	2,007.26	2,187.79
Number of cases with deferment	44 (23.8%)	69 (22.3%)	71 (27.7%)	113 (30.3%)	175 (33.7%)
O/w: - 12 months	37	57	56	81	132
- 24 months	7	12	12	27	38
- 36 months and longer	0	0	3	5	5
Number of cases with a guaranteed term	151 (81.6%)	250 (80.9%)	208 (81.3%)	310 (83.1%)	416 (80.0%)
O/w: - 5 years	1	3	2	5	8
- 10 years	89	149	120	175	217
- 15 years	53	82	70	104	138
- 20 years and longer	5	16	16	26	41
Joint Life					
Number	670	1,069	823	973	763
Average Age of Males	57.66	56.92	57.77	57.64	59.42
Average Age of Females	55.17	54.39	54.94	55.01	56.73
Average Age difference (male age less female age) in years	2.49	2.53	2.83	2.62	2.69
Average Purchase Price (UF)	2,085.47	1952.69	2237.30	2202.07	2705.19
Number of cases with deferment	148 (22.1%)	240 (22.5%)	222 (27.0%)	274 (28.2%)	219 (28.7%)
O/w: - 12 months	121	202	170	224	161
- 24 months	24	36	47	43	51
- 36 months and longer	3	2	5	7	7

(continued)

Table A1.3. Summary Statistics of Dataset by Subgroups *(Continued)*

	1999	*2002*	*2003*	*2004*	*2005*
Number of cases with a guaranteed term	504 (75.2%)	839 (78.4%)	655 (79.6%)	742 (76.3%)	602 (78.9%)
O/w: - 5 years	9	11	11	6	8
- 10 years	293	484	335	409	301
- 15 years	181	286	247	249	198
- 20 years and longer	14	58	62	78	75

Source: SVS and staff analysis.

The high share of guaranteed annuities in the case of single male and single female annuities reflects primarily a bequest motive, with the main beneficiary accepting a discount in exchange for the guarantee of some value to his/her heirs in the event of his/her death. The increase in the share of TWs and deferred annuities reveals the consumers' preference for larger payments in the early phases of retirement and may reflect the use of TWs and deferments as a substitute for the loss of informal access to lump sums through commission rebates.

Analysis of Money's Worth Ratios

As mentioned before, most empirical studies present estimates of MWRs computed with two mortality tables (the annuitant and the population tables) and with two discount rates (the Government and the corporate bond rate). Moreover, these four estimates are presented separately for single male, single female, and joint annuities. Some studies present MWRs of guaranteed annuities, whenever such information is available. In the very few countries that offer indexed annuities, such estimates are presented as well.

The lack of a reliable and updated population table for Chile reduces the value of the traditional exercise of comparing MWRs with population and annuitant tables to estimate the impact of adverse selection. Moreover, even if a reliable and current mortality table for the population were available, the exercise would still have limited value, as only 60 percent of the Chilean population is on average covered by the pension system, a much lower coverage ratio than the ratios of OECD countries for which MWRs have been computed. The uncovered segment of the population is the segment with the lowest incomes and probably the lowest life expectancies. Therefore, an exercise of this type would produce exaggerated measures of adverse selection in the Chilean case. A more relevant exercise in the Chilean case would involve a comparison of MWRs for the annuitant and the PW populations, but there is no reliable information on the mortality of PW holders at this time.

On the other hand, the availability of a larger dataset of individual annuities in the Chilean case allows a much more detailed examination of MWRs across different types of annuitants. This section analyzes in detail the MWRs computed with the risk-free rate and the cohortized RV-04 table, as these estimates are considered the most relevant in the Chilean case. The analysis includes the examination of the MWRs for the main classes of annuities, an econometric investigation of the individual MWRs against individual annuitant characteristics, and an analysis of dispersion of MWRs. The next section compares MWRs for annuitants in Chile with those estimated for annuitants in other countries, computed both with the risk-free rate and a higher discount rate.

An Overview of the Results

Table A1.4 presents estimates of MWRs for March of 1999, 2002, 2003, 2004, and 2005, using the cohortized version of the most updated mortality table for the annuitant population (the RV-04), and the risk-free yield curve.[6] The table shows the overall averages for each of the five

Table A1.4. Money's Worth Ratios in 1999, 2002, 2003, 2004, and 2005, Computed with the Risk-Free Rate and an Update Cohort Annuitant Table

	March 1999	*March 2002*	*March 2003*	*March 2004*	*March 2005*
All cases	0.978	1.079	1.036	1.064	1.062
- maximum	1.148	1.222	1.181	1.276	1.223
- minimum	0.755	0.872	0.872	0.876	0.706
Male Single Life	0.987	1.086	1.044	1.061	1.054
Female Single Life	1.009	1.111	1.063	1.097	1.086
Joint Life	0.968	1.070	1.026	1.052	1.046
Male Single Life age 55	0.981	1.075	1.034	1.049	1.042
Male Single Life age 65	0.996	1.117	1.069	1.086	1.067
Female Single Life age 55	0.994	1.101	1.049	1.076	1.064
Female Single Life age 60	1.021	1.131	1.077	1.105	1.083
Joint Life – Male 65 and Female 60	0.998	1.083	1.050	1.078	1.069
Purchase Price up to UF 1,000	0.980	1.078	1.045	1.068	1.067
Purchase Price above UF 3,000	0.997	1.099	1.047	1.075	1.071
Without guaranteed term	0.990	1.092	1.045	1.071	1.073
With guaranteed term	0.974	1.076	1.033	1.062	1.059
Without deferment	0.979	1.079	1.035	1.063	1.061
With deferment	0.974	1.080	1.036	1.067	1.064

Source: Authors' calculations.

years, the maximum and the minimum, and the averages for well-defined categories, including type, age, gender, size of the premium, and the presence of guaranteed and deferred periods. It must be emphasized that these are MWRs computed for indexed annuities.

The first thing to note is that the average MWR in 1999 is slightly lower than one, a value that is usually taken to indicate a fairly priced annuity. In 2002 and the following years average MWRs are all higher than one, and also higher than MWRs estimated for other countries—as shown in more detail in the next section, MWRs of nominal annuities estimated with similar assumptions usually range from 0.9 to levels slightly above 1.0 and are much lower in the case of indexed annuities.

Second, there is a significant variation in individual MWRs, as indicated by the wide difference between maximum and minimum values. Maximum values range roughly from 1.15 to 1.25 and minimum values range from 0.75 to 0.85. These variations reflect to a good extent price differentiation by providers based on the individual characteristics of annuitants, but they may also reflect inefficiencies, as discussed below.

Third, the MWRs of joint annuities are lower than those of single annuities, and the MWRs of single male annuities are lower than those of females. One possible explanation for the lower MWRs of joint annuities (the bulk of the annuities market) is their longer expected duration and consequent greater mortality and reinvestment uncertainty relative to single life annuities. Greater uncertainty would justify an increase in premiums for a given value of benefits, and therefore a lower MWR. However, the same argument would apply to single female annuities relative to males, and yet the MWRs of females turn out to be higher. A possible further explanation is the larger average premium of single female annuitants relative to single male annuitants (Table A1.3), but it is also recognized that the number of single life male cases is small. The relationship between MWRs and premiums will be discussed further below.

Fourth, MWRs of older annuitants are systematically higher than those of younger annuitants, regardless of gender. This positive relationship between MWRs and age can be explained by the greater mortality and reinvestment uncertainty associated with annuities issued to younger ages, and the inclusion of a risk premium (a smaller annuity relative to the premium) by the provider. This result contrasts with those produced by Mitchell et al. (2001) and Brown et al. (2001) for the U.S. and the U.K., respectively, but is consistent with those reported by James, Martinez, and Iglesias (2006) for Chile.

Fifth, there is a positive relationship between MWRs and the size of the premium. This result could be due to the lower unit costs and higher profit margins associated with larger premiums—insurance companies may pay better rates for larger annuity premiums just like banks pay higher interest rates for larger deposits. The positive association could also reflect the more sophisticated market search by educated consumers with higher incomes and larger premiums. These two effects probably offset the longevity effect, which would produce a negative relationship—retirees with higher incomes and larger premiums tend to have higher life expectancies and expose providers to greater risks due to the longer expected duration of their annuities.

Sixth, MWRs of guaranteed annuities are smaller than those of non-guaranteed annuities. The interpretation of this result is confused by the fact that the guarantee can alter the duration, and therefore the reinvestment risk, positively or negatively depending on the length of the guarantee relative to the life expectancy of the annuitant. Long periods of guarantee tend to increase duration, especially at older ages. Finkelstein and Poterba (1999) obtain exactly opposite results for the U.K., and interpret these results as evidence of adverse selection in the U.K. annuity market. According to the argument, individuals who expect to be longer-lived would self-select into non-guaranteed annuities, while individuals who are concerned about the potential for early death would self-select into guaranteed annuities (to leave a bequest or guarantee larger payments for the surviving spouse). If this interpretation is correct, the results in Table A1.4 would suggest the absence of adverse selection in Chile.

Finally, deferment periods seem to make little difference in the value offered to the customer. However, this result may be simply due to the preponderance of very short deferments in the Chilean market.

Econometric Analysis of MWRs

Most empirical studies examine the differences of MWRs across different classes of annuities without testing whether these differences are significant. The large dataset of individual annuities in Chile enables a more formal examination of the main determinants of MWRs, and the testing of whether the relationships identified above are significant. For this purpose we specify the MWR as a function of individual annuitant characteristics, as in equation (3):

$$MWR_{i,t} = f\,(\text{gender}_{i,t}, \text{age}_{i,t}, \text{premium}_{i,t}, \text{guarantee}_{i,t}, \text{deferment}_{i,t}) \qquad (3)$$

Where MWR_i is the money's worth ratio of the annuity bought by individual i at time t, gender and age are the age and gender of the annuitant, respectively, premium is the size of the annuity premium (expressed in logs), and guarantee and deferment are the guaranteed and deferment periods, respectively. Since the bulk of the market is constituted by joint annuities, the equation was estimated using this type of annuity as the base variable and dummies included for single male and single female annuities. Likewise, 1999 was considered as the base year and dummies were included for 2002, 2003, 2004, and 2005. Table A1.5 shows the results obtained through least squares with robust standard errors. This particular specification was selected after conducting a number of specification tests, including the White test for heteroskedasticity of the residuals.

Equation (3) explains about 65 percent of the variations of MWRs within the pooled sample, and the results confirm the signs and significance of all the relationships examined above. MWRs are positively and significantly related to age, in contrast with the results of other researchers for the U.K. and the U.S., indicating that the risk associated with younger ages and longer durations is an important factor in annuity pricing in Chile. MWRs are also positively and significantly related to the size of the premium, indicating that the cost and market search effects offset the longevity effect. MWRs are negatively associated with longer periods of guarantee, again providing support to the hypothesis that

Table A1.5. Main Determinants of MWRs, Pooled Data

Dependent Variable: 100*MWR; Least Squares with Robust Standard Errors

Pooled Data for 1999, 2002, 2003, 2004, and 2005; Observations: 6526

Variable	*Coefficient*	*Std. Error*	*t-Statistic*	*Prob.*
C	62.39024	0.722912	86.30404	0.0000
AGE	0.410145	0.008974	45.70317	0.0000
LOG(PREMIUM)	1.618070	0.073313	22.07059	0.0000
GUARANTEE	−0.134448	0.008383	−16.03824	0.0000
DEFERMENT	0.016582	0.007399	2.241063	0.0251
Male	1.345882	0.206458	6.518928	0.0000
Female	4.023704	0.089566	44.92436	0.0000
2002	10.66352	0.149209	71.46677	0.0000
2003	5.699579	0.152080	37.47739	0.0000
2004	8.253581	0.150549	54.82318	0.0000
2005	6.507061	0.156551	41.56508	0.0000
R-squared	0.639507		Mean dependent var	104.9609
Adjusted R-squared	0.638954		S.D. dependent var	5.600486
S.E. of regression	3.365172		Akaike info criterion	5.266519
Sum squared resid	73778.36		Schwarz criterion	5.277954
Log likelihood	−17173.65		F-statistic	1155.747
Durbin-Watson stat	1.754037		Prob(F-statistic)	0.000000

Source: Authors' estimations on SVS data.

longer durations imply greater risk for the provider and have a negative impact on MWRs.

As mentioned before, the negative coefficient for the guarantee variable could reveal the absence of adverse selection effects in the Chilean annuities market. Alternatively, it could reflect the net result of two different effects. Maybe higher income members with longer life expectancies self-select into non-guaranteed annuities and members with shorter life expectancies self-select into guaranteed ones, but the longevity risk is outweighed by the reinvestment risk. James, Martinez, and Iglesias (2006) examine actual/expected death ratios of guaranteed and non-guaranteed annuitants and show lower ratios for members with non-guaranteed annuities, indicating that individuals with longer life expectancies self-select into these annuities. Although their results are overestimated by the use of outdated mortality tables (the RV-85 and the RV-98), this is a more direct test of self-selection and provides evidence of some adverse selection in the Chilean annuities market. Therefore, the coefficient of the guarantee variable may not provide a robust test for adverse selection.

The positive and significant coefficient for the deferment variable is perhaps surprising, although this result should not be emphasized, given the very short length of deferments in Chile. Moreover, this was the only variable that proved non-significant at the 5 percent level when the equation was estimated separately for each year (these results are shown below). Finally, the signs of the male an female dummy variables are consistent with the relationships among the average MWRs for joint, single male, and single female annuities, although the sign of the female dummy coefficient does not have an obvious explanation.

Overall, the major conclusions to be drawn from this analysis is that, in Chile, there is evidence that annuities with longer expected durations get lower MWRs than annuities with shorter durations, and that larger premiums get better value on average than smaller ones. This is consistent with the view that insurers are concerned with the higher reinvestment and mortality risks presented by long durations and, in the case of size, the effect of fixed expense loadings is more significant in the Chilean market than attempts to differentiate mortality between annuitants of different income levels. An additional factor, the relevance of niche marketing and more sophisticated and price sensitive customers at higher premiums, may also be an explanation.

Additional insights on individual annuity pricing can also be gained by examining the pairs of correlation coefficients across these variables. As shown in Table A1.6, the relationship between premium size and age is positive

Table A1.6. Variable Correlation Matrix

	MWR	*Age*	*Premium*	*Deferment*	*Guarantee*
MWR	1				
Age	0.4626*	1			
Premium	0.1744*	0.0297	1		
Deferment Period	0.0277	−0.0490*	0.0729*	1	
Guaranteed Period	−0.1713*	−0.1455*	0.2077*	0.0962*	1

Source: Authors' calculations.
* Statistically significant correlations.

but not statistically significant. A positive correlation would be expected, as older retirees would have more time to accumulate a higher balance. However, this positive association is weakened by the strong association between annuitization and early retirement in Chile, caused in good part by early retirement rules that facilitate retirement by higher income workers with larger premiums, and also the influence of brokers, who induce early retirement.

The relationship between deferment and age is negative, suggesting that older retirees are less likely to opt for TWs than younger retirees. Given the relatively small volume of such cases, however, and the rational desire for flexibility for younger retirees, this is understandable. The negative and significant relationship between guarantee periods and age suggests a strong reaction by early retirees to the risk of reduction on reversion after the first death, or a stronger bequest motive

Table A1.7. Main Determinants of MWRs, 1999
Dependent Variable: 100*MWR; Least Squares with Robust Standard Errors; Observations: 937

Variable	*Coefficient*	*Std. Error*	*t-Statistic*	*Prob.*
C	60.86516	2.100710	28.97362	0.0000
AGE	0.406372	0.023248	17.47959	0.0000
LOG(PREMIUM)	1.854153	0.227955	8.133850	0.0000
GUARANTEE	−0.136101	0.023538	−5.782169	0.0000
DEFERMENT	−0.006032	0.022320	−0.270278	0.7870
Male	1.639658	0.522999	3.135107	0.0018
Female	4.316622	0.286877	15.04697	0.0000
R-squared	0.407434		Mean dependent var	97.81531
Adjusted R-squared	0.403611		S.D. dependent var	4.899386
S.E. of regression	3.783611		Akaike info criterion	5.506677
Sum squared resid	13313.61		Schwarz criterion	5.542855
Log likelihood	−2572.878		F-statistic	106.5742
Durbin-Watson stat	1.903532		Prob(F-statistic)	0.000000

Source: Authors' calculations.

Table A1.8. Main Determinants of MWRs, 2002
Dependent Variable: 100*MWR; Least Squares with Robust Standard Errors;
Observations: 1,517

Variable	*Coefficient*	*Std. Error*	*t-Statistic*	*Prob.*
C	65.91515	1.296474	50.84185	0.0000
AGE	0.499496	0.016820	29.69642	0.0000
LOG(PREMIUM)	1.862513	0.144434	12.89526	0.0000
GUARANTEE	−0.118013	0.016261	−7.257291	0.0000
DEFERMENT	0.025761	0.015423	1.670247	0.0951
Male	1.352054	0.394186	3.429992	0.0006
Female	4.419103	0.179380	24.63540	0.0000
R-squared	0.536716	Mean dependent var		107.9591
Adjusted R-squared	0.534875	S.D. dependent var		4.709875
S.E. of regression	3.212139	Akaike info criterion		5.176355
Sum squared resid	15579.93	Schwarz criterion		5.200924
Log likelihood	−3919.265	F-statistic		291.5563
Durbin-Watson stat	1.614660	Prob(F-statistic)		0.000000

Source: Authors' calculations.

Table A1.9. Main Determinants of MWRs, 2003
Dependent Variable: 100*MWR; Least Squares with Robust Standard Errors;
Observations: 1,191

Variable	*Coefficient*	*Std. Error*	*t-Statistic*	*Prob.*
C	70.19722	1.505577	46.62479	0.0000
AGE	0.406500	0.018254	22.26915	0.0000
LOG(PREMIUM)	1.356398	0.142582	9.513102	0.0000
GUARANTEE	−0.133558	0.016452	−8.117811	0.0000
DEFERMENT	0.020258	0.013499	1.500708	0.1337
Male	2.042872	0.376537	5.425418	0.0000
Female	3.864239	0.220587	17.51798	0.0000
R-squared	0.478898	Mean dependent var		103.5660
Adjusted R-squared	0.476257	S.D. dependent var		4.219287
S.E. of regression	3.053501	Akaike info criterion		5.076315
Sum squared resid	11039.46	Schwarz criterion		5.106187
Log likelihood	−3015.945	F-statistic		181.3513
Durbin-Watson stat	1.269357	Prob(F-statistic)		0.000000

Source: Authors' calculations.

among early retirees. The positive association between premiums and the length of guarantee periods indicates that higher income annuitants are more willing and capable of buying the guarantee, i.e., accepting a discount in the early payments relative to the premium in exchange for larger payments for the surviving spouse.

Table A1.10. Main Determinants of MWRs, 2004
Dependent Variable: 100*MWR; Least Squares with Robust Standard Errors;
Observations: 1,490

Variable	*Coefficient*	*Std. Error*	*t-Statistic*	*Prob.*
C	74.47563	1.466312	50.79111	0.0000
AGE	0.380927	0.018095	21.05134	0.0000
LOG(PREMIUM)	1.335759	0.146455	9.120596	0.0000
GUARANTEE	−0.141260	0.017002	−8.308617	0.0000
DEFERMENT	0.018659	0.014863	1.255400	0.2095
Male	0.896550	0.455371	1.968831	0.0492
Female	4.289322	0.172651	24.84389	0.0000
R-squared	0.465397	Mean dependent var		106.3872
Adjusted R-squared	0.463234	S.D. dependent var		4.509411
S.E. of regression	3.303790	Akaike info criterion		5.232704
Sum squared resid	16186.98	Schwarz criterion		5.257634
Log likelihood	−3891.365	F-statistic		215.1699
Durbin-Watson stat	1.798048	Prob(F-statistic)		0.000000

Source: Authors' calculations.

Table A1.11. Main Determinants of MWRs, 2005
Dependent Variable: 100*MWR; Least Squares with Robust Standard Errors;
Observations: 1,391

Variable	*Coefficient*	*Std. Error*	*t-Statistic*	*Prob.*
C	72.51743	1.879981	38.57349	0.0000
AGE	0.347256	0.024670	14.07629	0.0000
LOG(PREMIUM)	1.667719	0.165144	10.09859	0.0000
GUARANTEE	−0.137314	0.019536	−7.028687	0.0000
DEFERMENT	0.017231	0.016807	1.025200	0.3054
Male	0.847786	0.554230	1.529663	0.1263
Female	3.600156	0.184605	19.50199	0.0000
R-squared	0.407568	Mean dependent var		106.1712
Adjusted R-squared	0.405000	S.D. dependent var		4.506864
S.E. of regression	3.476427	Akaike info criterion		5.334907
Sum squared resid	16726.39	Schwarz criterion		5.361265
Log likelihood	−3703.427	F-statistic		158.6889
Durbin-Watson stat	2.027204	Prob(F-statistic)		0.000000

Source: Authors' calculations.

Tables A1.7 through A1.11 present the results obtained for individual years, showing that equation (3) explains 40–50 percent of the variations in MWRs in each year. The coefficients have the same signs as those obtained in the pooled sample and are significant, except for the deferment variable, which proved non-significant at the 5 percent level in all individual years.

Analysis of Dispersion of MWRs

An efficient and transparent annuities market should produce similar prices (or MWRs) for customers with similar characteristics. The results above indicate that annuity pricing is influenced by the characteristics of the annuitant such as age and gender, but the regression does not explain a relatively large share of the variations of MWRs across individual annuitants and over time. The unexplained variations in MWRs could be simply due to the absence of key explanatory variables, such as the level of education of individual annuitants and their geographical location, as well as variables capturing provider characteristics. These limitations could not be overcome, as the dataset on individual annuities used to compute MWRs does not provide information on providers or further information on the characteristics of annuitants, beyond those explored above.

The dispersion of MWRs could also be due to institutional and regulatory inefficiencies, such as the lack of a transparent pricing system and the excessive influence of brokers. The influence of these factors may be examined, because during this period there were substantial efforts to improve market transparency. As mentioned in Chapters 2 and 5, a major development in the annuities market was the passage of a new Pensions Law in 2004 that, among other factors, introduced a cap on broker's commissions and an electronic quotation system that allows easy and transparent comparisons of annuity and PW prices. The draft of the Pensions Law was first submitted to Congress in 2000, and it is possible that the market started changing behavior in anticipation of the Law's approval. Such change in behavior was observed in the sharp reduction in broker's commissions after 1999 (Chapters 2 and 5). If annuity rates became the main element of price competition, as opposed to marketing activity and sales tactics that included cash rebates to annuitants, it would be reasonable to expect less dispersion of MWRs.

As shown in Table A1.12, there was indeed a significant reduction in the dispersion of MWRs after 1999, measured by the decline in the coefficient of variation. Moreover, the reduction in dispersion was more pronounced in the bottom third of the market, i.e., for annuitants with lower premiums and incomes. Whereas in 1999 the coefficient of variation in the bottom third of the market was roughly equal to that of the whole market, in 2004 and 2005 it was significantly lower. The decline in the coefficient of variation was not continuous over the whole period (it was lowest in 2002 for the bottom third and lowest in 2003 for the whole market), but this is probably due to the fact that MWRs were computed only for

Table A1.12. Mean, Standard Deviation, and Coefficient of Variation of MWRs in Different Years

	March 1999		*March 2002*		*March 2003*		*March 2004*		*March 2005*	
	Bottom Third	*All MWRs*	*Bottom Third*	*All MWRs*	*Bottom Third*	*All MWRs*	*Bottom Third*	*All MWRs*	*Bottom Third*	*All MWRs*
Mean	0.980	0.980	1.077	1.080	1.034	1.036	1.060	1.064	1.055	1.062
Std. Dev.	0.049	0.049	0.041	0.047	0.043	0.042	0.042	0.045	0.041	0.045
Coef. Var.	4.956	5.009	3.807	4.363	4.137	4.074	3.942	4.239	3.928	4.245

Source of raw data: SVS.

the months of March of each year, and not for the whole year, and there were probably specific factors affecting MWRs in those particular months.

The reduction in the dispersion of MWRs after 1999 is also illustrated in Figure A1.1, which shows the residuals around a simple regression of MWRs against individual premiums in 1999 and 2005. It is also apparent in Figure A1.1 that the reduction in the dispersion of MWRs was stronger at the lower end of the market. Overall, these results are consistent with the sharp decline in broker's commissions after 1999 and probably also reflect a change in the behavior of market participants after the submission of the new Pensions Law to Congress in 2000.[7] The fact that the reduction in the dispersion of MWRs was more pronounced for lower premiums is a positive development, as these MWRs are generally related to lower income annuitants without complementary sources of retirement income.

Whereas the dispersion of MWRs declined after the submission of the draft Pensions Law to Congress in 2000, the effects of the actual approval and implementation of the Law in 2004 are less clear. As shown in Table A1.12, the coefficient of variation declined further in the bottom third of the market in March of 2005, relative to March 2004, but increased slightly for the whole market in the same period. This is somewhat surprising, as the actual implementation of the Law in mid-2004 seems to have generated further efficiency gains, as indicated by the further decline in broker's commissions and evidence that annuity pricing has been based on the best quotes produced by the new quotation system (Chapters 2 and 5). Therefore, it would be reasonable to expect a further reduction in the dispersion of MWRs in 2005.[8]

It is possible that the lack of clear evidence on the reduced dispersion of MWRs in 2005 is simply due to the limited amount of information,

Figure A1.1. MWRs and Premiums in 1999 and 2005

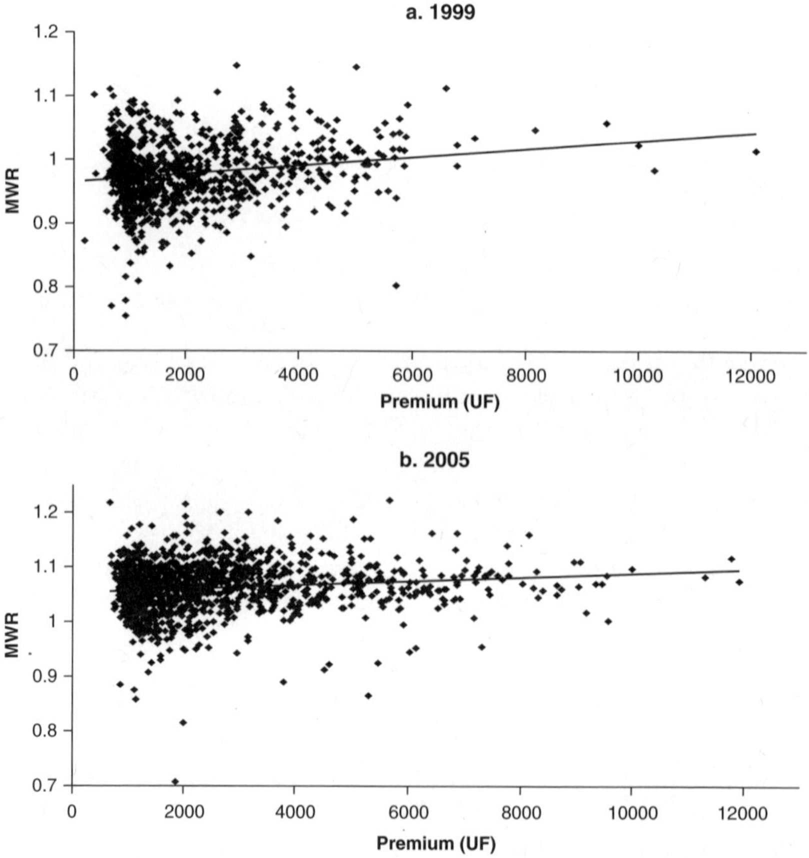

Source: Authors' calculations.

based only on one month. Moreover, the coefficient of variation is a limited statistic, as it does not control for changes in the individual determinants of MWRs. The White test for heteroskedasticity of the residuals controls for such changes and provides some evidence, albeit limited, that dispersion declined in 2005. As shown in Table A1.13, the coefficients of the year dummies were all negative and significant, except for 2002, indicating that the dispersion of MWRs declined relative to 1999, the base year. Moreover, the coefficient of the 2005 dummy is higher than the 2004 dummy in absolute value, indicating that the dispersion of MWRs

Table A1.13. White Heteroskedasticity Test

*Obs*R-squared*	*241.1479*	*Probability*	*0.00000*

Test Equation Dependent Variable: RESID^2; Least Squares
Pooled Data for 1999, 2002, 2003, 2004, and 2005; Observations: 6526

Variable	*Coefficient*	*Std. Error*	*t-Statistic*	*Prob.*
C	141.1213	79.19219	1.782010	0.0748
AGE	−7.339350	1.377755	−5.327035	0.0000
AGE^2	0.069465	0.011813	5.880583	0.0000
LOG(PREMIUM)	17.71593	17.36348	1.020298	0.3076
(LOG(PREMIUM))^2	−1.177378	1.138494	−1.034154	0.3011
GUARANTEE	−1.416413	0.228646	-6.194797	0.0000
GUARANTEE^2	0.068083	0.012801	5.318755	0.0000
DEFERMENT	0.243182	0.151408	1.606134	0.1083
DEFERMENT^2	0.008477	0.006064	1.398003	0.1622
Male	11.85092	1.736567	6.824335	0.0000
Female	−2.340857	1.155242	−2.026291	0.0428
2002	−2.758191	1.621989	−1.700499	0.0891
2003	−4.945800	1.704210	−2.902108	0.0037
2004	−3.741583	1.629701	−2.295870	0.0217
2005	−3.841310	1.688727	−2.274677	0.0230

R-squared	0.036952	Mean dependent var	11.30530
Adjusted R-squared	0.034881	S.D. dependent var	39.62918
S.E. of regression	38.93189	Akaike info criterion	10.16380
Sum squared resid	9868670.	Schwarz criterion	10.17939
Log likelihood	−33149.48	F-statistic	17.84465
Durbin-Watson stat	1.947129	Prob(F-statistic)	0.00000

Source: Authors' calculations.

declined from 2004 to 2005, after controlling for changes in the determinants of MWRs, albeit by a limited amount.

More research on MWRs is merited, because price dispersion in March of 2005 still seemed significant, and a closer inspection of the sample revealed several cases where the annuitants' age, gender, premium, and terms of the annuity purchased were similar, but MWRs were different. As mentioned before, there is separate evidence that the new quotation system has enhanced the transparency of the Chilean annuities market and has ensured that pricing is effectively based on the best quotes (Chapter 5). The systematic computation of MWRs would provide further evidence as to whether the new quotation system is indeed eliminating market inefficiencies and reducing differences that cannot be explained by individual risk characteristics.

Comparisons with Other Empirical Studies

Comparisons with MWR Estimates for Other Countries

Comparing MWRs in Chile with those estimated by other researchers for other countries provides many additional insights into the performance of the Chilean annuities market. Such a comparison is done in two steps. The first involves a comparison of MWRs calculated with cohort annuitant tables and the risk-free rate. As mentioned before, this is the measure that reflects most accurately the value of the annuity to the average consumer (the annuitant), and the one most commonly used for international comparisons. The second step involves a comparison of MWRs also calculated with the cohort annuitant table, but discounted with the corporate bond rate. This measure captures more accurately the cost of the annuity to providers.

Table A1.14 shows a selected number of MWRs in Chile, estimated for annuities issued in March 2004. The MWRs are computed with the most updated cohort annuitant table (the cohortized RV-04) and two discount rates—the risk-free rate and the corporate bond rate.[9] Tables A1.15 and A1.16 summarize the results obtained for other countries by other researchers, using similar parameters. Most MWRs computed for other countries are nominal, i.e., they related to nominal annuities. This reflects the absence of indexed annuities in most countries – the United Kingdom is the only country in this sample that has developed indexed annuities as well. Table A1.15 also shows indexed MWRs for the U.S., based on quotations of indexed annuities by a life insurance company (ILONA). These annuities have not been sold in the U.S. market, but are also shown for purposes of illustration.

Table A1.14. Money's Worth Ratios in Chile, March 2004, Computed with Cohort Annuitant Tables and Alternative Discount Rates

	Risk-Free Rate	*Corporate Bond Rate*
All cases	1.064	0.904
- maximum	1.276	1.146
- minimum	0.876	0.740
Male, Age 55	1.049	0.897
Male, Age 65	1.086	0.955
Female, Age 55	1.076	0.905
Female, Age 65	1.105	0.971
Joint (65–60)	1.078	0.892

Source: Authors' calculations.

Table A1.15. Money's Worth Ratios in Selected Countries Computed with Cohort Annuitant Table and Risk-Free Rate

	Australia (James)	*Canada (James)*	*Switzerl (James)*	*UK[1] (James)*	*UK (Cannon)*	*UK[2] (James)*	*UK[3] (Brown)*
Nominal Annuities							
Male, Age 55	–	–	–	–	–	0.921	0.934
Male, Age 65	1.013	0.981	1.046	–	0.977	0.908	0.927
Female, Age 55	–	–	–	–	–	0.928	0.937
Female, Age 65	1.002	0.976	1.036	-	0.979	0.907	0.927
Joint	0.988	0.980	0.985	0.981	0.987	–	0.929
Indexed Annuities							
Male, Age 55	–	–	–	–	–	0.867	–
Male, Age 65	–	–	–	–	0.887	0.854	0.822
Female, Age 55	–	–	–	–	–	0.876	–
Female, Age 65	–	–	–	–	0.877	0.857	0.782
Joint	–	–	–	–	0.880	–	–

Sources: Brown et al. (2001) ; James, Song, and Vittas (2001) ; Cannon and Tonk (2004).
Notes: 1 Cannon and Tonks' estimate is the overall average; 2 For males 60 and 65 and females 60 and 65; 3 MWR for indexed annuities in the U.S. relate to annuities offered by Irish Life of North America (ILONA), which have never been sold.

Table A1.16. Money's Worth Ratios in Selected Countries Computed with Cohort Annuitant Table and Corporate Bond Rate

	Australia (James)	*Canada (James)*	*Switzerl (James)*	*UK[1] (James)*	*UK (Cannon)*	*UK[2] (James)*	*UK[3] (Brown)*
Nominal Annuities							
Male, Age 55	–	–	–	–	–	–	0.840
Male, Age 65	0.896	0.879	0.944	–	0.879	–	0.853
Female, Age 55	–	–	–	–	–	–	0.838
Female, Age 65	0.865	0.864	0.916	–	0.860	–	0.847
Joint	0.846	0.868	0.875	–	0.873	–	0.841
Indexed Annuities							
Male, Age 55	–	–	–	–	–	–	–
Male, Age 65	–	–	–	–	0.784	–	–
Female, Age 55	–	–	–	–	–	–	–
Female, Age 65	–	–	–	–	0.747	–	–
Joint	–	–	–	–	–	–	–

Notes and sources: See Table A1.11.

As shown in Tables A1.14 and A1.15, the average MWRs estimated for Chile are higher than the average nominal MWRs estimated for all other countries, across all classes of annuitants. The differences between the

Chilean MWRs and the MWRs of indexed annuities in the U.K. and the U.S. are striking, amounting to roughly 20 percent. The average MWRs in the U.S. and U.K. decline with age, unlike the Chilean case. The MWRs for males and females tend to be very similar in other countries, unlike the Chilean case. MWRs of joint annuities are very similar or lower than single annuities, more similar to the pattern in Chile.

The first conclusion from a comparison of Tables A1.14 and A1.15 is that Chilean annuitants have got a better deal than annuitants in other countries, especially considering that Chilean annuities are indexed. Buyers of indexed annuities in the United Kingdom get a much lower annuity value of 86 percent of the premium, and pay a charge of about 5 percent of the premium to obtain inflation protection. The cost of inflation protection in the United States is even higher, amounting to more than 20 percent of the premium. This result is in part explained by the large supply of indexed instruments in the Chilean case—unlike their British and American counterparts, Chilean providers have access not only to indexed Government bonds, but also to many other higher yield instruments indexed to inflation, and that allows them to hedge inflation risk while obtaining more attractive returns.

Workers who retire early get lower MWRs in Chile. As mentioned before, this result is explained by the higher reinvestment and mortality risks associated with annuities with longer expected duration. The opposite result in the U.K. and the U.S. cannot be easily interpreted. Longer expected duration also explains the lower MWRs of joint annuities in Chile, and it is noteworthy that joint annuities have similar or lower MWRs in other countries as well. On the other hand, the differences between MWRs of single male and single female annuities in Chile cannot be easily explained. The larger premiums in the case of single females partly explain the higher MWRs, but even controlling for this factor, MWRs of single female annuities remain higher than those of males, as noted above. It is possible that these results are due to the small number of single male annuities.

An important question that arises in the Chilean case is whether these high MWRs are sustainable. The increase in MWRs to levels higher has been accompanied by negative spreads vis-á-vis the risk-free rate, raising the issue as to whether providers are able to generate profits in the annuity business. As shown in Figure A1.2, the average annuity rate reported by providers was lower than the average risk-free rate in 1999, but since the early 2000s the average annuity rate has exceeded the risk-free rate, a result that is unusual by international comparison. For example, Brown

Figure A1.2. Annuity Rate and Interest Rates on Central Bank Bonds and Corporate Bonds (% p.a.), 1993–2005

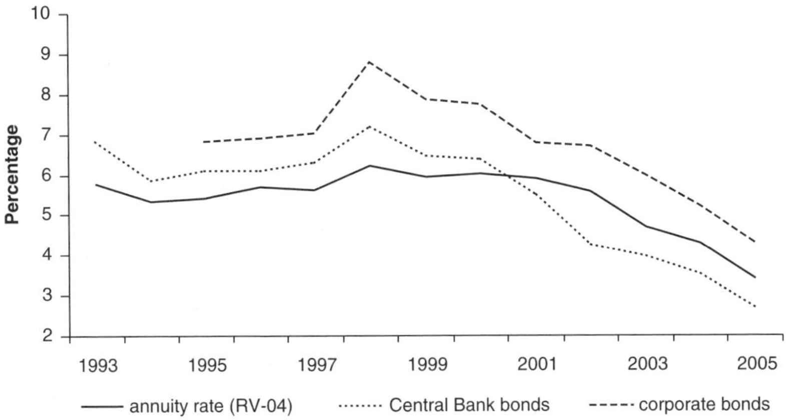

Source: Staff analysis on SVS data.

et al. (2001) compute the internal rates of return on U.S. annuities and obtains rates ranging from 5.9 to 6.5 percent p.a., lower than the yields of 10- and 30-year Treasury bonds, which were 7.1 and 7.3 percent p.a. in the same period. James, Song, and Vittas (2001) perform the same exercise for several countries and obtain similar results.[10]

Annuity providers can still achieve positive financial spreads and generate profits investing in higher yield paper, and Figure A1.2 indicates that a portfolio of corporate bonds would have generate returns exceeding the annuity rate by 100–120 basis points in 2002–2005. However, this strategy implies excessive concentration of risks in one asset class. Moreover, providers also have to pay for brokers' commissions, cover their operating costs, make an allowance for several risks such a default risk, and generate an adequate return on equity. Therefore, both the MWRs and the spreads estimated for recent years indicate a situation that may not be sustainable.

An international comparison of MWRs estimated with a higher discount rate yields similar conclusions. As shown in Table A1.14, the average MWR for 2004 drops from 1.06 to 0.9 when it is computed with the corporate bond rate. However, MWRs for representative classes of annuities in Chile remain significantly higher than the corresponding averages for other countries, as shown in Table A1.16. This suggests thin margins for Chilean providers on a present value basis, possibly making some providers unable to cover all costs and risks and still generate a positive profit margin. As discussed in Chapter 2, it is possible that the high MWRs observed in recent years reflect aggressive pricing strategies by some providers and that MWRs computed with the risk-free rate will eventually decline to levels closer to one with the ongoing industry consolidation.

Comparisons with Other Estimates for Chile

This section compares the MWRs estimated in this report with those estimated by James, Iglesias, and Martinez (2005). Their study computes MWRs using data on quoted annuities from four insurance companies in March 1999 and March 2003. The MWRs are calculated using three alternative mortality tables, two different discount rates, and two different premium levels. The mortality tables are the RV-85 and the RV-98 in period form, and the RV-98 in a cohort form using rates of mortality improvement from the Canadian Institute of Actuaries. The two discount rates used are the risk-free rate and the corporate bond rate. The MWRs are estimated for premiums of UF 1,000 and UF 4,000. Table A1.17 reproduces their MWRs for 1999 and 2003 while Table A1.18 reproduces our estimates for the same years to facilitate comparisons.

As shown in Tables A1.17 and 18, our MWRs computed with the risk-free rate for 1999 are roughly equal to those presented by James et al. for joint annuities, only slightly higher in the case of single males age 65, and higher in the case of single females age 60. The results are somewhat surprising, especially for single male and joint annuities, because the differences between the period RV-98 and the cohort RV-04 (see Table A1.1) should lead to larger differences between MWRs. Moreover, our MWRs

Table A1.17. Money's Worth Ratios for Chile Estimated by James, Martinez, and Iglesias (2006) for 1999 and 2003

	March 1999	*March 2003*			
	RV-98 Period Risk-free rate UF1, 000 Premium	*RV-98 Period Risk-free rate UF1, 000 Premium*	*RV-98 Cohort Risk-free rate UF1, 000 Premium*	*RV-98 Cohort Risk-free rate UF4, 000 Premium*	*RV-98 Cohort Corp. bond rate UF1, 000 Premium*
Male, 65	0.979	0.981	1.012	1.013	0.905
Male, 55	–	0.941	0.976	0.999	0.879
Female, 60	0.963	0.925	0.958	0.992	0.845
Female, 55	–	0.899	0.929	0.977	0.810
Joint	1.000	0.977	1.008	1.025	0.883

Source: James, Martinez, and Iglesias 2006.

Table A1.18. Money's Worth Ratios for Chile Estimated by This Report, 1999 and 2003

	March 1999	*March 2003*	
	RV-04 Cohort Risk-free rate Average	*RV-04 Cohort Risk-free rate Average*	*RV-04 Cohort Corporate bond rate Average*
Male, 65	0.996	1.069	0.955
Male, 55	0.981	1.049	0.897
Female, 60	1.021	1.077	0.971
Female, 55	0.994	1.049	0.905
Joint	0.998	1.050	0.892

Source: Authors' calculations.

are estimated from the total universe of actual sales, while James et al. use a sample of quoted annuities from four companies. Since annuity sales tend to reflect the best quotes, MWRs based on sales should be higher than those estimated from quotes.

Our MWRs computed with the risk-free rate for 2003 are higher than those presented by James et al. for the same year, with the differences ranging from 3 to 10 percent. Again, the differences are larger in the case of females. These differences are more consistent with the differences between the mortality tables, especially regarding female mortality rates, as well as the differences between annuity sales and annuity quotes. However, it is noteworthy that our MWRs increase between 1999 and 2003 while the MWRs estimated by James et al. remain stable or even decrease. This stability of MWRs is at odds with the behavior of the risk-free rate-annuity rate differential in the same period. As shown in Figure A1.2, the relation between the risk-free rate and the annuity rate would only be consistent with MWRs lower than one in 1999 and higher than one in subsequent years, including 2003.

The main conclusion of James et al., namely, that Chilean MWRs are high by international comparison and that Chilean annuitants have a good deal for their money is the same as the one reached in this report, but their numbers probably underestimate the true MWRs in March 2003. In addition to the use of an outdated mortality table, it is possible that their results are also being affected by a small and nonrepresentative sample of annuity quotes. The risk-free yield curve used for discounting is probably different and may also be contributing to the different results.

Conclusions

By any measure, the results in Chile indicate good value for consumers. In part, this can be explained by the larger supply of assets indexed to consumer prices in Chile, including higher yield indexed instruments such as mortgage, corporate, and infrastructure bonds. (Annex 2 provides separate evidence that the annuity rate is positively correlated with the share of higher yield assets in the portfolios of providers.) In other countries, providers are either exposed to inflation risk, due to the absence of indexed instruments, or can only access lower yield indexed instruments such as indexed Government bonds.

The high MWRs may also reflect aggressive pricing behavior in a very competitive annuities market. It is interesting to note that the *structure* of MWRs suggests efficient risk differentiation—MWRs are higher for customers that present relatively lower reinvestment and mortality risk to the provider. That is, annuities with a shorter expected duration tend to have higher ratios than those with a longer duration. However, the overall *levels* of MWRs seem excessive, suggesting that providers may be either counting on future increases in interest rates, or deliberately accepting temporary losses to drive competitors out of the market and gain market share. (Annex 2 provides separate evidence that the annuity rate increases with the level of competition, and decreases for larger firms with established market share.)

Although individual annuitant characteristics explain a significant share of variations in MWRs, a large share of these variations remains unexplained. The dispersion of MWRs \has decreased since March 1999, reflecting the threat imposed by the submission of the draft Pension Law to Congress. There is evidence, albeit limited, that dispersion of MWRs declined further in March 2005, possibly reflecting the approval and implementation of the Pensions Law in 2004, especially the new electronic quotation system. More research on MWRs is merited, to confirm whether the new quotation system has indeed resulted in the elimination of price inefficiencies and a reduction in price dispersion. More generally, the new system is an important and welcome innovation, and its outcomes should be closely and frequently monitored by regulators in Chile and other countries.

Notes

1. As noted in Chapters 2 and 5, the Pension Law approved in 2004 has allowed other types of annuities, but all the MWRs presented

in this report refer to annuities fixed in UFs, i.e., annuities indexed to prices.

2. See, e.g., Brown et al. (2001); and James, Song, and Vittas (2001).
3. A standard battery of statistical tests is set out in Benjamin and Pollard (2001) and has been applied to the RV-2004 tables separately for male and female tables. In the case of each test, the representative table used in these calculations is found to pass the test - that is, the table reflects the underlying mortality experience.
4. The authors of the report are grateful to the assistance provided by Messrs. Klaus Schmidt-Hebel and Jorge Perez of the Central Bank of Chile. The Central Bank adjustments result in higher yields than those generated by the direct application of the RiskAmerica software. The adjustments and the averaging still resulted in negative real interest rates for very short maturities in some years, but the results did not change significantly when the MWRs were estimated imposing minimum real interest rates of 0 percent.
5. This problem is recognized by Cannon and Tonks (2004).
6. The month of March was selected simply to allow comparisons with previous estimates made by other researchers.
7. Annex 2 provides an econometric analysis of the annuity rate with company data and shows through formal econometric testing that there were structural shifts in the annuities market after submission of the draft Pensions Law to Congress in 2000.
8. In general, market anticipations of a future event reflect the probability that such an event will take place in the future. The drop in broker's commissions after 2000 reveals that the draft Law was credible and the effects of its future approval were being strongly anticipated by market participants. However, the full adjustment of the market could only be expected after the realization of the expected event, that is, the approval of the Law in August 2004 and its implementation in the following months.
9. The conclusions would not be substantially affected if 2002, 2003, or 2005 were used as the basis for comparisons. The year 2004 was chosen because it was the last year for which MWRs were computed both with the risk-free rate and the higher corporate bond rate.
10. The annuity rate in this report is defined as the internal rate of return on the annuity contract, thus comparable with the results in Brown et al., and with the yield on financial instruments. Other researchers (Orszag [2001], Cannon and Tonks [2004]) define the annuity rate as the ratio of the annuity payment over the premium. This indicator is much higher than the internal rate of return on annuities—in

Chile this indicator exceeds the annuity rate by more than 200 basis points. It is a useful indicator that can be easily computed and used to track the annuity rate (the two series are highly correlated), but is not directly comparable to the yield of financial instruments. The ratio of payments to the principal is only equal to the internal rate of return in the case of perpetuities or consols.

ANNEX 2

An Econometric Analysis of the Annuity Rate in Chile*

Introduction

This annex examines the main determinants of annuity rates in Chile, based on data reported by life insurance companies to the Insurance Supervisory Agency—the *Superintendencia de Valores y Seguros* (SVS). The analysis of annuity rates presented in this annex complements the analysis of money's worth ratios presented in the previous annex by introducing company-level data. The analysis in Annex 1 is based on a sample of individual annuities, which contains information on the individual annuitant such as age and gender, but does not contain information on the annuity provider. The analysis in Annex 2, on the other hand, is based on company-level data, which contain information on the provider but not information on individual annuitants. Ideally, money's worth ratios and annuity rates should be both examined combining individual and provider characteristics, but there is no database that contains such information.[1]

*Marco Morales coauthored this annex with Roberto Rocha and Craig Thorburn. Sara Zervos and Ying Lin provided valuable inputs in the early stages of the analysis.

This annex is structured as follows. The next section presents a heuristic model of the supply and demand for annuities, and discusses the main determinants of the annuity rate. The third section provides an analysis of the data used in the regressions. The fourth section presents a number of preliminary tests designed to identify the most appropriate estimation model. This includes tests for non-stationarity, model specification, and autocorrelation. The fifth section presents and discusses the estimation results. Finally, the sixth and last section summarizes the main findings and conclusions.

A Heuristic Model of the Annuity Rate

The annuity rate (defined as the internal rate of return on annuities, as in the remainder of the report) is determined by the interaction of the flow demand and flow supply of annuities. The theoretical derivation of the flow demand and supply of annuities would require solving models of intertemporal maximization for consumers and providers and is beyond the scope of this annex. Instead, this section follows a heuristic approach, examining the most important determinants of the annuity rate based on the factors that may affect the flow demand and supply of this product, both at the aggregate and at the company levels.

The aggregate flow demand for annuities in any given period of time (e.g., a year) is determined by five major groups of factors: (i) the retirement rules, combined with the demographic structure of the working population; (ii) the history of contributions and the return performance of pension funds during the accumulation phase; (iii) the menu of retirement instruments, including lump sums; (iv) the rate of return on annuities vis-à-vis alternative retirement instruments; (v) the risk profile and preferences of retiring workers. Each of these major groups of determinants is briefly examined below.

Retirement rules and the demographic structure of the working population together define the number of workers eligible for retirement in any given year, and the universe of potential annuitants in that year. For example, an increase in the normal retirement age, or more stringent conditions for early retirement produce a decline in the number of retiring workers and a resulting contraction in the flow demand for all retirement products, including annuities.

The historic performance of pension funds (and the history of contributions) also affects the demand for annuities because it defines the size of the pension balance for any given cohort. For example, a prolonged and sustained period of higher returns results in larger pension balances, possibly leading several cohorts to anticipate retirement and increase the demand for all retirement products, including annuities. By contrast, large capital losses and negative returns on pension savings in the years preceding retirement may lead several workers to postpone retirement in order to achieve their target retirement income. A sharp drop in returns may also cause many retirees to fail to meet legal criteria for early retirement.

The menu of retirement products is also a very important determinant of the aggregate demand for annuities. When lump sums are allowed, the demand for annuities may be weak due to the adverse selection effect that has been extensively examined in the literature. The demand for annuities may be particularly weak if retiring workers are already covered by a social security benefit, i.e., if they are already substantially "annuitized." However, Chilean retirees do not receive a separate social security benefit, and lump sums are severely restricted. These restrictions appear to increase the potential demand for annuities in the Chilean case.

The aggregate demand for annuities also depends on the level of the annuity rate vis-à-vis the return on PWs, which is the only alternative retirement instrument in the Chilean case—if lump sums were allowed, retiring workers could also try to manage their own accumulated savings and produce their own retirement income outside the annuity market, but this is not possible as indicated above. Finally, the demand for annuities depends on behavioral parameters such as the degree of risk aversion and the desire of retiring cohorts to leave bequests. However, these factors are important at the individual level but less important at the aggregate level, because it is unlikely that they change significantly across different retiring cohorts.

The aggregate flow supply of annuities is derived from a long-run profit maximization process of all annuity providers that takes into consideration the current and expected returns on financial assets, annuity rates, operating costs, and proper consideration of all the complex risks involved in the annuity business, including longevity, reinvestment, and credit risk. Like banks, annuity providers also operate with intermediation spreads and attempt to maximize this spread adjusted for risk. The difference lies in the much longer time horizon involved in the annuity business and the greater complexity of the risks in the annuity contract.

Figure A2.1 provides a useful starting point for analyzing the interaction of the flow aggregate demand and flow aggregate supply of annuities in Chile, and its impact on the annuity rate. The aggregate flow demand for annuities is shown as the upward sloping curve in Figure A2.1.

Figure A2.1. Supply and Demand for Annuities

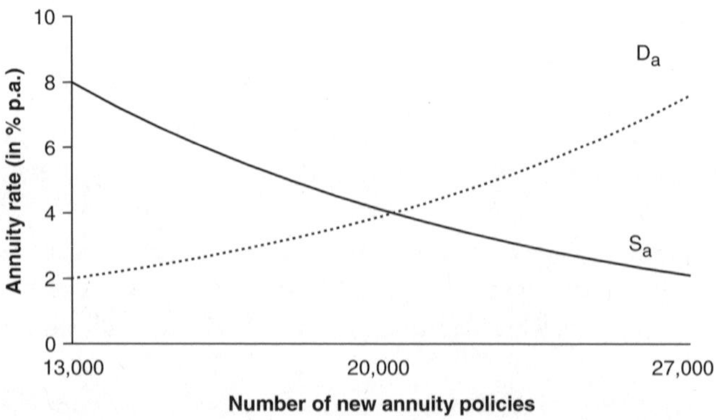

Source: Authors' schematic.

A reduction in the annuity rate results, other things being held constant, in a decline in the demand for annuities (measured by the number of new annuity policies in a given period of time) for two reasons. First, PWs (the alternative retirement product) become more attractive, leading new retirees to choose this instrument at the expense of annuities. Second, workers eligible for retirement may decide to postpone retirement, hoping for an increase in the annuity rates in subsequent years. They may also decide to retire but defer the annuity, also hoping for an increase in annuity rates.

As mentioned before, stricter conditions for retirement or poor pension fund performance in the preretirement period would both cause a reduction in the flow demand for annuities—in Figure A2.1 the demand curve would shift to the left. More interesting to the purpose of the exercise is the analysis of changes in interest rates and other market conditions. A general increase in interest rates vis-à-vis the annuity rate would imply an increase in PW returns and lead to a contraction in the aggregate demand for annuities.[2] Other factors that could affect the aggregate demand for annuities include a move by all annuity providers towards riskier portfolio strategies or increased leverage. The perception of greater risk associated with annuities could lead potential annuitants to demand a risk premium, also shifting the demand curve to the left.

The aggregate flow supply of annuities is shown as the downward sloping curve in Figure A2.1. The aggregate supply is downward sloping because the annuity rate is the basic cost of issuing new annuity contracts.

An increase in annuity rates relative to the interest rates on financial assets implies a reduction in intermediation spreads and profit margins for annuity providers, and a loss of enthusiasm in issuing new annuity policies. A general increase in interest rates for the same annuity rate implies an increase in spreads and profit margins and would lead to a supply expansion—in Figure A2.1 the aggregate supply would shift to the right. Changes in market structure resulting in greater industry concentration and increased monopoly power would lead to a contraction in the aggregate supply—in Figure A2.1 the aggregate supply would shift to the left.

Market equilibrium is illustrated in Figure A2.1 with an annuity rate of 4 percent and 20,000 new annuities issued within one year (these are roughly the figures for 2003). A general increase in interest rates would lead to a contraction in demand and an expansion in supply, with ambiguous effects on the flows of new annuities, but producing an unambiguous increase in annuity rates. This simple framework also allows the analysis of the impact of other variables on the annuity rate. For example, a general portfolio shift from Government bonds to higher yield corporate bonds could result in an expanded supply of annuities and a higher annuity rate. Providers would expand supply and increase the annuity rate if they could extract an increase in the risk-adjusted return. This would be possible if the yield on corporate bonds contained a liquidity premium. If annuitants perceive an increase in risk and demand a risk premium, the aggregate demand would contract, reinforcing the increase in the annuity rate. Again, the effect on the new flows of annuities is ambiguous, but the impact on the annuity rate is unambiguously positive.

The equilibrium depicted in Figure A2.1, where the market is cleared by one annuity rate, admittedly simplifies the structure and organization of annuity markets. First, the market comprises several types of annuities and rates. Second, adverse selection may restrict severely the overall size of the market and for some risk segments there may not be a market clearing annuity rate. In a scenario of high and volatile interest rates the market may also collapse, as providers may require very high spreads or even refuse to take the underwriting risk. However, if the potential annuitant population is large, because the private pension system is mandatory, adverse selection is reduced by restrictions on lump sums, and macroeconomic conditions are stable—the conditions observed in Chile during the 1990s and early 2000s—this simple framework can be applied as the basis for an empirical analysis of the annuity rate.

In the case of Chile, therefore, it seems possible to specify an annuity rate equation as a reduced form equation of an underlying structural model of the demand for and the supply of annuities. Introducing company-level characteristics, such a reduced form equation can be written as:

$$AR_{j,t} = f(\overset{+}{RF_t}, \overset{+}{ROFI_t}, \overset{+}{SOFI_{j,t}}, \overset{+}{ROA_{j,t}}, \overset{+}{SOA_{j,t}}, \overset{+-}{LEV_{j,t}}, \overset{-}{MIS_{j,t}}, \overset{+-}{MSHARE_{j,t}}, \overset{+-}{AP_{j,t}} \overset{-}{CR_{j,t}}, \overset{-}{HER_t}) \qquad (1)$$

Where: AR is the average annuity rate of the annuities offered by company j at time t (the subscripts j and t will not be repeated hereafter); RF is the risk-free rate; ROFI is the rate of return on other fixed income instruments; SOFI is the share of other fixed income assets in the fixed income portfolio of providers; ROA is the rate of return on other assets; SOA is the share of other assets in the portfolio of providers; LEV is the financial leverage; MIS is the duration mismatch; MSHARE is the market share measured by the stock of technical reserves; AP is the average annuity premium; CR is the commission rate; and HER is the degree of industry concentration measured by the Herfindahl index. The variables RF, ROFI, ROA, and HER are common to all the companies, whereas the others are company-specific. The equation also shows the expected sign of the coefficient.

An increase in RF, the risk-free rate, leads to an increase in the annuity rate, for the reasons already elaborated above. The risk-free rate, measured by the interest rate on Government or Central Bank bonds, is one of the most important determinants of the annuity rate, as it is the key reference rate for both annuitants and providers—it captures the basic opportunity cost for potential annuitants and the basic return on assets for annuity providers.

An increase in the rate of return on other fixed income instruments, ROFI, (measured by the interest rates on corporate and mortgage bonds), or on other assets, ROA (measured by the return on equity and foreign exchange assets), for the same levels of RF, could also lead to an increase in the annuity rate, although such an increase would arguably have to happen on a risk-adjusted basis—if agents are taking risk properly into account, an increase in the rates of return on financial assets due entirely to risk could have little impact on the demand or supply of annuities. It is unlikely that *changes* in ROFI and ROA relative to RF reflect other factors in addition to risk. Even if they did, there would still be a problem in utilizing these variables due to their correlation with RF.

A more promising route to test the impact of portfolio variables on the annuity rate is to use the share of the main classes of privately issued assets in the overall portfolio. The share of other fixed income assets, SOFI, and other assets, SOA, may capture the portfolio strategies of annuity providers and their attempts to extract additional returns and remain competitive in the annuities market. An increase in these shares would imply an increase in expected average portfolio returns *for the same levels* of ROFI, ROA, and RF. If this increase in the average expected return reflects factors other than risk, competitive pressures could lead providers to share them with annuitants. This would be possible if the spread of corporate bonds over Government bonds reflects not only default risk but also other factors such as a liquidity premium.[3] If potential annuitants perceive an increase in risk associated with a higher share of these assets they would demand a risk premium and the impact on the annuity rate would be stronger. In any case, the impact of SOFI and SOA on the annuity rate would seem unambiguously positive. An increase in LEV, or the financial leverage of providers, should also have a positive impact on the annuity rate, given the higher levels of risk involved.

Walker (2003a) examines the impact of different portfolios and leverage ratios on the annuity rate under a stylized Modigliani-Miller framework, and concludes that an increase in the share of risky assets or an increase in leverage could have a positive impact on the annuity rate. The impact of an increase in financial leverage on the annuity rate would be modest if providers held primarily risk-free assets, but could be significant if providers held a significant share of riskier assets.[4]

The variable MIS measures the mismatch in the duration of provider assets and liabilities. As indicated in the main report, the average duration mismatch in Chile has ranged from three to four years, with some variations across companies and over time. Such a duration mismatch penalizes providers in at least two ways. First, it exposes providers to changes in interest rates, or more specifically to reinvestment risk. Second, it also penalizes providers through reserve regulations, which impose larger reserves the greater the duration of the mismatch. Therefore, an increase in the mismatch, either across providers or over time, should lead to a contraction in supply and lower annuity rates.

The variable MSHARE represents the market share of each company, measured by the stock of technical reserves, and can have multiple and conflicting effects on the annuity rate. A large market share captures absolute size and should reflect the capacity of companies to achieve lower costs through economies of scale. Companies with lower operating costs should be able to compete more effectively and offer higher annuity rates. At the same time, a large market share may also be associated with reputation and brand name in the market, allowing companies to pay lower annuity rates, relative to less-known newcomers attempting to gain market share. A large market share may also be a proxy for the size of the sales force and the number of branches and distribution channels. Companies with better distribution channels may also be able to attract customers paying lower annuity rates and lower commission rates (the role of brokers in the annuity market is further elaborated below).[5]

The impact of the average premium, AP, on the annuity rate cannot be determined a priori. On the one hand, the size of the annuity premium is associated with levels of worker wealth and education, which are positively correlated with expected longevity. From this aspect, a higher annuity premium should lead to lower annuity rates (when annuity rates are measured with the same mortality table, as is the case). However, life insurance companies value customers with larger annuity premiums, just like commercial banks value customers with larger deposits, because they involve lower unit costs and higher unit profits for the providers. Therefore, annuity providers may be willing to pay higher annuity rates for larger premiums, just like banks pay higher interest rates for larger deposits. In fact, some annuity providers seem to specialize in the upscale annuity market, just like some banks specialize in the corporate sector or in the upscale consumer market, avoiding the higher costs associated with retail banking, for the same levels of scale, and being able to pay higher rates for better educated, higher income consumers.[6]

The variable CR measures the commission rate, defined as the ratio of broker commissions to the premium. In Chile as in other countries, annuities can be sold either by sales agents, which are employees of an insurance company, or by independent brokers. As discussed in the report, commission rates were about 3 percent in the early 1990s, increased continuously to 6 percent in 1999, and then declined rapidly in the early 2000s to 3 percent again, as a result of political and supervisory pressures. The increase in commissions during the 1990s was to a large extent related to the increase in cash rebates to customers—the broker would charge a large commission of, say, 5 percent of the premium, and transfer the excess over 2.5 or 3 percent to the customer's bank account.

An increase in the commission rate has an unambiguously negative impact on the annuity rate, due to several factors operating both on the side of demand and the side of supply of annuities—under the heuristic model outlined above a higher commission rate leads simultaneously to an expansion in the demand and a contraction in the supply of annuities. These effects are further elaborated below.

The level of commissions reflects the broker's efforts to search for new customers and induce eligible workers to retire. In general, it is likely that the intensity of broker activity replaces the annuity rate as marketing device, leading eligible workers to buy an annuity without a complete market search. In some cases the broker may provide services that are valued by the consumer, such as the verification of the conditions for retirement, the certification of outstanding recognition bonds and their transfer to the retiree's account, and the remaining paperwork. The eligible worker may be more willing to sacrifice market search when these services are provided. There is an even more direct and powerful substitution effect between the commission rate and the annuity rate when the former is partly shared with retiring workers. The illegal practice of sharing the commission was a loophole in the system that allowed several middle income workers de facto access to a modest lump sum. These workers may be willing to accept a lower annuity rate in exchange for such an informal lump sum.

An increase in commission leads to a contraction in supply because it implies an increase in a company's costs. The company needs to issue an annuity based on a smaller premium net of commissions. If interest rates, operating costs, and all other variables remain constant, the only way to preserve profit margins is to reduce annuity payments and the annuity rate. From another angle, the company will try to maintain constant the adjusted annuity rate, which is the annuity rate plus the capitalized value of the commission.

Finally, the variable HER captures the degree of industry concentration, as measured by the Herfindahl index. An increase in the Herfindahl index due to a reduction in the number of market participants should reflect the greater monopoly power of incumbents and be accompanied by a contraction in aggregate supply and ultimately a lower annuity rate.

Data

The sample is based on pooled quarterly data of active annuity providers over the 1993–2003 period. The sample starts in the first quarter of 1993 and ends in the third quarter of 2003, yielding a total of 43 quarters. The number of active providers ranged from 17 to 24 during the period under examination. This yields a total of 693 observations. The time unit is the quarter because of some limitations on monthly data. First, balance sheet data on the providers such as the portfolio composition, reserves, and leverage are only available quarterly. Second, some series such as annuity rates and commissions are available monthly, but suffer from discontinuities, due to the fact that many active providers do not sell annuities every month. All the flow variables were constructed by computing averages of the monthly figures within the quarter. The stock variables are end of quarter figures. The SVS is the source of most of the raw data used in the analysis. Market interest rates were obtained from the Central Bank of Chile.

$AR_{j,t}$ is the average annuity rate of each company during the quarter, computed by the average of monthly rates, weighted by the premiums. Each company needs to calculate the annuity rate of every annuity issued (the *tasa de venta*), based on a regulated mortality table (which was the RV-85 during the sample period).[7] The SVS databank provides a breakdown of annuity rates by type of policy, i.e., early retirement, normal age retirement, disability, and survivors of deceased members. The empirical analysis focuses on the annuity rates for early retirement policies AR(EARLY), and normal age retirement policies, AR(OLD).

The risk-free rate, RF, was measured by the interest rate on 20-year indexed bonds issued by the Central Bank of Chile (PRC-20). The instrument was discontinued in 2002, but secondary market quotations are available after that date and were used to complete the series. Monthly data on interest rates on corporate and mortgage bonds are available from the SVS, but only since 1995, and reflecting instruments with varying maturities, possibly resulting in some consistency problems. Estimates of the returns of other risky assets such as equity can be obtained, but there are no direct data on the returns on foreign assets held by annuity providers.

The share of other fixed income assets, SOFI was measured by the combined share of corporate bonds, mortgage bonds, endorsable mortgages, and other fixed income assets in the total fixed income portfolio. The share of other assets, SOA, was measured by the combined shares of variable income and foreign assets in the total portfolio. Leverage, LEV, was measured by the ratio of technical reserves to equity. The duration mismatch, MIS, was measured by the coefficient CP(9) computed for the calculation of reserves under the CALCE rule (Chapter 6). Market share, MSHARE, was measured by dividing the technical reserves of each company by total technical reserves in the system. Note that technical reserves account for a large share of the balance sheet and also constitute a good proxy for scale.

The average premium for each company, AP, is directly available from the SVS databank, broken down by class of annuity, including old age AP(OLD) and early retirement policies, AP(EARLY). The quarterly figure is simply the average of the monthly figures. The commission rate was computed by dividing the payments to brokers by the total premium. Finally, the Herfindahl index was constructed on the basis of company premia (or annuity sales). As in the case of average premium, the Herfindahl index was also constructed separately for early retirement policies, HER(EARLY), and normal old age policies, HER(OLD).

Econometric Results

The econometric analysis of the annuity rate involves the following preliminary steps. First, the series are tested for non-stationarity through a set of unit root tests, and a solution to deal with non-stationarity is elaborated. Second, several specification tests are conducted, involving pooled OLS versus Fixed Effects, pooled OLS versus Random Effects, and Fixed versus Random Effects. Third, after identifying the best estimating model, a test of autocorrelation is performed to select an appropriate robust variance-covariance matrix estimator and conduct inference about estimated coefficients.

Unit Root Testing

Table A2.1 presents a summary of the unit root tests performed for each series. All the tests considered have a unit root process as the null hypothesis, either a common one for all the companies or a specific process for each company. The figures in Table A2.1 correspond to asymptotic p-values for each test statistic. Therefore, a number lower than 0.05 means that the null hypothesis of a unit root is rejected at the 5 percent significance level.

The first test statistic (LLC) is due to Levin, Lin, and Chu (2002). In this case, the null hypothesis is a common unit root process for all the cross-section units. The statistic is based on a basic ADF specification for each cross-section, but with the same AR(1) coefficient for all of them. The test is a modified t-statistic for the coefficient of interest (1 minus the autoregressive parameter) from a pooled regression involving standardized variables. For the specification of the ADF regressions, an information criterion is required (such as AIC or BIC) to select the optimum number of lags and capture the autocorrelation in the series. In addition, to modify the standard t-statistic, a kernel-based spectral density estimator

Table A2.1. Panel Unit Root Tests (p-values)

	LLC		*IPS*		*FISHER(ADF)*	
	Const.	*+Trend*	*Const.*	*+Trend*	*Const.*	*+Trend*
AR(EARLY)	0.9894	1.0000	0.5757	1.0000	0.0240	0.9997
AR(OLD)	0.0048	0.0004	0.2611	0.7633	0.0000	0.7318
RF	0.9994	0.9947	0.9998	0.9778	0.9996	0.9775
SOFI	0.9527	0.8834	0.9997	0.1185	0.9953	0.0008
SOA	0.9231	1.0000	0.9260	0.8663	0.9703	0.2582
LEV	0.0061	0.9875	0.0000	0.0412	0.0000	0.0064
MIS	0.7051	0.0000	0.0487	0.0000	0.0000	0.0000
MSHARE	0.0000	0.0001	0.0013	0.9666	0.0000	0.0000
AP(EARLY)	1.0000	1.0000	0.4185	0.8368	0.4600	0.5527
AP(OLD)	1.0000	1.0000	0.5273	0.0203	0.1218	0.0000
CR	0.9990	0.9999	0.9997	0.9997	0.9998	0.7720
HER(EARLY)	1.0000	1.0000	0.9988	1.0000	0.9983	0.9122
HER(OLD)	0.0018	0.9918	0.0000	0.0000	0.0000	0.0000

Source: Authors' calculations.

at frequency zero is computed (by using the corresponding bandwidth truncation selection method). Under the null of a common unit root process, the final test statistic is asymptotically distributed as N(0,1).

The second statistic (IPS) was proposed by Im, Pesaran, and Shin (2003). In this case, the null hypothesis is a specific unit root process for each individual cross-section unit. To compute the unit root test statistic, an ADF regression is specified for each cross-section, and then the average t-statistic for the individual coefficients is adjusted by using the expected mean and variance of the individual t-statistics. As in the previous test, an optimum lag order is required for the construction of the ADF regressions. The IPS test also has an asymptotic N(0,1) distribution.

Finally, the Fisher (ADF) statistic proposed by Maddala and Wu (1999), and Choi (2001), is based on the idea of Fisher (1932) of combining p-values from individual unit root tests. Again, for a Fisher test based on ADF specifications for each cross-section unit, information criteria are required to choose the required lag order to have white noise residuals. The combined test statistic is asymptotically distributed as a Chi-square with 2N degrees of freedom.

All the three test statistics are constructed using the Modified Akaike Information Criterion (MAIC), proposed by Ng and Perron (2001), which reduces the well-known size distortions commonly present in unit root tests when the autocorrelation structure is characterized by high negative MA components. When required, the long-run variance is estimated through a Quadratic Spectral Kernel with automatic bandwidth selection method proposed by Andrews (1991). As deterministic components, both fixed effects and fixed effects plus a time trend are considered for each test statistic.

As shown in Table A2.1, the null hypothesis of a unit root is rejected for the two annuity rates, SOFI, LEV, AP(OLD), MIS, and MSHARE. The non-rejection of unit roots in the other variables seems to be related to the presence of a structural change in the intercept of their deterministic trend, which occurs at the end of the sample. As stated by Perron (1989), unit root tests are not consistent against the alternative hypothesis of trend stationary processes when the trend contains a shift in the slope. Moreover, although the tests are consistent when the shift is in the level of the trend (intercept), their power is remarkably lower. Therefore, breaks in the deterministic function of a trend stationary series are likely to produce the non-rejection of the null of a unit root.

If the series are considered as trend-stationary and some of them affected by a discrete change in the intercept of their deterministic trend, this deterministic non-stationarity can be addressed by including in the regressions a time trend plus an additive dummy variable. According to the Frisch-Waugh-Lovell theorem (Frisch and Waugh 1933; Lovell 1963), the numeric value of the coefficients of interest are the same, either if the regression includes detrended variables (the residual from the regression of the original variable on a constant, the additive dummy, and a time trend) or if the dummy and trend are included as additional explanatory variables in the regression. Finally, with the annuity rate (AR) considered as a stationary process, the inclusion of a potential non-stationary independent variable is not longer a big concern, since in this case there is no possibility of spurious correlation.

Specification Testing

There are three alternative models to consider in the estimation of the annuity rate. First, a pooled OLS regression where no heterogeneity is allowed. Second, a Fixed Effects model where a specific constant term for each cross-section unit is considered. Finally, a Random Effects specification which assumes that the heterogeneity comes in the form of an error component model (as part of the individual disturbance terms). The testing procedure is conducted as follows. First, the pooled OLS model is tested against the Fixed Effects specification. Second, the pooled OLS is compared to the Random Effects model. Finally, these two alternative specifications are compared to select the way to model the cross-section heterogeneity.

In the first case, the null hypothesis of pooled OLS is strongly rejected in favor of a Fixed Effects model, based on both an F-statistic and a Likelihood Ratio test. The values of the statistics are 5.8 and 128.1, respectively, while the corresponding critical 5 percent significance level for the F and Chi-squared distributions are 1.5 and 35.2, respectively. The null hypothesis of a pooled OLS model is also rejected in favor of a Random Effects specification, based on the results of the Breusch-Pagan (BP) Lagrange Multiplier test. The value of the BP statistic is 59.8, compared to the value of the Chi-squared distribution with 1 degree of freedom of 3.8. This conclusion is supported by the more powerful test proposed by Honda (1985), where the alternative hypothesis is one sided (considering that the variance components are non-negative) and also robust to non-normality. The value of the Honda statistic is 7.7, compared with a 1.6 value for the standard Normal distribution for a 5 percent significance level.

Given the rejection of the pooled OLS model against both the Fixed and Random Effects, it is possible to compare the two alternatives by a Hausman's-type test. The main idea behind this statistic is that under the null hypothesis (individual effects are independent from the exogenous variables), both the Fixed and Random Effects specifications are consistent (and the GLS estimator is efficient), given that individual effects are not correlated with the exogenous variables in the model. However, under the alternative hypothesis (individual effects are correlated with the exogenous variables), the Random Effects model is inconsistent. This way, a large Wald statistic comparing the two estimated parameter vectors (weighted by the inverse of the difference of their variance-covariance matrices), should be taken as evidence in favor of the Fixed Effects specification.

The Hausman statistic is constructed following Ahn and Low (1996), by using an artificial regression of the GLS residuals ($\tilde{e}_{it}$) on cross-sectional demeaned exogenous variables (that is, (X^*_{it}) the same transformation applied to independent variables to compute the Fixed Effects estimator) and their corresponding means($\bar{X}_i$). The test statistic is finally computed as NT (number of effective observations) by the R-squared from the artificial regression above, and distributed as Chi-squared with as many degrees of freedom as exogenous variables in the original model. Under these conditions, the Hausman statistic has a value of 66.9, while the asymptotic critical value at the 5 percent significance level is 16.9. Hence, these tests favor the Fixed Effects specification to model the cross-section heterogeneity.

Autocorrelation Testing

Given the long time series dimension of the panel utilized, autocorrelation could be a more serious problem than heteroskedasticity. To test for AR(1) autocorrelation under Fixed Effects, it is possible to use an extension of the Breusch-Godfrey (BG) Lagrange Multiplier statistic. To compute the BG test, the first step is to run an auxiliary regression of the residuals from the Fixed Effects model on the independent variables and the first lagged residual. The R-squared from this regression is then multiplied by the number of observation in the sample. The BG statistic takes a value of 38.5, while the asymptotic Chi-squared distribution with 1 degree of freedom at the 5 percent significance level corresponds to 3.8. Therefore, the null hypothesis of no first order serial correlation under Fixed Effects is strongly rejected.

In order to ensure an appropriate inference about estimated coefficients, a heteroskedasticity-autocorrelation consistent covariance matrix for estimated parameters is required if the disturbance term is not a white noise process. Given that the Fixed Effects estimator is unbiased and consistent, but inefficient under non-spherical errors, an adjusted variance-covariance matrix for estimated parameters is enough to make consistent inference about the model. As suggested by Arellano (1987), an estimate of the asymptotic variance for the Fixed Effects estimator, which is valid under heteroskedasticity and serial correlation of arbitrary forms, is given by

$$V(\hat{\beta}_{FE})=\left(\sum_{i=1}^{N} X_i^{*\prime}X_i^{*}\right)^{-1}\left(\sum_{i=1}^{N} X_i^{*}e_i^{*}e_i^{*\prime}X_i^{*}\right)\left(\sum_{i=1}^{N} X_i^{*\prime}X_i^{*}\right)^{-1} \qquad (2)$$

Even though this asymptotic variance is consistent for relative small T and large N, for the unbalanced panel at hand, where some cross-section units have just a few effective observations (and on average there are 28 observations per unit), its use seems appropriate. The number of cross-section units considered for estimation is 24.

Estimation Results

The analysis of the estimation results focuses on the regressions with the annuity rate of early retirement policies as the dependent variable, because early retirement annuities constitute the bulk of the annuities market—as shown in Chapter 2, they represent 60 percent of the whole stock of annuities and 70 percent of the flows of new annuities. Excluding disability and survivor annuities, their shares in the stock and the new flows of annuities are both around 80 percent. The regressions with the annuity rate of normal old age policies are shown at the end of the section.

Table A2.2 shows the estimates of equation (1) with the fixed effects model, excluding ROFI and ROA. The interest rate on other fixed income assets, ROFI, was excluded because it turned out to be non-significant, due to the strong colinearity with the risk-free rate—the correlation coefficients between the interest rates on PRC20, corporate bonds and mortgage bonds were 0.86 and 0.92, respectively. The interest rate on other assets, ROA, was excluded because it could not be computed, due to the lack of data on the return on foreign assets. The quarterly return on equity can be computed but also turned to be non-significant. As mentioned before, these results are expected and do not affect the exercise, because the shares of other fixed income assets and other assets, capture the expected return of the portfolio of annuity providers.

As shown in Table A2.2, the regression explains about 80 percent of the annuity rate across companies and over time, the coefficients of all explanatory variables have the expected signs (or signs that can be reasonably explained in the cases where it could be either positive or negative)

Table A2.2. Fixed Effects Estimation

Dependent Variable: AR(EARLY)

Sample: 1993Q1–2003Q3; Cross-Sections Included: 24

Total Panel Observations (Unbalanced): 693

R^2 = 0.7968; Adj. R^2 = 0.7854; F-Statistic = 69.4348 ; P-Value (F-Statistic) = 0.0000

Variable	*Coefficient*	*Std. Error*	*t-Statistic*	*Prob.*
C	3.0257	0.1803	16.7840	0.0000***
RF	0.3652	0.0166	21.9809	0.0000***
SOFI	0.0029	0.0010	2.9696	0.0031***
SOA	0.0083	0.0031	2.6801	0.0075***
LEV	0.0115	0.0046	2.5309	0.0116**
MIS	−0.0208	0.0548	−0.3800	0.7041
MSHARE	−3.7609	0.7187	−5.2331	0.0000***
AP(EARLY)	0.0002	$2.46 \times e^{-5}$	7.2057	0.0000***
CR	−0.0437	0.0074	−5.9007	0.0000***
HER(EARLY)	−4.6728	0.9512	−4.9128	0.0000***
TREND	0.0002	0.0019	0.0997	0.9206
D	−1.2189	0.2011	−6.0609	0.0000***
RF × D	0.4163	0.0382	10.8874	0.0000***
AP(EARLY) × D	−0.0001	$3.39 \times e^{-5}$	−4.0003	0.0001***
CR × D	−0.0884	0.0264	−3.3444	0.0009***

Source: Authors' calculations.

*** = significant at the 1% level; ** = significant at the 5% level.

and are significant, with the exception of MIS. The coefficient of the risk-free rate is 0.37, only slightly higher than the value obtained by Walker (2003a) in a regression of the annuity rate against the lagged risk-free rate using monthly data. This coefficient looks low, as one would expect a tighter relationship between the annuity rate and the key interest rate, and possibly a coefficient close to 1. The relationship between the annuity rate and the risk-free rate will be further examined below.

The coefficients of SOFI and SOA are positive and significant, capturing the impact of portfolio strategies on the annuity rate. During the sample period there were two major portfolio shifts, namely, a reduction in the share of equity from 10 percent in 1995 to about 3 percent in all the following years, and a sharp increase in the share of mortgage and corporate bonds, from 37 percent in 1995 to 66 percent in 2003. The share of Central Bank bonds decreased proportionately. The decline in the share of equity happened as insurance companies (and pension funds) sold their equity holdings to foreign strategic investors in the mid-1990s at attractive prices. These prices reflected the large capital gains accumulated in previous years and possibly a control premium. It is clear that asset managers decided not to rebuild their equity portfolio after that event, possibly perceiving that the period of exceptional equity returns was over. This perception may have resulted in an overall downward adjustment of average expected portfolio returns and a commensurate adjustment of the annuity rate.

During the same period annuity providers initiated a move towards higher yield fixed income assets, first through mortgage instruments and bonds of financial institutions, and after 2000 through corporate bonds. The increase in the holdings of corporate bonds has been particularly impressive—the share of this instrument increased from 10 percent in 2000 to 30 percent in 2003. The positive coefficient of SOFI may reflect the strategy of annuity providers to extract an increase in risk-adjusted returns by capturing the liquidity premium in corporate bonds and mortgages, which tend to be less traded and have lower liquidity than Central Bank and Government bonds. These institutional investors can afford to hold these less liquid assets given their longer time horizon. By capturing the liquidity premium and investing only in high rated bonds (most corporate bonds are rated AA or higher), annuity providers may have felt that they were able to compete more aggressively in the annuities market while maintaining the degree of portfolio risk at acceptable levels. It is possible that the coefficients of both SOFI and SOA also reflect a higher degree of portfolio risk and a higher risk premium demanded by annuitants.

The coefficients of SOFI and SOA are admittedly small, indicating that portfolio shifts have had only a moderate impact on the annuity rate (an increase of 10 basis points in the case of SOFI). These results are consistent with several scenarios, including a small liquidity premium, and/or a partial and delayed sharing of higher returns with annuitants. In any case, it is noteworthy that higher portfolio returns tend to be at least partially shared with annuitants.

The coefficient of LEV is positive and significant, reflecting the perception of higher risk involved in the combination of a riskier portfolio, large fixed liabilities, and a declining capital buffer. This result is consistent with the existence of a risk premium in the annuity rates of more leveraged companies, and has been obtained despite the fact that leverage ratios should be ideally measured at economic values, not book values. As discussed in Chapter 6, it is possible that leverage ratios measured at economic and book values have not differed too much, after all the proper adjustments are considered. The existence of an annuity guarantee would tend to weaken the impact of bankruptcy risk on the annuity rate, but the fact that the guarantee is partial may explain the result.

The coefficient of MIS was not significant, however. A larger duration mismatch implies more exposure of the provider to reinvestment risk, which should have a negative impact on the annuity rate. This result may be due simply to a deficient proxy for the duration mismatch. It may also be due to the negative correlation between the mismatch and the share of risk-free assets (or equivalently the positive correlation between MIS and SOFI—see the correlation matrix in Table A2.8 at the end of this annex.). Some companies indicated in interviews that there were still not sufficient corporate bonds with long duration, and in order to reduce the duration mismatch they needed to invest more in risk-free assets with long duration and sacrifice yield.

The coefficient of MSHARE is negative and significant, suggesting that reputation, brand name, and the existence of a large distribution network have had a more powerful impact on the annuity rate than the pure scale effect during the period covered by the sample. It may also reflect the strategy of some small companies to gain market share by offering higher annuity rates, even at the expense of positive financial results. Equation (1) was re-estimated replacing MSHARE by the stock of technical reserves in order to explore further the existence of a scale effect, but the results did not change significantly (the correlation coefficient between two variables is 0.7, as shown in Table A2.8.).

The coefficient of the average premium, AP(EARLY), is positive and significant, indicating that the unit cost effect is more important than the longevity effect. This result is consistent with the regression results obtained for money's worth ratios based on a sample of individual annuities. As shown in Annex Table A1.5, a regression of money's worth ratios against a number of individual annuitant characteristics such as age, sex, and the size of the premium also yields a positive and significant coefficient for the premium.

The coefficient of the commission rate, CR, has the expected negative sign and is significant. This result confirms the important role that brokers have played in the marketing of annuities in Chile, and will be further examined below. Finally, the coefficient of the Herfindahl index, HER(EARLY) is also negative and significant, confirming that a more concentrated annuities market tends to have a negative effect on the annuity rate. It is interesting to note that in the case of Chile the reverse happened during the sample period—HER(EARLY) declined as the annuities market became much more competitive during the 1990s, with the entry of several new companies, and resulting in the adoption of more aggressive pricing strategies.

As shown in Table A2.2, the regression also includes a dummy variable taking value 0 for the period 1993Q1–2001Q2, and value 1 for the rest of the sample, to control for a structural change in the annuities market during this period. The dummy was also multiplied by each of the right-hand-side variables in the model, to capture structural breaks in the individual coefficients. Based on t-statistics, the null hypothesis of no change in the slope was rejected for the variables RF, CR, and AP. Therefore, the final regression reported in Table A2.2 includes only the general dummy and the multiplicative dummies for only these three variables.[8]

The possibility of a structural break was first raised by Walker (2003a), based on the observation that the scandal of large commissions and illegal rebates in the 1990s had prompted the Government to submit a new draft pension law to Congress at the end of 2000. The draft law proposed, among other measures, an electronic quotation system and controls on broker's commissions. The draft pension law was only approved in 2004, but the threat of these legal changes may have changed dramatically the behavior of annuity brokers and providers. Walker (2003a) tested the hypothesis of a structural break in the coefficient of the risk-free rate and of a unitary long-run coefficient at the end of the sample, and was not able to reject either of the two hypotheses. He concludes that the annuity rate became progressively the key instrument of competition in recent years. These tests were performed through regressions of the annuity rate against lagged values of the risk-free rates and the annuity rate using monthly series of the two variables.

The results in Table A2.2 are largely consistent with Walker's and supportive of a structural break in the regression. It is interesting to note that two of the three coefficients that experienced a structural break are precisely those related to the risk-free rate and the commission rate. Taking into consideration the multiplicative dummy, the coefficient of the risk-free rate increases from 0.37 to 0.71. The hypothesis of a unitary long-run coefficient at the end of the sample period was tested by means of a Wald statistic including the lagged dependent variable plus two lagged values for the risk-free rate on the right-hand-side of the equation. The calculated value for the test was 0.65, with a p-value of 0.42. Therefore, the null hypothesis of a unitary long-run coefficient at the end of the sample cannot be statistically rejected at conventional significance levels.

Equation (1) was re-estimated by the Fixed Effects model, but with the consistent asymptotic variance described above, with the results shown in Table A2.3. All the variables remain significant, although the share of other risky assets, SOA, only remains significant at the 10 percent level. Considering that the coefficient for the MIS variable is statistically not different from 0, equation (1) was re-estimated again by the Fixed

Table A2.3. Fixed Effects Estimation, with Robust Standard Errors—Dependent Variable: AR(EARLY)

Sample: 1993Q1–2003Q3; Cross-Sections Included: 24
Total Panel Observations (Unbalanced): 693
$R^2 = 0.7968$; Adj. $R^2 = 0.7854$; F-Statistic = 69.4348 ; P-Value(F-Statistic) = 0.0000

Variable	*Coefficient*	*Std. Error*	*t-Statistic*	*p-value*
C	3.0257	0.2270	13.3270	0.0000***
RF	0.3652	0.0217	16.8099	0.0000***
SOFI	0.0029	0.0009	3.1631	0.0016***
SOA	0.0083	0.0046	1.7966	0.0729*
LEV	0.0115	0.0040	2.9086	0.0038***
MIS	−0.0208	0.0489	−0.4260	0.6703
MSHARE	−3.7609	0.6535	−5.7550	0.0000***
AP(EARLY)	0.0002	$2.79 \times e^{-5}$	6.3559	0.0000***
CR	−0.0437	0.0180	−2.4237	0.0156**
HER(EARLY)	−4.6728	0.7214	−6.4778	0.0000***
TREND	0.0002	0.0021	0.0900	0.9283
D	−1.2189	0.2703	−4.5093	0.0000***
RF × D	0.4163	0.0491	8.4727	0.0000***
AP(EARLY) × D	−0.0001	$5.53 \times e^{-5}$	−2.4490	0.0146**
CR × D	−0.0884	0.0410	−2.1565	0.0314**

Source: Authors' calculations.
*** = significant at the 1% level; ** = significant at the 5% level; * = significant at the 10% level.

Effects model with Robust Standard Errors, but excluding the MIS variable. As shown in Table A2.4, the exclusion of the MIS variable generally improves the t-statistics of all estimated coefficients, including the coefficient of SOA.

Tables A2.5 through A2.7 show the estimates of equation (1) with the annuity rate on normal old age policies as the dependent variable, replicating the same steps and procedures followed above. The coefficients have the right sign and their values are similar to the ones obtained with the annuity rate on early retirement policies, although some of them become marginally non-significant at the 10 percent level, when estimated with robust standard errors. It is possible that these differences are simply due to a much smaller sample—as mentioned before, the number of new annuities classified as normal old age (i.e., bought by males and females above 65 and 60 years of age) is only 20 percent of total flow of new annuities, excluding disability and survivor annuities.

Summary of Findings and Conclusions

This annex formulated and estimated an equation for the annuity rate in Chile, based on a heuristic model of the demand and supply of annuities

Table A2.4. Fixed Effects Estimation, with Robust Standard Errors, Excluding MIS Variable—Dependent Variable: AR(EARLY)
Sample: 1993Q1–2003Q3; Cross-Sections Included: 24
Total Panel Observations (Unbalanced): 725
$R^2 = 0.7995$; Adj. $R^2 = 0.7890$; F-Statistic = 76.2162 P-Value(F-Statistic) = 0.0000

Variable	*Coefficient*	*Std. Error*	*t-Statistic*	*p-value*
C	3.0760	0.2187	14.0668	0.0000***
RF	0.3639	0.0209	17.4077	0.0000***
SOFI	0.0029	0.0009	3.1772	0.0016***
SOA	0.0086	0.0038	2.2509	0.0247**
LEV	0.0110	0.0039	2.7967	0.0053***
MSHARE	−3.4900	0.5727	−6.0937	0.0000***
AP(EARLY)	0.0002	$2.57 \times e^{-5}$	6.8931	0.0000***
CR	−0.0441	0.0180	−2.4431	0.0148**
HER(EARLY)	−5.1390	0.7219	−7.1191	0.0000***
TREND	−0.0005	0.0020	−0.2244	0.8225
D	−1.2547	0.2437	−5.1479	0.0000***
RF × D	0.4118	0.0457	9.0149	0.0000***
AP(EARLY) × D	−0.0001	$3.95 \times e^{-5}$	−3.0191	0.0026***
CR × D	−0.0808	0.0351	−2.3035	0.0215**

Source: Authors' calculations.
*** = significant at the 1% level; ** = significant at the 5% level.

that incorporates company-level data. The estimated equation explains 80 percent of the variations of the annuity rate across companies and over time, and most of the coefficients have the expected sign, or signs that can be reasonably explained, and are significant.

The results of the exercise are consistent with the analysis and conclusions developed in Annex 1 and in other parts of the report, indicating the existence of a very competitive market for annuities in Chile. During the period under examination market competition took place through the annuity rate and broker activity. The illegal provision of increasing cash rebates to annuitants (made possible by increasing commissions) became a powerful element of competition in the 1990s, and the results confirm the substitutability between annuity rates and commissions (which included the rebates) as two elements of price competition. The reduction in broker commissions and rebates in the 2000s translated into higher annuity rates and enhanced the role of the annuity rate as the main instrument of competition. The role of brokers has possibly been reduced but has not been eliminated.

During the past decade there were significant changes in the portfolio strategies of annuity providers. Most noticeably, there has been a marked shift from Government bonds and towards higher yield fixed income assets, especially corporate bonds. It is possible that annuity providers have been able to generate an increase in risk-adjusted returns, as the corporate and mortgage bonds held in their portfolios have been issued primarily by highly rated companies (implying a low credit risk), and these instruments are usually held to maturity, allowing providers to extract the liquidity premium. Competitive pressures may have led providers to share the increased returns with annuitants, and the results confirm the small but positive impact of the share of higher yield assets on the annuity rate. However, it is possible that the coefficient reflects a risk premium as well.

Other portfolio variables such as financial leverage also have a positive impact on the annuity rate, but this result should reflect only the presence of a risk premium demanded by annuitants. The presence of an annuity guarantee would tend to reduce the need for a risk premium, due either to higher portfolio risk or to higher leverage, but the result can still be explained, because the annuity guarantee in Chile is not total—75 percent of the value of the annuity above the minimum pension guarantee.

The coefficient of the Herfindahl index and the market share variable were both negative and significant, reflecting the high degree of competitiveness of the annuities market during the period under examination.

Table A2.5. Fixed Effects Estimation—Dependent Variable: AR(OLD)
Sample: 1993Q1–2003Q3; Cross-Sections Included: 24;
Total Panel Observations (Unbalanced): 675
$R^2 = 0.7909$; Adj. $R^2 = 0.7787$; F-Statistic = 65.1110; P-Value (F-Statistic) = 0.0000

Variable	*Coefficient*	*Std. Error*	*t-Statistic*	*p-value*
Constant	2.7371	0.1741	15.7198	0.0000***
RF	0.3961	0.0182	21.8170	0.0000***
SOFI	0.0030	0.0011	2.7053	0.0070***
SOA	0.0070	0.0035	1.9727	0.0490**
LEV	0.0121	0.0051	2.3558	0.0188**
MIS	0.0247	0.0589	0.4187	0.6756
MSHARE	−2.0611	0.8026	−2.5680	0.0105**
AP(OLD)	0.0001	$1.87 \times e^{-5}$	7.8900	0.0000***
CR	−0.0280	0.0087	−3.2029	0.0014***
HER(OLD)	−3.4204	0.6212	−5.5066	0.0000***
TREND	0.0055	0.0018	3.1318	0.0018***
D	−1.8350	0.2148	−8.5421	0.0000***
RF × D	0.5536	0.0406	13.6334	0.0000***
AP(OLD) × D	−0.0001	$3.80 \times e^{-5}$	−3.4935	0.0005***
CR × D	−0.1340	0.0310	−4.3171	0.0000***

Source: Authors' calculations.
*** = significant at the 1% level; ** = significant at the 5% level.

Table A2.6. Fixed Effects Estimation, with Robust Standard Errors—Dependent Variable: AR(OLD)
Sample: 1993Q1–2003Q3; Cross-Sections Included: 24
Total Panel Observations (Unbalanced): 675
$R^2 = 0.7933$; Adj. $R^2 = 0.7821$; F-Statistic = 71.3020; P-Value (F-Statistic) = 0.0000

Variable	*Coefficient*	*Std. Error*	*t-Statistic*	*p-value*
Constant	2.7371	0.1976	13.8525	0.0000***
RF	0.3961	0.0196	20.2453	0.0000***
SOFI	0.0030	0.0018	1.6559	0.0982*
SOA	0.0070	0.0039	1.7942	0.0733*
LEV	0.0121	0.0057	2.1144	0.0349**
MIS	0.0247	0.0648	0.3810	0.7033
MSHARE	−2.0611	0.9332	−2.2088	0.0275**
AP(OLD)	0.0001	$1.67 \times e^{-5}$	8.8551	0.0000***
CR	−0.0280	0.0158	−1.7696	0.0773*
HER(OLD)	−3.4204	0.5765	−5.9336	0.0000***
TREND	0.0055	0.0024	2.2893	0.0224**
D	−1.8350	0.2995	−6.1268	0.0000***
RF × D	0.5536	0.0490	11.3063	0.0000***
AP(OLD) × D	−0.0001	$5.85 \times e^{-5}$	−2.2645	0.0239**
CR × D	−0.1340	0.0329	−4.0739	0.0001***

Source: Authors' calculations.
*** = significant at the 1% level; ** = significant at the 5% level; * = significant at the 10% level.

Table A2.7. Fixed Effects Estimation, with Robust Standard Errors, Excluding MIS Variable—Dependent Variable: AR(OLD)

Sample: 1993Q1–2003Q3; Cross-Sections Included: 24

Total Panel Observations (Unbalanced): 675

$R^2 = 0.7909$; Adj. $R^2 = 0.7787$; F-Statistic = 65.1110; P-Value (F-Statistic) = 0.0000

Variable	*Coefficient*	*Std. Error*	*t-Statistic*	*p-value*
Constant	2.7150	0.1973	13.7634	0.0000***
RF	0.3987	0.0189	21.0905	0.0000***
SOFI	0.0031	0.0020	1.5814	0.1143
SOA	0.0075	0.0032	2.3210	0.0206**
LEV	0.0122	0.0059	2.0549	0.0403**
MSHARE	−1.5149	0.9939	−1.5242	0.1279
AP(OLD)	0.0001	$1.63 \times e^{-5}$	8.8935	0.0000***
CR	−0.0273	0.0157	−1.7313	0.0839*
HER(OLD)	−3.5768	0.5652	−6.3288	0.0000***
TREND	0.0050	0.0025	2.0480	0.0410**
D	−1.8897	0.2834	−6.6676	0.0000***
RF × D	0.5483	0.0446	12.3071	0.0000***
AP(OLD) × D	−0.0001	$5.03 \times e^{-5}$	−2.1317	0.0334**
CR × D	−0.1257	0.0289	−4.3552	0.0000***

Source: Authors' calculations.

*** = significant at the 1% level; ** = significant at the 5% level; * = significant at the 10% level.

Table A2.8. Pairwise Correlation Matrix

	RF	*SOA*	*SOFI*	*MSHARE*	*LEV*	*HER(EARLY)*	*AP(EARLY)*	*CR*	*MIS*	*ROFI(B)*	*ROFI(M)*
RF	1.00										
SOA	−0.39	1.00									
SOFI	−0.55	0.38	1.00								
MSHARE	−0.06	0.17	−0.18	1.00							
LEV	−0.05	0.06	0.05	0.03	1.00						
HER(EARLY)	−0.58	0.06	0.20	0.07	−0.07	1.00					
AP(EARLY)	−0.16	0.36	0.17	0.26	0.06	0.00	1.00				
CR	0.42	−0.02	−0.18	−0.09	0.05	−0.44	−0.11	1.00			
MIS	−0.22	0.13	0.33	−0.16	−0.11	0.09	0.00	−0.01	1.00		
ROFI(B)[a]	0.86	−0.23	−0.37	−0.07	0.05	−0.59	0.00	0.43	−0.15	1.00	
ROFI(M)[a]	0.92	−0.30	−0.44	−0.08	0.04	−0.68	−0.04	0.47	−0.19	0.97	1.00
RES	−0.43	0.52	0.30	0.71	0.09	0.18	0.42	−0.16	−0.01	−0.26	−0.32

Source: Authors' calculations.

a. ROFI(B) and ROFI(M) are the rates of return on corporate and mortgage bonds, respectively.

The Herfindahl concentration index declined significantly during the 1990s with the entry of several new providers, and although it increased recently due to the exit of three firms, it remains substantially lower than at the beginning of the decade. Finally, the significance of the market share variable suggests that market reputation and a more extensive distribution network may allow larger companies to pay lower annuity rates and remain competitive. It may also reflect the attempts of smaller companies to gain market share through aggressive price strategies.

Notes

1. Note that money's worth ratios and annuity rates are closely related and are determined by essentially the same set of variables.
2. An increase in interest rates could also reduce the demand for new annuities by producing a capital loss in the accumulated pension balance.
3. Most empirical studies on corporate bond spreads conclude that default risk does not explain all the observed spread, and that taxes, liquidity, and market risk factors may help explain the difference. See, e.g., Duffee (1999), Deliandes and Geske (2001), and Elton, Gruber, Agrawal, and Mann (2001).
4. Walker (2003b) makes these predictions but does not test them empirically. Such an empirical analysis is provided below.
5. Market share cannot be constructed using the flows of new annuity policies or flows of annuity premiums, because these are essentially the endogenous quantity variable in the heuristic model outline above, and cannot be included in a reduced form equation.
6. Most studies of economies of scale in banking and other areas of the financial sector involve the estimation of a cost function that includes a measure of scale such as assets or the number of accounts, complemented by a variable measuring the average balance. Average costs are shown to decline both with larger scale and larger average balances.
7. Companies are free to use their own mortality tables for pricing annuities, but they have to report annuity rates based on regulated mortality tables.
8. The Fixed Effects model also includes dummies for each company but these are not reported.

ANNEX 3

Statistical Tables

Table A3.1. Assets of Insurance Companies and Pension Funds as Percentage of GDP, Chile and Selected Benchmarks

Country	*Insurance*			*Pension funds*	*Insurance + Pension funds*
	Total	*Life*	*Non-Life*		
Latin America					
Argentina	4.6			13.5	14.1
Brazil	4.2			17.0	21.2
Chile (2003)	20.1	19.6	0.5	59.2	79.3
Colombia	3.6			9.8	13.4
Mexico	2.3			4.3	6.6
Peru	2.1			10.6	12.7
Uruguay	3.0			11.4	14.4
High income OECD (2001)					
Australia	40.5	28.7	11.8	67.4	107.9
Austria	25.3	23.3	2.0	3.8	29.1
Belgium	45.5	35.8	9.7	5.6	51.1
Canada	29.1	23.8	5.3	48.2	77.3
Denmark	58.1	49.3	8.8	23.8	81.9
Finland	24.4	17.1	7.2	3.4	27.8
France	69.0	53.8	15.2	..	..
Germany	41.3	27.0	14.3	3.3	44.6
Greece	5.0	2.1	2.9	..	..
Iceland	9.9	..	..	87.3	97.2
Italy	22.3	16.9	5.4	4.4	26.7
Japan	60.3	53.2	7.1	18.5	78.8
Korea	38.9	30.6	8.3	3.2	42.1
Luxembourg	117.2	108.0	9.2	..	..
Netherlands	61.8	61.8	..	105.1	166.9
Norway	31.8	25.5	6.3	5.6	37.4

(Continued)

Table A3.1. Assets of Insurance Companies and Pension Funds as Percentage of GDP, Chile and Selected Benchmarks *(Continued)*

Country	*Insurance*			*Pension funds*	*Insurance + Pension funds*
	Total	*Life*	*Non-Life*		
Portugal	22.4	..	..	11.3	33.7
Spain	22.8	..	..	8.2	31.0
Sweden	76.1	61.1	15.0	3.7	79.8
Switzerland	87.1	63.5	23.6	113.5	200.6
United Kingdom	97.1	89.6	7.5	66.4	163.5
United States	40.5	31.9	8.6	63.0	103.5

Sources: SVS, OECD, SAFP, ASSAL.

Table A3.2. Insurance Premiums in Chile and Selected Benchmarks as Percentage of GDP, 2003

Region	*Country*	*Life*	*Non-life*	*Total*
Latin America	Argentina	0.71	1.82	2.53
	Bahamas	4.46	3.66	8.10
	Barbados	3.30	6.30	9.60
	Brazil	1.28	1.68	2.96
	Chile	2.62	1.48	4.09
	Colombia	0.70	1.86	2.56
	Costa Rica	0.16	1.71	1.87
	Dominican Republic	0.21	2.30	2.50
	Ecuador	0.17	1.53	1.70
	El Salvador	0.69	1.64	2.33
	Guatemala	0.20	0.93	1.13
	Jamaica	2.47	3.37	5.86
	Mexico	0.70	1.10	1.80
	Panama	1.15	2.37	3.53
	Peru	0.60	0.83	1.43
	Trinidad and Tobago	3.48	1.62	5.10
	Uruguay	0.47	1.68	2.16
	Venezuela, R. B. de	0.09	2.79	2.88
High income	Australia	4.42	3.57	7.98
	Austria	2.58	3.30	5.88
	Belgium	6.91	4.21	11.12
	Canada	2.63	4.19	6.82
	Denmark	5.19	2.75	7.93
	Finland	6.79	1.88	8.66
	France	5.99	3.31	9.31
	Germany	3.17	3.89	7.06
	Greece	0.93	1.17	2.10
	Iceland	0.28	2.85	3.14
	Ireland	6.02	5.53	11.55
	Italy	4.86	2.71	7.57

(Continued)

Table A3.2. Insurance Premiums in Chile and Selected Benchmarks as Percentage of GDP, 2003 *(Continued)*

Region	*Country*	*Life*	*Non-life*	*Total*
	Japan	8.61	2.20	10.81
	Korea, Rep. of	6.76	2.86	9.62
	Luxembourg	28.52	4.41	32.93
	Netherlands	4.93	4.83	9.76
	New Zealand	1.39	4.83	6.22
	Norway	2.79	2.55	5.34
	Portugal	4.14	3.17	7.30
	Singapore	6.11	3.71	9.82
	Spain	2.38	3.20	5.58
	Sweden	4.73	2.23	6.97
	Switzerland	7.72	5.01	12.74
	United Kingdom	8.62	5.11	13.73
	United States	4.38	5.23	9.61

Sources: Sigma Swiss Life, SVS.

Table A3.3. Number of Pensions and Average Amount Paid (UF) in the New System, by Instrument, 1982–2004

	PW		*Annuities*		*TW*		*TW*	
Year	*Number*	*Amount*	*Number*	*Amount*	*Number*	*Amount*	*Number*	*Amount*
1982	4,343	—	—	—	—	—	4,343	—
1983	2,020	—	1	3.68	—	—	2,021	3.68
1984	5,709	1.97	27	8.27	—	—	5,736	2.00
1985	7,373	1.84	236	7.87	—	—	7,609	2.03
1986	10,386	2.05	1,120	6.96	—	—	11,506	2.53
1987	13,257	2.01	2,757	6.82	—	—	16,014	2.84
1988	18,134	2.61	5,642	7.45	8	17.11	23,784	3.76
1989	27,444	3.15	11,267	7.38	9	17.44	38,720	4.38
1990	36,696	2.85	20,275	7.43	148	27.73	57,119	4.54
1991	48,794	3.36	32,908	7.65	1,019	24.08	82,721	5.32
1992	56,998	3.89	44,191	7.58	2,303	24.55	103,492	5.93
1993	68,268	3.97	57,906	7.55	2,852	24.41	129,026	6.03
1994	85,205	4.78	72,719	7.49	4,898	24.47	162,822	6.58
1995	98,699	5.36	84,898	7.39	6,803	20.96	190,400	6.82
1996	105,941	4.89	102,130	7.54	7,377	23.37	215,448	6.78
1997	113,251	5.03	122,250	7.48	7,974	23.95	243,475	6.88
1998	117,462	4.50	146,310	7.58	5,063	23.59	268,835	6.54
1999	128,391	4.92	167,743	7.78	5,364	27.19	301,498	6.91
2000	147,532	5.32	189,801	7.92	6,632	26.82	343,965	7.17
2001	162,516	5.31	213,431	8.15	6,829	28.04	382,776	7.30
2002	171,899	5.07	234,117	8.31	5,257	27.68	411,273	7.20
2003	184,860	5.15	254,363	8.31	5,981	26.04	445,204	7.24
2004	197,525	5.10	320,039	9.25	6,132	27.53	523,696	7.90

Source: SVS.

Table A3.4. Number of Pensions and Average Amount Paid (UF) in the New System, 1982–2004

Year	*Old age*		*Early retirement*		*Disability*		*Survivorship*		*Others*		*Total*	
	Number	*Amount*	*Number*	*Amount*	*Number*	*Amount*	*Number*	*Amount*	*Number*	*Amount*	*Number*	*Amount*
1982	—	—	—	—	749	14.0	3,536	2.6	58	3.2	4,343	4.6
1983	393	2.9	—	—	348	3.1	1,256	0.8	24	0.8	2,021	1.6
1984	1,730	3.2	—	—	906	3.4	3,033	0.9	67	0.9	5,736	2.0
1985	2,647	3.1	—	—	1,226	3.0	3,661	0.9	75	0.7	7,609	2.0
1986	4,835	3.6	—	—	1,721	3.5	4,839	1.1	111	1.1	11,506	2.5
1987	7,980	3.8	—	—	2,334	3.6	5,567	1.2	133	1.0	16,014	2.8
1988	11,819	4.3	772	9.5	3,294	5.3	7,703	1.7	196	1.7	23,784	3.7
1989	17,129	4.8	2,824	8.3	5,181	6.7	13,213	2.1	373	1.9	38,720	4.4
1990	23,876	4.9	5,790	8.6	6,785	6.9	20,052	2.3	616	2.2	57,119	4.6
1991	30,141	5.5	15,673	9.4	6,942	7.6	29,040	2.5	925	2.2	82,721	5.3
1992	35,763	5.8	26,054	9.7	7,196	7.7	33,347	2.9	1,132	2.4	103,492	5.9
1993	43,089	5.6	37,521	9.7	7,301	7.2	39,660	2.9	1,455	2.5	129,026	6.0
1994	51,440	6.0	53,354	10.2	8,295	7.7	47,853	3.1	1,880	2.5	162,822	6.6
1995	55,591	6.1	69,537	10.1	10,409	8.2	52,667	3.2	2,196	2.6	190,400	6.8
1996	61,374	6.0	80,576	10.0	11,931	7.7	58,989	3.1	2,578	2.3	215,448	6.8
1997	67,405	6.2	94,116	10.0	13,413	7.6	65,571	3.1	2,970	2.3	243,475	6.9
1998	71,161	6.0	106,177	9.2	15,875	7.4	72,215	3.1	3,407	2.4	268,835	6.5
1999	80,968	6.4	117,559	9.7	19,069	7.7	80,047	3.4	3,855	2.8	301,498	6.9
2000	93,152	6.6	132,221	10.2	20,281	8.1	93,650	3.5	4,661	2.9	343,965	7.2
2001	103,138	6.7	149,603	10.3	23,388	8.1	101,455	3.5	5,192	2.9	382,776	7.3
2002	109,804	6.6	159,888	10.1	26,809	8.1	109,022	3.5	5,750	2.7	411,273	7.2
2003	118,839	6.7	175,039	10.1	29,826	8.1	115,350	3.5	6,150	2.7	445,204	7.2
2004	134,207	7.2	221,201	10.4	34,199	8.4	126,020	4.3	8,069	3.3	523,696	7.9

Source: SAFP, SVS.

Table A3.5. Age Distribution of Old Age Pensioners

Age	*Percentage of men*	*Percentage of women*
60		56.5
61		13.9
62		6.9
63		4.6
64		3.5
65	60.3	3.0
66	13.6	2.2
67	6.1	1.7
68	3.9	1.2
70	5.9	2.0
72	3.8	1.4
74	2.4	1.0
76	1.5	0.6
77+	2.5	1.4
Total	**100.0**	**100.0**

Source: SAFP.

Table A3.6. Number and Average Amount of Old Age Pensions Paid (UF) in the New System, by Instrument, 1983–2004

	PW		*Annuities*		*TW*		*TW*	
Year	*Number*	*Amount*	*Number*	*Amount*	*Number*	*Amount*	*Number*	*Amount*
1983	392	2.9	1	3.7	—	—	393	2.9
1984	1,721	3.2	9	8.5	—	—	1,730	3.2
1985	2,501	2.8	146	8.4	—	—	2,647	3.1
1986	4,021	2.9	814	7.3	—	—	4,835	3.6
1987	5,801	2.6	2,179	7.0	—	—	7,980	3.8
1988	8,385	3.0	3,433	7.7	1	9.3	11,819	4.3
1989	12,423	3.7	4,705	7.9	1	9.3	17,129	4.8
1990	16,852	3.4	6,972	8.2	52	32.2	23,876	4.9
1991	21,469	4.3	8,428	8.3	244	21.5	30,141	5.5
1992	25,590	4.6	9,599	8.0	574	22.9	35,763	5.8
1993	30,868	4.5	11,529	7.7	692	22.1	43,089	5.6
1994	37,465	5.0	13,261	7.8	714	22.2	51,440	6.0
1995	40,777	5.2	14,162	7.9	652	19.9	55,591	6.1
1996	43,653	4.9	16,736	8.3	985	20.4	61,374	6.0
1997	46,482	5.0	19,723	8.3	1,200	21.6	67,405	6.2
1998	48,490	4.6	21,761	8.6	910	20.2	71,161	6.0
1999	52,575	4.9	27,696	8.7	697	26.8	80,968	6.4
2000	61,678	5.2	30,726	8.8	748	24.9	93,152	6.6
2001	68,069	5.2	34,090	9.1	979	26.0	103,138	6.7
2002	71,857	5.1	37,169	9.3	778	25.8	109,804	6.6
2003	77,831	5.2	40,066	9.4	942	24.4	118,839	6.7
2004	84,528	5.1	48,472	10.4	1,207	25.4	134,207	7.2

Source: SVS.

Table A3.7. Number and Average Amount of Early Retirement Pensions Paid (UF) in the New System, by Instrument, 1988–2004

	PW		*Annuities*		*TW*		*TW*	
Year	*Number*	*Amount*	*Number*	*Amount*	*Number*	*Amount*	*Number*	*Amount*
1988	5	12.9	766	9.4	1	26.2	772	9.5
1989	33	20.5	2,791	8.2	—	—	2,824	8.3
1990	41	17.9	5,717	8.4	32	29.8	5,790	8.6
1991	230	15.8	14,792	8.6	651	24.5	15,673	9.4
1992	934	15.6	23,461	8.4	1,659	24.7	26,054	9.7
1993	2,288	13.5	33,127	8.4	2,106	25.1	37,521	9.7
1994	5,572	14.8	43,750	8.3	4,032	24.9	53,354	10.2
1995	10,276	14.5	53,382	8.1	5,879	20.8	69,537	10.1
1996	10,818	13.3	63,831	8.2	5,927	24.0	80,576	10.0
1997	12,177	13.6	75,626	8.2	6,313	24.5	94,116	10.0
1998	11,964	10.7	90,443	8.4	3,770	24.7	106,177	9.2
1999	14,146	11.3	99,127	8.7	4,286	27.4	117,559	9.7
2000	15,032	14.1	111,720	8.9	5,469	27.3	132,221	10.2
2001	16,612	13.8	127,636	9.1	5,355	28.7	149,603	10.3
2002	17,057	12.8	139,049	9.3	3,782	28.3	159,888	10.1
2003	19,208	12.9	151,494	9.3	4,337	26.4	175,039	10.1
2004	20,102	11.5	196,984	9.9	4,115	28.3	221,201	10.4

Source: SVS.

Table A3.8. Number and Average Amount of Disability Pensions Paid (UF) in the New System, by Instrument, 1982–2004

	PW		Annuities		TW					
Year	*Number*	*Amount*	*Number*	*Amount*	*Number*	*Amount*	*Total number*	*Average amount*	*Special number*	*System amount*
1982	749	14.0	—	—	—	—	749	14.0	42	14.0
1983	348	3.1	—	—	—	—	348	3.1	1,924	13.5
1984	888	3.3	18	8.2	—	—	906	3.4	3,152	11.7
1985	1,136	2.7	90	7.0	—	—	1,226	3.0	4,503	10.7
1986	1,415	3.0	306	6.0	—	—	1,721	3.5	6,258	10.5
1987	1,756	2.8	578	6.0	—	—	2,334	3.6	8,286	10.3
1988	2,426	4.5	867	7.8	1	50.0	3,294	5.3	9,492	10.6
1989	3,487	5.2	1,692	9.8	2	43.6	5,181	6.7	9,207	10.7
1990	4,095	4.4	2,645	10.5	45	30.2	6,785	6.9	8,992	10.7
1991	3,970	4.8	2,886	10.5	86	33.3	6,942	7.6	8,549	11.0
1992	4,193	5.3	2,953	10.5	50	44.0	7,196	7.7	8,240	10.9
1993	4,256	5.2	3,005	10.0	40	26.9	7,301	7.2	7,995	11.0
1994	4,923	6.0	3,241	9.5	131	25.3	8,295	7.7	7,800	11.2
1995	6,834	6.5	3,322	10.1	253	27.1	10,409	8.2	7,567	11.4
1996	7,593	5.7	3,910	10.0	428	22.6	11,931	7.7	7,372	11.2
1997	8,475	5.7	4,530	9.9	408	22.6	13,413	7.6	7,130	11.3
1998	10,183	5.5	5,349	10.1	343	21.7	15,875	7.4	6,116	11.4
1999	11,834	5.6	6,880	10.4	355	26.2	19,069	7.7	6,042	11.3
2000	12,045	6.0	7,840	10.4	396	24.4	20,281	8.1	5,612	11.5
2001	14,119	6.0	8,802	10.6	467	25.6	23,388	8.1	5,397	11.5
2002	15,901	5.7	10,243	10.8	665	26.5	26,809	8.1	5,315	11.6
2003	17,779	5.8	11,369	10.8	678	24.9	29,826	8.1	5,152	11.6
2004	20,141	5.6	13,274	11.5	776	26.8	34,199	8.4	4,993	12.0

Source: SVS.

Table A3.9. Number and Average Amount of Survivorship Pensions Paid (UF) in the New System, by Instrument, 1982–2004

	PW		*Annuities*		*TW*					
Year	*Number*	*Amount*	*Number*	*Amount*	*Number*	*Amount*	*Total number*	*Average amount*	*Special number*	*System amount*
1982	3,536	2.6	—	—	—	—	3,536	2.6	138	2.6
1983	1,256	0.8	—	—	—	—	1,256	0.8	7,086	2.6
1984	3,033	0.9	—	—	—	—	3,033	0.9	10,972	2.3
1985	3,661	0.9	—	—	—	—	3,661	0.9	13,979	2.3
1986	4,839	1.1	—	—	—	—	4,839	1.1	17,440	2.3
1987	5,567	1.2	—	—	—	—	5,567	1.2	21,077	2.3
1988	7,127	1.6	571	3.2	5	10.3	7,703	1.7	22,472	2.4
1989	11,156	2.0	2,051	3.2	6	10.1	13,213	2.2	20,830	2.6
1990	15,176	1.8	4,857	3.5	19	6.4	20,052	2.3	20,241	2.7
1991	22,318	2.2	6,685	3.6	37	12.2	29,040	2.5	20,846	2.6
1992	25,294	2.6	8,034	3.6	19	9.0	33,347	2.9	18,725	2.8
1993	29,610	2.6	10,037	3.8	13	24.8	39,660	2.9	17,638	3.2
1994	35,628	2.9	12,204	3.8	21	15.9	47,853	3.1	16,728	3.1
1995	38,904	3.0	13,744	3.7	19	25.2	52,667	3.2	15,719	3.3
1996	41,689	2.8	17,265	4.0	35	17.6	58,989	3.1	14,995	3.5
1997	43,683	2.7	21,836	3.9	52	18.5	65,571	3.1	14,318	3.7
1998	44,166	2.6	28,009	3.9	40	16.1	72,215	3.1	14,525	3.9
1999	46,910	3.0	33,111	4.0	26	20.1	80,047	3.4	13,941	4.2
2000	55,229	3.1	38,402	4.1	19	22.0	93,650	3.5	13,061	4.5
2001	59,754	3.1	41,675	4.2	26	20.9	101,455	3.6	12,536	4.7
2002	62,726	3.0	46,265	4.3	31	21.0	109,022	3.5	11,885	4.9
2003	65,422	3.1	49,905	3.9	23	21.6	115,350	3.5	11,392	5.1
2004	67,746	3.1	58,242	5.7	32	16.1	126,020	4.3	10,934	5.4

Source: SVS.

Table A3.10. Number and Average Amount of Programmed Withdrawal Pensions Paid under the New System, 1982–2004

	Old Age		*Early Retirement*		*Disability*		*Survivorship*		*Others*		*Total*	
Year	*Number*	*Amount*	*Number*	*Amount*	*Number*	*Amount*	*Number*	*Amount*	*Number*	*Amount*	*Number*	*Amount*
1982	—	—	—	—	749	14.0	3,536	2.6	58	3.2	4,343	4.5
1983	392	2.9	—	—	348	3.1	1,256	0.8	24	0.8	2,020	1.6
1984	1,721	3.2	—	—	888	3.3	3,033	0.9	67	0.9	5,709	2.0
1985	2,501	2.8	—	—	1,136	2.7	3,661	0.9	75	0.7	7,373	1.8
1986	4,021	2.9	—	—	1,415	3.0	4,839	1.1	111	1.1	10,386	2.1
1987	5,801	2.6	—	—	1,756	2.8	5,567	1.2	133	1.0	13,257	2.0
1988	8,385	3.0	5	12.9	2,426	4.5	7,127	1.6	191	1.8	18,134	2.6
1989	12,423	3.7	33	20.5	3,487	5.2	11,156	1.9	345	1.7	27,444	3.2
1990	16,852	3.4	41	17.9	4,095	4.4	15,176	1.8	532	1.9	36,696	2.9
1991	21,469	4.3	230	15.8	3,970	4.8	22,318	2.2	807	1.9	48,794	3.4
1992	25,590	4.6	934	15.6	4,193	5.3	25,294	2.6	987	2.1	56,998	3.9
1993	30,868	4.5	2,288	13.5	4,256	5.2	29,610	2.6	1,246	2.2	68,268	4.0
1994	37,465	5.0	5,572	14.8	4,923	6.0	35,628	2.9	1,617	2.2	85,205	4.8
1995	40,777	5.2	10,276	14.5	6,834	6.5	38,904	3.0	1,908	2.4	98,699	5.4
1996	43,653	4.9	10,818	13.3	7,593	5.7	41,689	2.8	2,188	2.1	105,941	4.9
1997	46,482	5.0	12,177	13.6	8,475	5.7	43,683	2.7	2,434	2.0	113,251	5.0
1998	48,490	4.6	11,964	10.7	10,183	5.5	44,166	2.6	2,659	2.0	117,462	4.5
1999	52,575	4.9	14,146	11.3	11,834	5.6	46,910	2.9	2,926	2.2	128,391	4.9
2000	61,678	5.2	15,032	14.1	12,045	6.0	55,229	3.1	3,548	2.5	147,532	5.3
2001	68,069	5.2	16,612	13.8	14,119	6.0	59,754	3.1	3,962	2.4	162,516	5.3
2002	71,857	5.1	17,057	12.8	15,901	5.7	62,726	3.0	4,358	2.2	171,899	5.1
2003	77,831	5.2	19,208	12.9	17,779	5.8	65,422	3.1	4,620	2.3	184,860	5.2
2004	84,528	5.1	20,102	11.5	20,141	5.6	67,746	3.1	5,000	2.3	197,525	5.1

Source: SVS.

Table A3.11. Number and Average Amount of Annuities Pensions Paid under the New System, 1983–2004

	Old Age		*Early retirement*		*Disability*		*Survivorship*		*Others*		*Total*	
Year	*Number*	*Amount*	*Number*	*Amount*	*Number*	*Amount*	*Number*	*Amount*	*Number*	*Amount*	*Number*	*Amount*
1983	1	3.7	—	—	—	—	—	—	—	—	1	3.7
1984	9	8.5	—	—	18	8.2	—	—	—	—	27	8.3
1985	146	8.4	—	—	90	7.0	—	—	—	—	236	7.9
1986	814	7.3	—	—	306	6.0	—	—	—	—	1,120	7.0
1987	2,179	7.0	—	—	578	6.0	—	—	—	—	2,757	6.8
1988	3,433	7.7	766	9.4	867	7.8	571	3.2	5	1.6	5,642	7.5
1989	4,705	7.9	2,791	8.2	1,692	9.8	2,051	3.2	28	4.5	11,267	7.4
1990	6,972	8.2	5,717	8.4	2,645	10.5	4,857	3.5	84	4.2	20,275	7.4
1991	8,428	8.3	14,792	8.6	2,886	10.5	6,685	3.6	117	3.9	32,908	7.7
1992	9,599	8.0	23,461	8.4	2,953	10.5	8,034	3.6	144	4.0	44,191	7.6
1993	11,529	7.7	33,127	8.4	3,005	10.0	10,037	3.8	208	4.5	57,906	7.5
1994	13,261	7.8	43,750	8.3	3,241	9.5	12,204	3.8	263	4.4	72,719	7.5
1995	14,162	7.9	53,382	8.1	3,322	10.1	13,744	3.7	288	4.1	84,898	7.4
1996	16,736	8.3	63,831	8.2	3,910	10.0	17,265	4.0	388	3.9	102,130	7.5
1997	19,723	8.3	75,626	8.2	4,530	9.9	21,836	3.9	535	3.8	122,250	7.5
1998	21,761	8.6	90,443	8.4	5,349	10.1	28,009	3.8	748	4.0	146,310	7.6
1999	27,696	8.7	99,127	8.7	6,880	10.4	33,111	4.0	929	4.6	167,743	7.8
2000	30,726	8.8	111,720	8.9	7,840	10.4	38,402	4.1	1,113	4.4	189,801	7.9
2001	34,090	9.1	127,636	9.1	8,802	10.6	41,675	4.2	1,228	4.4	213,431	8.2
2002	37,169	9.3	139,049	9.3	10,243	10.8	46,265	4.3	1,391	4.4	234,117	8.3
2003	40,066	9.4	151,494	9.3	11,369	10.8	49,905	3.9	1,529	3.8	254,363	8.3
2004	48,472	10.4	196,984	9.9	13,274	11.5	58,242	5.7	3,067	3.7	320,039	9.3

Source: SVS.

Table A3.12. Number and Average Amount of Temporary Withdrawal Pensions Paid (UF) under the New System, 1988–2004

	Old Age		*Early retirement*		*Disability*		*Survivorship*		*Others*		*Total*	
Year	*Number*	*Amount*	*Number*	*Amount*	*Number*	*Amount*	*Number*	*Amount*	*Number*	*Amount*	*Number*	*Amount*
1988	1	9.3	1	26.2	1	50.0	5	10.3	—	—	8	17.1
1989	1	9.3	—	—	2	43.6	6	10.1	—	—	9	17.4
1990	52	32.2	32	29.8	45	30.2	19	6.4	—	—	148	27.7
1991	244	21.5	651	24.5	86	33.3	37	12.2	1	6.4	1,019	24.1
1992	574	22.9	1,659	24.7	50	44.0	19	9.0	1	6.4	2,303	24.6
1993	692	22.1	2,106	25.1	40	26.9	13	24.8	1	10.3	2,852	24.4
1994	714	22.2	4,032	24.9	131	25.3	21	15.9	—	—	4,898	24.5
1995	652	19.9	5,879	20.8	253	27.1	19	25.2	—	—	6,803	21.0
1996	985	20.4	5,927	24.0	428	22.6	35	17.6	2	14.9	7,377	23.4
1997	1,200	21.6	6,313	24.5	408	22.6	52	18.5	1	6.9	7,974	23.9
1998	910	20.2	3,770	24.7	343	21.7	40	16.1	—	—	5,063	23.6
1999	697	26.8	4,286	27.4	355	26.2	26	20.1	—	—	5,364	27.2
2000	748	24.9	5,469	27.3	396	24.4	19	22.0	—	—	6,632	26.8
2001	979	26.0	5,355	28.7	467	25.6	26	20.9	2	10.5	6,829	28.0
2002	778	25.8	3,782	28.3	665	26.5	31	21.0	1	24.9	5,257	27.7
2003	942	24.4	4,337	26.4	678	24.9	23	21.6	1	6.4	5,981	25.9
2004	1,207	25.4	4,115	28.3	776	26.8	32	16.1	2	7.0	6,132	27.5

Source: SVS.

Table A3.13. Number of New Annuity Policies, by Type, 1990–2004

Year	*Normal old age*	*Early retirement*	*Disability*	*Survivorship*	*Total*
1990	2,424	3,989	1,054	1,189	8,656
1991	1,981	8,695	337	806	11,819
1992	2,022	11,795	72	662	14,551
1993	2,956	11,950	110	1,060	16,076
1994	2,575	14,824	396	941	18,755
1995	2,531	17,557	579	972	21,667
1996	4,290	15,722	1,016	2,017	23,082
1997	4,540	17,023	957	2,224	24,771
1998	5,372	11,475	1,429	2,843	21,154
1999	3,689	15,412	1,162	1,996	22,322
2000	3,899	20,411	1,318	1,824	27,528
2001	4,271	21,109	1,324	1,675	28,515
2002	3,827	14,814	1,665	1,732	22,223
2003	3,683	16,188	1,789	1,641	23,301
2004	4,270	14,038	1,739	1,603	21,650

Source: SVS.

Table A3.14. Average Premiums by Type of Pension, 1990–2004 (in UF)

Year	*Normal old age*	*Early retirement*	*Disability*	*Survivorship*	*Total*
1990	1,290	1,424	2,016	1,656	1,490
1991	1,309	1,551	1,829	1,624	1,523
1992	1,105	1,431	1,424	1,454	1,387
1993	1,187	1,471	1,419	1,531	1,422
1994	1,106	1,463	1,522	1,362	1,411
1995	1,103	1,402	1,442	1,393	1,367
1996	1,345	1,567	1,567	1,487	1,518
1997	1,347	1,585	1,582	1,429	1,527
1998	1,540	1,783	1,714	1,497	1,678
1999	1,681	1,934	1,760	1,526	1,847
2000	1,604	1,837	1,819	1,579	1,786
2001	1,822	1,841	1,937	1,714	1,835
2002	1,857	1,994	2,091	1,670	1,952
2003	1,918	2,028	2,123	1,811	2,002
2004	2,211	2,329	2,338	1,963	2,279

Source: SVS.

Table A3.15. Average Annuity Rates on Each Type of Pension, 1990–2004 (in %)

Year	*Normal old age*	*Early retirement*	*Disability*	*Survivorship*	*Total*
1990	5.65	5.30	5.72	5.48	5.48
1991	5.15	4.97	5.21	5.05	5.01
1992	5.22	5.11	5.03	5.01	5.12
1993	5.33	5.13	5.25	5.11	5.16
1994	4.88	4.74	4.85	4.68	4.76
1995	4.97	4.82	4.93	4.76	4.83
1996	5.24	5.07	5.15	4.96	5.09
1997	5.17	5.00	5.02	4.86	5.01
1998	5.73	5.54	5.56	5.37	5.56
1999	5.52	5.28	5.38	5.16	5.31
2000	5.58	5.34	5.38	5.18	5.37
2001	5.45	5.23	5.33	5.07	5.26
2002	5.11	4.95	4.96	4.80	4.97
2003	4.23	4.17	4.26	4.04	4.17
2004	3.33	3.42	3.50	3.36	3.40

Source: SVS.

Table A3.16. Average Value of New Annuities, 1990–2004 (in UF)

Year	*Normal old age*	*Early retirement*	*Disability*	*Survivorship*	*Total*
1990	8.82	8.52	12.56	13.14	9.73
1991	8.62	8.93	11.19	12.40	9.18
1992	7.47	8.37	8.75	11.09	8.37
1993	8.04	8.63	9.20	12.14	8.76
1994	7.38	8.28	9.25	10.80	8.31
1995	7.31	7.88	8.86	11.14	7.99
1996	9.23	9.12	9.81	12.38	9.46
1997	9.13	9.15	9.75	11.69	9.40
1998	10.86	10.92	11.00	13.22	11.22
1999	11.60	11.41	11.16	13.18	11.59
2000	11.00	10.89	11.39	13.13	11.08
2001	12.35	10.76	12.15	14.34	11.28
2002	12.29	11.36	12.50	13.79	11.80
2003	11.69	10.62	11.97	13.61	11.09
2004	12.43	12.22	12.68	16.09	12.64

Source: SVS.

Table A3.17. Portfolio Composition of Chilean Pension Funds (%), 1983–2004

	1983	*1990*	*1994*	*2000*	*2002*	*2003*	*2004*
Claims on the public sector	**42.1**	**44.1**	**39.7**	**35.7**	**30.0**	**24.7**	**18.7**
Government bonds	16.5	1.5	0.2	0.0	0.0	0.3	1.2
Central Bank bonds	25.6	42.5	38.5	31.9	24.4	19.1	12.6
Other	—	0.1	1.0	3.8	5.6	5.3	4.9
Claims on the financial sector	**55.8**	**33.4**	**20.1**	**35.6**	**35.0**	**27.3**	**29.5**
Mortgage bonds	42.9	16.1	13.7	14.4	11.1	8.8	6.8
Time deposits/CDs	16.2	16.3	4.8	18.7	21.2	15.0	19.4
Other	0.7	1.0	1.6	2.5	2.7	3.5	3.4
Claims on the corporate sector	**2.0**	**22.4**	**39.3**	**17.6**	**18.4**	**24.0**	**24.4**
Shares	—	11.3	32.1	11.1	9.0	13.5	14.7
Bonds	2.0	11.1	6.3	4.0	7.1	7.7	6.8
Other	—	—	0.9	2.5	2.3	2.8	2.9
Claims on the foreign sector	—	—	**0.9**	**10.9**	**16.4**	**23.8**	**27.2**
Quotas of mutual funds	—	—	—	8.9	11.9	20.4	24.4
Other	—	—	—	2.0	4.5	3.4	2.8
Total	**100.0**	**100.0**	**100.0**	**100.0**	**100.0**	**100.0**	**100.0**
Memo items:							
Total variable income	—	11.3	33.1	23.1	24.2	37.8	42.8
Total assets/GDP	5.6	22.0	38.0	50.4	55.8	59.9	59.1

Source: SAFP.

Table A3.18. Average Age, Income, Balance, and Size of Different Funds, Dec. 2004

	Fund A	*Fund B*	*Fund C*	*Fund D*	*Fund E*
Average age (years)	32	28	42	57	45
Average wage (1,000 Pesos)	489	306	343	355	404
Average balance (1,000 Pesos)	6,447	1,776	5,033	6,638	12,008
Number of members (1,000)	385	3,083	3,175	702	80
Number of active contributors (1,000)	249	1,271	1,265	198	54

Source: SAFP.

Table A3.19. Portfolio Composition of Pension Funds, by Type of Portfolio, December 2004

	A	*B*	*C*	*D*	*E*	*F*
Claims on the public sector	**6.1**	**12.4**	**18.7**	**29.9**	**46.0**	**18.7**
Central Bank of Chile	3.8	8.4	12.6	20.8	28.3	12.6
Government	0.6	0.9	1.3	1.4	3.0	1.2
Recognition bonds	1.6	3.2	4.9	7.6	14.7	4.9
Claims on the financial sector	**14.5**	**26.4**	**31.1**	**37.1**	**32.3**	**29.5**
Mortgage bonds	1.8	4.7	7.3	9.2	14.2	6.8
Time deposits	8.7	18.1	20.2	25.7	15.8	19.4
Bonds of financial institutions	0.1	0.6	1.4	0.7	1.2	1.0
Shares of financial institutions	1.3	1.2	1.1	0.7	0.0	1.0
Forwards	2.6	1.8	1.2	0.8	1.1	1.4
Claims on the corporate sector	**23.7**	**26.2**	**25.7**	**19.5**	**13.6**	**24.4**
Shares	19.8	18.8	14.4	9.5	0.0	14.7
Bonds	1.9	4.4	8.0	7.8	13.3	6.8
Units of investment funds	2.0	3.0	3.1	1.7	0.0	2.7
Commercial paper	0.1	0.2	0.2	0.4	0.3	0.2
Claims on the foreign sector	**55.5**	**34.8**	**24.3**	**13.2**	**7.7**	**27.2**
Units of mutual funds and shares	54.6	33.9	21.1	9.2	0.0	24.4
Indirect investments abroad	0.4	0.4	0.5	0.2	0.0	0.4
Debt instruments	0.5	0.6	2.7	3.8	7.7	2.4
Other						0.0
Other assets	**0.2**	**0.1**	**0.1**	**0.3**	**0.3**	**0.1**
Total assets	**100.0**	**100.0**	**100.0**	**100.0**	**100.0**	**100.0**
Total assets (US$ million)	**5,455**	**12,646**	**32,205**	**8,698**	**1,802**	**60,806**
Memo item: Variable income	**77.7**	**56.9**	**39.7**	**21.1**	**0.0**	**42.8**

Source: SAFP.

Table A3.20. Real Rates of Returns of Individual AFPs (% p.a.), 1999–2004

	1999	*2000*	*2001*	*2002*	*2003*	*2004*
Cuprum	16.3	4.4	6.6	2.8	12.8	9.6
Habitat	16.3	4.4	7.0	4.1	11.3	9.3
Magister	18.4	4.2	7.0	3.6	10.1	—
Planvital	16.1	4.4	6.9	3.3	11.1	9.0
Provida	16.2	4.5	6.4	3.3	11.7	8.9
Santa Maria	16.0	4.5	7.0	3.1	11.5	8.3
Summa Bansander	16.3	4.2	6.9	3.5	13.3	9.3
System	16.3	4.4	6.7	3.4	11.9	9.1

Source: SAFP.

Table A3.21. Real Rates of Return of Each Portfolio Managed by the AFPs (% p.a.), 2004

	A	*B*	*C*	*D*	*E*
Cuprum	13.50	11.36	9.32	6.71	5.68
Habitat	12.87	10.39	8.97	7.19	5.80
Planvital	11.94	9.68	8.99	6.91	5.02
Provida	12.73	9.98	8.82	6.60	5.18
Santa Maria	12.27	9.59	8.05	6.54	4.38
Summa Bansander	12.61	10.16	9.02	7.16	5.84
System	12.86	10.26	8.86	6.80	5.44

Source: SAFP.

Table A3.22. Expenses as Percent of Assets for LICOs in High Income OECD Countries

	1996	*1997*	*1998*	*1999*	*2000*	*2001*
Australia	1.6	2.4	2.3	2.1	2.6	2.7
Austria	2.6	—	—	—	—	—
Belgium	1.6	1.4	1.4	1.1	1.1	1.1
Canada	—	3.7	3.6	2.1	2.1	1.9
Denmark	0.4	0.5	—	—	—	0.6
Finland	1.8	—	1.2	1.1	1.0	0.9
Germany	2.1	2.0	1.9	2.4	2.0	2.2
Ireland	2.8	—	—	—	—	—
Italy	0.7	0.7	—	—	—	—
Japan	—	—	—	—	2.0	2.0
Luxembourg	2.5	—	1.5	1.6	1.6	—
Netherlands	1.3	1.3	1.4	1.3	1.3	1.4
Portugal	2.8	2.6	2.5	1.9	1.7	1.6
Singapore	—	—	—	1.3	1.1	1.0
Sweden	0.6	0.6	0.6	0.5	0.6	0.6
Switzerland	0.9	—	—	—	—	—
United Kingdom	1.2	1.0	0.9	0.9	0.9	1.0
Average	1.6	1.6	1.7	1.5	1.5	1.4

Source: OECD.

— = not available.

Table A3.23. Pension Funds Investment Regulations in Chile

Limits instruments/Classes of instruments							Limits on issuers		
Bank deposits	*Bonds*	*Equity*	*Real estate*	*Investment funds*	*Loans*	*Foreign assets*	*Diversification requirements*	*Self-investment/ conflicts of interest*	*Ownership concentration limits*
Combined limits for time deposits, bonds, and other instruments of financial institutions: Fund A: 40% Fund B: 40% Fund C: 50% Fund D: 70% Fund E: 80%	Bonds issued by the State/ Central Bank: Fund A: 40% Fund B: 40% Fund C: 50% Fund D: 70% Fund E: 80% Bonds issued by financial institutions: see first column investment-grade bonds issued by public and private companies: Fund A: 30% Fund B: 30%	Individual domestic share approved by the CCR (90 shares approved): Fund A: 60% Fund B: 50% Fund C: 30% Fund D: 15% Fund E: 0% Overall floor and ceiling on all variable income instruments (domestic and foreign shares, domestic and foreign quotas of mutual equity funds:	Direct investments in property not allowed. Limits on mortgage bonds (see also second column): Fund A: 40% Fund B: 40% Fund C: 50% Fund D: 60% Fund E: 70%	Joint limits on investment and mutual fund shares and committed payments: Fund A: 40% Fund B: 30% Fund C: 20% Fund D: 10% Fund E: 0%	Fund A: 15% Fund B: 10% Fund C: 5% Fund D: 5% Fund E: 5%	30% overall limit on foreign investments. Additional limits on foreign currency exposure without exchange coverage Fund A: 37% Fund B: 22% Fund C: 18% Fund D: 13% Fund E: 9%	Several issuer limits expressed as a basic percentage of individual fund assets (Funds A to E) in each AFP. Limits vary depending on sectors (e.g., financial, corporate, and foreign); instruments type (e.g., shares, bonds), company type (e.g., general, leasing), and other parameters (e.g., companies with less than 3	1% of fund assets for all claims on individual companies related to the AFP; 5% of fund assets for all claims on all companies related to the AFP; Several limits on quotas of mutual funds whose managers are related to the AFP.	Several issuer limits expressed as a percentage of the sum of all AFP holdings of a given instrument on the total equity or assets of the issuing company. Limits also vary depending on sectors (e.g., financial, corporate, and foreign); instrument type (e.g., shares, bonds), and company

Fund C: 40% Fund D: 50% Fund E: 60% Investment grade commercial paper: Fund A: 10% Fund B: 10% Fund C: 10% Fund D: 20% Fund E: 30% Letters of Credit/ Mortgage bonds: Fund A: 40% Fund B: 40% Fund C: 50% Fund D: 60% Fund E: 70%	Fund A: 40–80% Fund B: 25-60% Fund C: 15–40% Fund D: 5–20% Overall ceiling on listed domestic shares not approved by the CCR: Fund A: 3% Fund B: 3% Fund C: 1% Fund D: 1% Fund E: 0%	years). This results in 21 different instruments subject to specific issuer limits. The basic percentages vary from 0.15% of fund assets for riskier shares to 5% for approved shares. 7% for debt instruments to 10% to debt instruments issued by banks.	type (e.g., general, leasing). This results in 13 different instruments subject to specific issuer limits. The basic percentage varies from 2.5% of total shares outstanding for bank shares to 7% for nonfinancial company shares to 35% for mutual fund quotas. In the case of debt instruments the percentages are defined by a separate set of single multiples that vary

(Continued)

Table A3.23. Pension Funds Investment Regulations in Chile *(Continued)*

	Limits Instruments/Classes of Instruments						*Limits on Issuers*		
Bank deposits	*Bonds*	*Equity*	*Real estate*	*Investment funds*	*Loans*	*Foreign assets*	*Diversification requirements*	*Self-investment/ conflicts of interest*	*Ownership concentration limits*
									depending on the instrument.
	Additional sublimits by bond type (convertibles) and by credit risk classification: BBB and N-3 rated bonds limited to: Fund A: 10% Fund B: 10% Fund C: 10% Fund D: 5% Fund E: 5% Further joint limits on fixed income	Additional sublimits for shares with low liquidity: Fund A: 10% Fund B: 8% Fund C: 5% Fund D: 2% Fund E: 0% Further joint limits on fixed income and equities, involving equities, funds, high risk and convertible bonds, issuers		Additional sublimits for mutual funds shares: (5% for Funds A to D and 0% for Fund E). Further joint limits on fixed income and equities, involving equities, funds, high risk and convertible bonds, issuers with a history of less than		Limit on other potential authorized instruments by the Central Bank (1%–5% for all funds). Numerous additional sublimits by instrument, groups of instruments, issuer, and related issuer are described in other sections.	The limits on individual issuers are reduced further through the product of the basic percentages by up to four reducing factors with values between zero and one: Risk Factor, Diversification Factor, Concentration Factor, and Liquidity Factor. There are further		There are additional limits on specific issues by the same company that vary between 20% and 35% of the issue. There are further issuer limits on connected companies and companies related to the AFP.

	and equities, involving equities, funds, high risk and convertible bonds, issuers with a history of less than 3 years	with a history of less than 3 years	3 years	issuer limits on connected companies and companies related to the AFP.

Source: Authors' analysis.

Table A3.24. Pension Funds Investment Regulations in OECD Countries

	Limits Instruments/Classes of Instruments							*Limits on Issuers*		
Countries	*Bank deposits*	*Bonds*	*Equity*	*Real estate*	*Investment funds*	*Loans*	*Foreign assets*	*Diversification requirements*	*Self-investment/ conflicts of interest*	*Ownership concentration limits*
Australia	No limits	No limits	No limits	No limits	No limits	No member-related loans	No limits	None	5% of fund assets	None
Canada	No limits	No limits	No limits	25%	No limits	No limits	30%	10% of fund assets for investments in securities, stocks, bonds, and notes issued by one company or person; 5% of fund assets for investments in one individual property, 15% of fund assets for investments in any resource property	10% of fund assets; Other conflict of interest rules also apply (related party rules)	30% of the voting shares issued by a single company
Ireland	No limits	No limits	No limits	No limits	No limits	No limits	No limits	10% of fund assets for holdings of single issues, for purposes of proving solvency	5% of fund assets for purposes of proving solvency, disclosure of exposures exceeding this level	None

Netherlands	No limits	No limits	No limits	No limits	No limits	No limits	No limits	General requirement for diversification	5% of funds assets until the level of technical provision, in case of exceeding assets (surplus), raised to 10% of fund assets	None
U.K.	No limits	No limits	No limits	No limits	No limits	No employer-related loans	No limits	General requirement for diversification	5% of fund assets	None
U.S.	No limits	No limits	No limits	No limits	No limits	No employer-related loans	Assets must be under the jurisdiction of US courts	General requirement for diversification	For all DB plans and some DC plans, 10% limit on investment in employer securities or real property; no transactions with parties in interest, unless an exemption applies	None

(Continued)

Table A3.24. Pension Funds Investment Regulations in the OECD *(Continued)*

	Limits Instruments/Classes of Instruments							*Limits on Issuers*		
Countries	*Bank deposits*	*Bonds*	*Equity*	*Real estate*	*Investment funds*	*Loans*	*Foreign assets*	*Diversification requirements*	*Self-investment/ conflicts of interest*	*Ownership concentration limits*
Denmark	No limits	No limits on Government bonds of OECD countries and mortgage bonds complying with certain criteria, 70% limit on other types of bonds of OECD countries, 10% limit otherwise	70%	70% on property and investment trust holdings	70%	No limits (if gilt-edged)	70% limit on all assets except Government and mortgage bonds of OECD countries, 10% limit otherwise, 80% minimum currency matching requirement; for EU currencies, up to 50% of liabilities can be covered by assets denominated in euros	2% of fund assets on instruments issued by a single company. 3% of fund assets when issued in stock exchange in OECD with equity capital over DKK250 million. 40% of fund assets on mortgage bonds and similars. 10% of fund assets on instruments issued by credit institutions in OECD	Limit of 2% of provisions for investment in any one enterprise (only relevant for company pension funds)	Prohibited to exercise controlling influence over the company in question
Portugal	No limits	No limits on listed instruments 15% joint limit on unlisted	No limits on listed instruments	50%	No limits on harmonized funds,	50%	No limits on OECD securities, 15% limit on listed equities and	10% of the fund's assets on all instruments issued by a single company	5% of fund assets additional limits on sponsors apply	10% of the shares or voting rights issued by a

		bonds and equities	15% joint limit on unlisted bonds and equities		5% limit on non-harmo-nized		bonds outside the OECD			single company. Sum of shares held by all pension funds managed by the same management company can-not exceed 20% of share capital or vot-ing rights
Spain	15%	No limits	No limits (listed) 10% limit (unlisted)	No limits	No limits	10% (if no mortgage guarantee)	No limits on OECD securities, 90% of assets must be invested in recognized markets. Deposits and other money market assets must be 1–15%	10% of fund's assets on all instruments is-sued by a single com-pany	10% of fund assets	5% of the mar-ket value of the securities issued by a single company
Switzer-land	No limits	See foreign asset column	30%	50%			Overall limit 30% sublimits; 20%	10% of the fund's assets on debt instruments issued by	10% of fund assets	None

(Continued)

Table A3.24. Pension Funds Investment Regulations in the OECD *(Continued)*

	Limits Instruments/Classes of Instruments							Limits on Issuers		
Countries	*Bank deposits*	*Bonds*	*Equity*	*Real estate*	*Investment funds*	*Loans*	*Foreign assets*	*Diversification requirements*	*Self-investment/ conflicts of interest*	*Ownership concentration limits*
							equities; 20% bonds; 50% domestic and foreign equity; 30% domestic and foreign bonds; 70% real estate and equity	a single company (except government, banks, and insurance companies (5% for foreign assets). 10% of the fund's assets for equity issued by a single company (5% foreign assets)		

Source: Authors' analysis.

Table A3.25. LICO Investment Regulations in Chile

1. Fixed income		2. Variable Income					
Bank deposits	*Loan*	*Equity*	*Investment funds*	*3. Foreign assets*	*4. Real estate*	*5. Other assets*	*6. Ownership concentration limits*
a) Securities issued or warranted by the State/Central Bank: No Limits b) Term deposits, bonds, mortgage bonds, and other instruments of financial institutions: No Limits c) Bonds or commercial paper issued by public and private companies: With Classification >=BBB: No Limits Not registered issuers, issuers registered without classification or with Classification below BBB or N–3: 5%	e) Participation in loan agreements with the participation of two or more financial institutions: 3% (TR + RC)	a) For individual domestic shares: no limit for shares with Presencia and a 5% (TR+RC)-ceiling on shares without presencia Overall ceiling on all domestic variable income instruments (domestic shares, domestic quotas of mutual funds, and	b) Limit on investment funds shares with assets invested in domestic securities or assets 10% (TR+RC). c) Mutual fund shares invested in domestic securities or assets: No limit Overall ceiling on all domestic variable income instruments (domestic shares, domestic quotas of mutual funds, and	a) Bonds, financial claims, and commercial paper issued by foreign States, Central Banks, or by foreign public and private companies or financial institutions with classification >=BBB: No limit Bonds and commercial paper issued by foreign States, Central Banks, or foreign public and private companies or financial institutions with classification <BBB: 5% (TR+RC) b) Shares of foreign corporations, mutual or investment funds, or domestic	a) Direct investments in inhabitable property: 20% (TR+RC) b) Mortgage bonds: no limits	Credit for unpaid insured premiums 100% RRC + 10% RC Unpaid (but informed) losses 100% R.SIN + 10%RC Credit for unpaid annuities and disability insured premiums 100% R.SIN Advancements to life insurance policy holders 100% of redemption value Credit for ceding insurers undisbursed premiums 100% RRC	Several issuer limits expressed as a percentage of the sum of all insurance companies holdings of a given instrument on the total equity of the issuing company. Limits also vary depending on sectors (e.g., financial and corporate); instrument type (e.g., shares, bonds). This results in 11 different instrument subject to specific issuer limits. The basic percentage vary from 13% of total shares outstanding for corporate shares to 20% for mutual or investment fund quotas. In the case of bonds and commercial

(Continued)

Table A3.25. LICO Investment Regulations in Chile *(Continued)*

1. Fixed income		*2. Variable Income*					
Bank deposits	*Loan*	*Equity*	*Investment funds*	*3. Foreign assets*	*4. Real estate*	*5. Other assets*	*6. Ownership concentration limits*
of Technical Reserve + Risk Capital d) Securitized mortgage instruments: 30% of TR + RC		investment funds) 40% (TR+RC)	investment funds) 40% (TR+RC)	Mutual or Investment funds with assets in-vested in 10% (TR+RC-Reserved Fund Value) c) Direct investments in foreign inhabitable property: 3% (TR+RC) Overall limit on foreign assets categories a) and B): 20% (TR+RC-Reserved Fund Value)		Credit for ceding insurers dis-bursed premi-ums 100% R.SIN.	paper issued by public and private companies the limit is 30% of the issue for companies with classification >=BBB and 20% for the rest. For financial institutions the limit is 10% of the deposits and 20% of the issued Mortgage bonds. For participation in loan agreements 20% of the credit and/or 1% of TR+RC to a single debtor
Share limit for instruments b) and c) with classification below BBB or N-3 or without classification 25% (TR+RC)	Share limit for fixed instru-ments b), c), and loan agreements and individual		Share limit for inversion and mutual funds administered by the same management	Share limit for bonds, commercial paper, and shares issued by the same company: 5% (TR+RC). Limit is reduced by half if the	Share limit for securitized mortgage instruments, domestic		

	domestic shares issued or guaranteed by companies in the same business group 15% (TR+RC). Limit is reduced by half if the company belongs to the business group. This limit is 10% for instruments issued by one company or it branches. Limit is reduced by half if the company belongs to the issuer group	company 10% (TR+RC)	issuer is related to the company	inversion funds with real state investment, direct investment in real state and bonds issued by securitized companies from real state sector: 40% (TR+RC)

Source: Authors' analysis.

Bibliography

Acuña, Rodrigo, and Augusto Iglesias. 2001. "Chile's Pension Reform after 20 Years." World Bank Social Protection Discussion Paper, No. 0129, December.

Ahn, S. C., and S. Low. 1996. "A Reformulation of the Hausman Test for Regression Models with Pooled Cross-Section Time-Series Data." *Journal of Econometrics* 71: 309–19.

Alier, Max, and Dimitri Vittas. 2001. "Personal Pension Plans and Stock Market Volatility." In *New Ideas about Social Security*, ed. Robert Holzman and Joseph Stiglitz. Washington, DC: World Bank.

Andersen, Carsten, and Peter Skjodt. 2006. "Pension Institutions and Annuities in Denmark." Unpublished manuscript, World Bank, Washington, DC.

Anderson, Ronald, and Suresh Sundaresan. 2000. "A Comparative Study of Structural Models of Corporate Bond Yields: An Exploratory Investigation." *Journal of Banking and Finance* 24: 255–69.

Andrews, D. W. K. 1991. "Heteroskedasticity and Autocorrelation Consistent Covariance Matrix Estimation." *Econometrica* 59: 817–58.

Arellano, M. 1987. "Computing Robust Standard Errors for Within-Group Estimators." *Oxford Bulletin of Economics and Statistics* 49: 431–34.

———. 2003. *Panel Data Econometrics*. Oxford, U.K.: Oxford University Press.

Baltagi, B. H. 2001. *Econometric Analysis of Panel Data*. New York: Wiley.

Bateman, Hazel, H. Doyle, and John Piggott. 1999. "Private Mandatory Retirement Provision: Design and Implementation Challenges." Institute for Economic Research, University of Tokyo.

Benjamin, B., and J. H. Pollard. 2001. *The Analysis of Mortality and Other Actuarial Statistics*. London: Institute of Actuaries and Faculty of Actuaries.

Benninga, Simon, Iddo Eliazar, and Avi Wohl. 2005. "(Only?) Stocks for the Long Run?" The Henry Crown Institute of Business Research in Israel, Working Paper No. 7, 16 pp.

Blake, David. 1999. "Annuity Markets: Problems and Solutions." *The Geneva Papers on Risk and Insurance* 24 (July): 358–75.

Blake, David, and Robert Hudson. 2000. "Improving Security and Flexibility in Retirement." The Pensions Institute, Birkbeck College, University of London.

Blume, Marshall E., Donald B. Keim, and Sandeep A. Patel. 1991. "Returns and Volatility of Low-Grade Bonds 1977–1989." *The Journal of Finance* 46 (1)(March): 49–74.

Bodie, Zvi. 1990. "Pensions as Retirement Income Insurance." *Journal of Economic Literature* XXVIII (March): 28–49.

__________. 1995. "On the Risk of Stocks in the Long Run." *Financial Analysts Journal* (May–June): 18–22.

Bodie, Zvi, Alex Kane, and Alan J. Marcus. 2005. *Investments*. New York: McGraw-Hill.

Bodie, Zvi, Robert Merton, and Paul Samuelson. 1992. "Labor Supply Flexibility and Portfolio Choice in a Lifecycle Model." *Journal of Economic Dynamics and Control*, Vol. 16.

Booth, Philip, and Yakoub Yakoubov. 1998. "Investment Policy for Defined-Contribution Pension Scheme Members Close to Retirement: An Analysis of the 'Lifestyle' Concept." *North American Actuarial Journal* 4(2).

Brown, Jeffrey R., Olivia S. Mitchell, and James M. Poterba. 2001. "The Role of Real Annuities and Indexed Bonds in an Individual Accounts Retirement Program." In *The Role of Annuity Markets in Financing Retirement*, ed. Jeffrey Brown, Olivia S. Mitchell, James M. Poterba, and Mark J. Warshawsky. Cambridge, MA: MIT Press.

Brown, Jeffrey R., and James M. Poterba. 2004. "Household Demand for Variable Annuities." CRR WP2004-08, Center for Retirement Research at Boston College, March.

Burtless, G. 1998. "Financial Market Risks of Individual Retirement Accounts: The Twentieth Century Record." The Brookings Institution, Washington, DC.

__________. 2000. "How Would Financial Risk Affect Retirement Income under Individual Accounts?" The Center for Retirement Research at Boston College, #5, October.

_________. 2003. "What Do We Know about the Risk of Individual Account Pensions? Evidence from Industrial Countries." *Implications of Risk for Public Pension Reform* 93 (2): 354–59.

Campbell, John Y., and Luis M. Viceira. 2002. *Strategic Asset Allocation: Portfolio Choice for Long-Term Investors*. Oxford: Oxford University Press.

Cannon, Edmund, and Ian Tonks. 2004. "U.K. Annuity Rates, Money's Worth and Pension Replacement Ratios 1957–2002." *The Geneva Papers on Risk and Insurance* 29(3) (July): 371–93.

Cardinale, Mirko, Alex Findlater, and Mike Orszag. 2002. "Paying Out Pensions: A Review of International Annuities Markets." Research Report 2002-RU07, Watson Wyatt, May.

Choi, I. 2001. "Unit Root Tests for Panel Data." *Journal of International Money and Finance* 20: 249–72.

Collin-Dufresne, Pierre, and Robert S. Goldstein. 2001. "Do Credit Spreads Reflect Stationary Leverage Ratios?" *The Journal of Finance* LVI(5) (October): 1929–57.

Collins, Sean. 2003. "The Expenses of Defined Benefit Pension Plans and Mutual Funds." In *Perspectives*, Vol. 9, No. 6 (December). The Investment Company Institute. Washington, DC.

Cornell, Bradford, and Kevin Green. 1991. "The Investment Performance of Low-Grade Bond Funds." *The Journal of Finance* 46(1) (March): 29–48.

Davis, E. Philip. 2000. "Issues in the Regulation of Annuities Markets." Center for Research on Pensions and Welfare Policies Working Paper 26/02.

Delianedis, Gordon, and Robert Geske. 2001. "The Components of Corporate Credit Spreads: Default, Recovery, Tax, Jumps, Liquidity, and Market Factors." *Finance*, December 1. Paper 22_01.

Doyle, S., and John Piggott. 1998. "Mandatory Annuity Design: A Preliminary Study." Paper prepared for the Society of Actuaries Conference "Retirement Needs Framework," Florida.

_________. 1999. "Retirement Payouts in a Mandatory Annuity Market." Paper presented to the University of Munich Welfare State Workshop, Venice International University.

Duffee, Gregory R. 1998. "The Relation between Treasury Yields and Corporate Bond Yield Spreads." *The Journal of Finance* LIII(6) (December).

_________. 1999. "Estimating the Price of Default Risk." *The Review of Financial Studies* 12(1) (Spring): 197–226.

Dus, Ivica, Raimond Maurer, and Olivia S. Mitchell. 2003. "Betting on Death and Capital Markets in Retirement: A Shortfall Risk Analysis of Life Annuities versus Phased Withdrawal Plans." MRRC Working Paper, WP2003-063.

Dushi, Irena, and Anthony Webb. 2004. "Annuitization: Keeping Your Options Open." CRR WP2004-04, Center for Retirement Research at Boston College, March.

Dynkin, Lev, Jay Hyman, and Prashant Vankudre. 1998. "Attribution of Portfolio Performance Relative to an Index." Lehman Brothers Fixed Income Research. Lehman Brothers, March.

Edwards, Gonzalo, and Carlos Diaz. 2000. "Beneficios del sistema previsional." In *AFP Chile: Logros y Desafíos,* ed. Trade Association of AFPs, Chile, January.

Elton, Edwin J., Martin J. Gruber, Deepak Agrawal, and Christopher Mann. 2001. "Explaining the Rate Spread on Corporate Bonds." *The Journal of Finance* LVI(1) (February).

Exley, John, S. J. B. Mehta, and A. D. Smith. 1997. "The Financial Theory of Defined Benefit Pension Schemes." Presented to the Institute of Actuaries, April.

__________. 2000. "Asset and Liability Modeling for Pension Funds." Presented to the Joint Institute and Faculty of Actuaries Investment Conference, June.

Financial Services Authority. 2005. *FSA Guide to Annuities and Income Withdrawal.* London: FSA.

Fabozzi, Frank J. 2000. *Bond Markets, Analysis and Strategies,* Fourth ed. Englewood Cliffs, N.J.: Prentice Hall.

Fabozzi, Frank, Sergio Focardi, and Caroline Jonas. 2005. "Market Experience with Modeling for Defined-Benefit Pension Funds: Evidence from Four Countries." *Journal of Pension Economics and Finance* 4 (3) (November).

Finkelstein, Amy, and James Poterba. 1999. "The Market for Annuity Products in the United Kingdom." NBER Working Paper no. 7168. National Bureau of Economic Research, Cambridge, MA.

Fisher, R. A. 1932. *Statistical Methods for Research Workers,* Fourth ed. Edinburgh: Oliver & Boyd.

Fornero, Elsa, and Elisa Luciano, ed. 2004. *Developing an Annuity Market in Europe.* Cheltenham, U.K.: Edward Elgar.

Frisch, R. and Waugh, F. 1933. Partial Time Regressions as Compared with Individual Trends. *Econometrica* 45: 939–53.

G-10. 2005. "Ageing and Pension System Reform: Implications for Financial Markets and Economic Policies." Unpublished manuscript, September.

Golub, Bennett W., and Leo M. Tilman. 1997. "Measuring Yield Curve Risk Using Principal Components Analysis, Value at Risk, and Key Rate Durations." *The Journal of Portfolio Management* (Summer): 72–84.

Grandes, Martin, and Marcel Peter. 2004. "The Determinants of Corporate Bond Yield Spreads in South Africa: Firm-Specific or Driven by Sovereign Risk?" OECD.

Green, W. 1997. *Econometric Analysis.* Englewood Cliffs, N.J.: Prentice Hall.

Honda, Y. 1985. "Testing the Error Components Model with Non-Normal Disturbances." *Review of Economic Studies* 52: 681–90.

Huang, Jing-Zhi, and Ming Huang. 2003. "How Much of the Corporate-Treasury Yield Spread is Due to Credit Risk?" Draft.

IAIS (International Association of Insurance Supervisors). 2006. "Roadmap for a Common Structure and Common Standards for the Assessment of Insurer Solvency." IAIS, Basel, February 16. Available at www.iaisweb.org.

Im, K. S., M. H. Pesaran, and Y. Shin. 2003. "Testing for Unit Roots in Heterogeneous Panels." *Journal of Econometrics* 115: 53–74.

Impavido, Gregorio, Craig W. Thorburn, and Mike Wadsworth. 2003. "A Conceptual Framework for Retirement Products: Risk Sharing Arrangements between Providers and Retirees." World Bank, Washington, DC.

International Actuarial Association. 2004. "A Global Framework for Insurer Solvency Assessment: Research Report of the Insurer Solvency Assessment Working Party, IAA, Canada." Available at www.actuaries.org.

Investment Company Institute. 2004. "The Cost of Buying and Owning Mutual Funds." *Fundamentals* 13(1) (February).

James, Estelle, Guillermo Martinez, and Augusto Iglesias. 2006. "The Payout Stage in Chile: Who Annuitizes and Why?" *Journal of Pension Economics and Finance* 5(2): 121–54.

James, Estelle, Xue Song, and Dimitri Vittas. 2001."Annuity Markets around the World: Money's Worth and Risk Intermediation." American Economic Association Meetings and CeRP Working Paper 16/01.

Jorion, Philippe. 2003. "The Long-Term Risks of Global Stock Markets." *Financial Management* 32(4): 27.

Kapur, Sandeep, and J. Michael Orszag. 2002. "Portfolio Choice and Retirement Income Solutions." Watson Wyatt Technical Report, Watson Wyatt Worldwide.

Knox, David M. 2000. "The Australian Annuity Market." Policy Research Working Paper 2495, World Bank, Washington, DC. November.

Levin, A., C. F. Lin, and C. Chu. 2002. "Unit Root Tests in Panel Data: Asymptotic and Finite-Sample Properties." *Journal of Econometrics* 108: 1–24.

Levy, Haim, and Allon Cohen. 1998. "On the Risk of Stocks in the Long Run: Revisited." *The Journal of Portfolio Management* (Spring).

Liu, Sheen, Howard Qi, and Chunchi Wu. 2004. "Taxes, Default Risk and Corporate Bond Yield Spreads: A Structural Approach." Draft, June.

Lovell, M. 1963. "Seasonal Adjustment of Economic Time Series." *Journal of the American Statistical Association* 58: 993–1010.

Mackenzie, G. A. Sandy. 2002. "The Role of Private Sector Annuities Markets in a Privatized Pension System." IMF Working Paper, WP/02/161. IMF, Washington, DC.

Maddala, G. S., and I. M. Kim. 1999. *Units Roots, Cointegration, and Structural Change*. Cambridge, U.K.: Cambridge University Press.

Maddala, G. S., and S. Wu. 1999. "A Comparative Study of Unit Roots with Panel Data and a New Simple Test." *Oxford Bulletin of Economics and Statistics* 61: 631–52.

Mendez-Vives, David. 2000. "Empirical Models of Interest Rate Risk: From Duration to Principal Components Analysis." International Fixed Income Research, Analytical Research Series, Lehman Brothers International, September.

Ministry of Labor. 2004. *Primera Encuesta de Protección Social* (First Survey of Social Protection). Santiago de Chile.

Mitchell, Olivia S. 2002. "Developments in Decumulation: The Role of Annuity Products in Financing Retirement." In *Ageing, Financial Markets and Monetary Policy*, ed. A. Auerbach and H. Herrman, pp. 97–125. Berlin: Springer-Verlag.

Mitchell, Olivia S., James M. Poterba, Mark J. Warshawsky, and Jeffrey R. Brown. 2001. "New Evidence on the Money's Worth of Individual Annuities." In *The Role of Annuity Markets in Financing Retirement*, ed. Jeffrey Brown, Olivia S. Mitchell, James M. Poterba, and Mark J. Warshawsky. Cambridge, MA: MIT Press.

Myners, Paul. 2001. *Institutional Investment in the United Kingdom: A Review*. London: HM Treasury.

Naldi, Marco. 2000. "Measuring the Risk of Treasury Positions: GARCH-PCA." Lehman Brothers International Fixed Income Research, Lehman Brothers, June.

Ng, S., and P. Perron. 2001. "Lag Length Selection and the Construction of Unit Root Tests with Good Size and Power." *Econometrica* 69: 1519–54.

Orszag, J. Michael. 2000. "Annuities: the Problems." Paper presented at the NAPF Annual Conference, May.

Orszag, Mike. 2001. "Retirement Income Decisions." Paper presented at IFID Conference, Fields Institute of Mathematical Sciences, Toronto, September.

Orszag, Mike, and Mirko Cardinale. 2002. "Paying Out Private Pensions in Latin America." Watson Wyatt Technical Report 2002-RU14, Watson Wyatt, December.

Palacios, Robert, and Rafael Rofman. 2001. "Annuity Markets and Benefit Design in Multipillar Pension Schemes: Experience and Lessons for Four Latin American Countries." World Bank Pension Reform Primer Paper, No. 107.

Perron, P. 1989. "The Great Crash, the Oil Price Shock and the Unit Root Hypothesis." *Econometrica* 57: 1361–1402.

Poterba, James M. 2001. "A Brief History of Annuity Markets." In *The Role of Annuity Markets in Financing Retirement*, ed. Jeffrey Brown, Olivia S. Mitchell, James M. Poterba, and Mark J. Warshawsky. Cambridge, MA: MIT Press.

Poterba, James M., and Mark J. Warshawsky. 2001. "The Costs of Annuitizing Retirement Payouts from Individual Accounts." In *The Role of Annuity Markets in Financing Retirement*, ed. Jeffrey Brown, Olivia S. Mitchell, James M. Poterba, and Mark J. Warshawsky. Cambridge, MA: MIT Press.

Rocha, R. 2005. "The Chilean Private Pension Sector: An Assessment." Unpublished manuscript, World Bank, Washington, DC.

Rocha, Roberto, Richard Hinz, and Joaquin Gutierrez. 2001. "Improving the Regulation and Supervision of Pension Funds: Are There Lessons from the Banking Sector?" In *New Ideas for Old-Age Security—Toward Sustainable Pension Systems in the 21st Century*, ed. Robert Holzman and Joseph Stiglitz. Washington, DC: World Bank.

Samuelson, Paul A. 1994. "The Long-Term Case for Equities and How It Can Be Oversold." *Journal of Portfolio Management* 21(1): 15–24.

Sarig, Oded, and Arthur Warga. 1989. "Bond Price Data and Bond Market Liquidity." *Journal of Financial and Quantitative Analysis* 24(3) (September): 367–78.

Scott, Jason, and Greg Stein. 2003. "Retirement Security in a DC World: Effectively Bridging the Expertise Gap." Pension Research Council Working Paper, The Wharton School, University of Pennsylvania.

Shiller, Robert J. 2005. "Life-Cycle Portfolios as Government Policy." *The Economists' Voice* 2(1) [A Special Issue on Social Security]: Article 14.

Siegel, Jeremy J. 1994. *Stocks for the Long Run: A Guide to Selecting Markets for Long Term Growth*. Irwin Professional Publishing.

Siegel, J. J., and Thaler, R. H. 1997. "Anomalies: The Equity Premium Puzzle." *Journal of Economic Perspectives* 11(1): 191–200.

Smink, Meye, and Robert Van der Meer. 1997. "Life Insurance Asset-Liability Management: An International Survey." The Geneva Papers on Risk and Insurance, Issues and Practice, No. 82 (January).

Society of Actuaries. 2003. "Professional Actuarial Specialty Guide: Asset-Liability Management." Schaumburg, IL.

Swiss Reinsurance Company. 2000. "Asset-Liability Management for Insurers." In Sigma Series, No. 6, Zurich.

Thorburn, Craig. 2004. "On the Measurement of Solvency of Insurance Companies: Recent Developments That Will Alter Methods Adopted in Emerging Markets." World Bank, Washington, DC, February.

Valdes-Prieto, Salvador. 1998. "Risks in Pensions and Annuities: Efficient Designs." Social Protection Discussion Paper Series 9804, World Bank, Washington, DC. February.

__________. 2000. "Do Investment Regulations Compromise Pension Fund Performance? Evidence from Latin America: A Comment." *Revista de Analisis Economico* 15(2) (November): 109–120.

Van der Meer, Robert, and Meye Smink. 1993. "Strategies and Techniques of Asset Liability Management: An Overview." The Geneva Papers on Risk and Insurance, Issues and Practice, No. 67 (April).

Wadsworth, Mike, and Alec Findlater. 2000. "Reinventing Annuities." Unpublished manuscript. Watson Wyatt Worldwide.

Walker, Eduardo. 2002. "The Chilean Experience in Completing Markets with Financial Indexation." In *Indexation, Inflation and Monetary Policy*, ed. Fernando Leford and Klaus Schmidt-Hebel. Central Bank of Chile.

__________. 2003a. "Portafolios Optimos Para Los Nuevos Sistemas De Pensiones de Paises Emergentes." Unpublished manuscript, Catholic University of Chile.

__________. 2003b. "Rentas Vitalicias, Tasas de Mercado y Competencia." Documento de Trabajo, Escuela de Administración, Pontificia Universidad Católica de Chile. Unpublished manuscript, Catholic University of Chile.

__________. 2005. "Annuity Markets: Competition, Regulation and Myopia?" December. Unpublished manuscript, Catholic University of Chile.

Warshawsky, Mark J. 2001. "Private Annuity Markets in the United States: 1919–1984." In *The Role of Annuity Markets in Financing Retirement*, ed. Jeffrey Brown, Olivia S. Mitchell, James M. Poterba, and Mark J. Warshawsky. Cambridge, MA: MIT Press.

Watson Wyatt Partners. 2002. "Modernizing Annuities." Watson Wyatt Worldwide.

Wolswijk, Guido, and Jakob de Haan. 2005. "Government Debt Management in the Euro Area: Recent Theoretical Developments and Changes in Practice." European Central Bank Occasional Paper No. 25, March.

Wooldridge, J. F. 2002. *Econometric Analysis of Cross Section and Panel Data*. Cambridge, MA: MIT Press.

Yazigi, Alejandro Ferreiro et al. 2002. *El Sistema Chileno de Pensiones Derivado de la Capitalizacion Individual*. Superintendencia de Administradoras de Fondos de Pensiones, Santiago, Chile.

Yermo, Juan. 2000. "The Performance of the Funded Pension Systems in Latin America." Background paper for a regional study on social security reform, Office of the Chief Economist, Latin America and Caribbean Region, World Bank.

Index

A

D

E

F

G

H

N

O

P

Q

R

ECO-AUDIT
Environmental Benefits Statement

The World Bank is committed to preserving endangered forests and natural resources. The Office of the Publisher has chosen to print ***Developing Annuities Markets: The Experience of Chile*** on recycled paper with 30 percent post-consumer waste, in accordance with the recommended standards for paper usage set by the Green Press Initiative, a nonprofit program supporting publishers in using fiber that is not sourced from endangered forests. For more information, visit www.greenpressinitiative.org.

Saved:
- 7 trees
- 5 million BTUs of energy
- 640 lbs. of CO_2-equivalent greenhouse gases
- 2,658 gallons of wastewater
- 341 lbs. of solid waste

green press INITIATIVE